CITY EATS
SAN FRANCISCO

50+ RECIPES FROM THE
BEST OF THE CITY BY THE BAY

TREVOR FELCH

CIDER MILL
PRESS

BOOK
PUBLISHERS

CITY EATS: SAN FRANCISCO

Copyright © 2024 by Cider Mill Press Book Publishers LLC.

This is an officially licensed book by Cider Mill Press Book Publishers LLC.

All rights reserved under the Pan-American and International Copyright Conventions.

No part of this book may be reproduced in whole or in part, scanned, photocopied, recorded, distributed in any printed or electronic form, or reproduced in any manner whatsoever, or by any information storage and retrieval system now known or hereafter invented, without express written permission of the publisher, except in the case of brief quotations in critical articles and reviews.

The scanning, uploading, and distribution of this book via the internet or via any other means without permission of the publisher is illegal and punishable by law. Please support authors' rights, and do not participate in or encourage piracy of copyrighted materials.

13-Digit ISBN: 978-1-64643-425-1
10-Digit ISBN: 1-64643-425-0

This book may be ordered by mail from the publisher. Please include $5.99 for postage and handling. Please support your local bookseller first!

Books published by Cider Mill Press Book Publishers are available at special discounts for bulk purchases in the United States by corporations, institutions, and other organizations. For more information, please contact the publisher.

Cider Mill Press Book Publishers
"Where good books are ready for press"
501 Nelson Place
Nashville, Tennessee 37214

cidermillpress.com

Typography: Casablanca URW, FreightSans Pro, FreightText Pro, Sackers Gothic Std

Printed in Malaysia

24 25 26 27 28 COS 5 4 3 2 1

First Edition

CONTENTS

INTRODUCTION

San Francisco is a city of abundant mystique, fun, funk, and folklore, as if the City by the Bay's defining personality is perpetually somewhat hidden by the region's frequent coastal fog. Everything here seems larger, quirkier, and steeper than anything else. Have you ever walked up Nob Hill? Somehow that "hill" really does feel like the most mountain-like hill you'll ever climb.

There's Alcatraz and its mystery as "The Rock," where the country's most notorious prisoners once resided on an island in the middle of San Francisco Bay. There's Lombard Street—a crazy, curvy street that literally would fit in a Dr. Seuss book. There are the ships supposedly buried under what is essentially now the Financial District, creating a place where a Bull, Bear, and Boat market meet. There's the fact that San Francisco's population is a little over 815,000 as of 2021, dwarfed by other major cities worldwide, and yet it still manages to be one of the most important, most visited, and most beloved large cities anywhere. There is a herd of buffalo in Golden Gate Park, a flock of parrots on Telegraph Hill, coyotes prowl through the Presidio, and seals in the bay almost always supervise the tourists, joggers, and cyclists on land along the Embarcadero.

Heck, even that near-constant (and always colder than you think!) San Francisco fog has a real name: Karl. That's San Francisco for you.

This mystique, fun, funk, and folklore really adds up to a city whose character is a beautiful series of complex puzzle pieces, each one having its own character. It's a city made up of fascinating residents and fascinating neighborhoods. What possibly can unite this crazy, mystical, fun, funky, bizarre, diverse, fog-covered, hill-filled kind of small city? Sure, the Muni public transit system technically connects all 49-ish square miles of San Francisco. Yes, it's very rare to find a corner of the city where there aren't banners supporting the Giants, 49ers, and Warriors.

But it's really one of the general big-picture topics that ultimately is the most intimate, critical element that unites all of those different, complex puzzle pieces of this city: food.

The San Francisco food scene is friendly and fun, yet it's also vast and intimidating. Like San Francisco itself, the city's past and present restaurants, food artisans, cafés, and food shops have their own grandeur and enchantment. Some people come to San Francisco to put a flower in their hair. A lot of people come to San Francisco to photograph the Golden Gate Bridge. But, stepping back a little bit and digging through the dense layers of this city, it's always remarkable how so many people—whether looking for work, for amusement, for exploring, for turning a new page in life, for Instagram—genuinely come to San Francisco because of the food. This is a city that truly eats. And eats. You might leave your heart in San Francisco. You'll probably leave your wallet in San Francisco. And, you'll definitely feel like you left your stomach in San Francisco because of how wonderful its unique dining scene is.

Given how many restaurants open and close each week, plus the uncertain number of pop-ups and food trucks that regularly operate in San Francisco, it's nearly impossible to get a perfect figure for the number of places to eat at any moment in the city. However, the general ballpark estimate from a somewhat official count (by the Golden Gate Restaurant Association) in 2021 was 3,974, according to an April 2022 article by *The San Francisco Standard*, after most of the pandemic-induced closings had happened. In general, the local media and hospitality industry, per my decade of journalism experience in the region, tends to run with a 4,000 active restaurants ballpark estimate. That's just brick-and-mortar restaurants—it does not include mobile food vendors/trucks, coffee shops with actual meal-level food, pop-ups, and much more. All in all, there are easily at least 5,000 options for satiating your appetite within 47 to 49 square miles (there are many disputed reports on the city's exact size and I haven't used a ruler and a blimp lately to measure the exact square mile value).

To make this delicious math even more complex, Golden Gate Park is about a thousand acres and the Presidio (a former military base turned part of the Golden Gate National Recreation Area) is about 1,500 acres, which is almost four square miles of parkland, so it's actually 43 to 45 square miles of San Francisco for restaurants with probably 5,000 or more options to eat. That's a lot of restaurants in a small amount of space.

Plus, here's the exclamation point at the end of this food math sentence—almost all of those places to eat are genuinely really good. Sure, everyone loves reading a snarky one-star Yelp review or seeing a newspaper critic write a full-on slam review of a restaurant like *The New York Times*' Pete Wells did in 2012 for Bay Area resident Guy Fieri's Times Square restaurant. But the reality on the ground is that San Francisco just doesn't have a lot of underachieving or simply "bad" restaurants because restaurants *can't* be bad in this city. The clientele is too discerning, the market is too expensive and competitive, and the bar is set too high for "not good" restaurants to generate sustainable revenue in San Francisco.

San Francisco deserves to be known as a world-class food city *because* it truly is one.

However, it certainly hasn't always been known as a destination for food. In fact, that reputation is a somewhat recent one. The path of San Francisco from being simply the gateway to the Golden Gate and Gold Country to being a culinary capital pretty closely mirrors the route and timing of the tech industry just to the city's south, in Silicon Valley. For the tech world, there's the pretty definitive historical line of Before Apple (which was founded in 1976, and, yes, kids, there were many, many years when people didn't have internet access on their cell phones or even cell phones . . . or even the internet!) and After Apple. For the San Francisco food world, this critical twentieth-century shift is usually referred to as the Before Chez Panisse era (the Berkeley restaurant founded by Alice Waters in 1971) and After Chez Panisse.

Yes, I understand that eyebrow raise just now—Chez Panisse isn't in San Francisco! It's across the bay! That's true. However, to downplay Chez Panisse's massive role in the formation of San Francisco's modern-day food renaissance would be completely incorrect. Chez Panisse was the San Francisco food scene's equivalent of Apple, or in the case of Chez Panisse's signature farm-to-table mentality, a bowl of Frog Hollow Farm apples at their sweet, juicy peak in September.

That being said, too many of my peers and culinary analysts say that Chez Panisse singularly changed the direction of food in San Francisco. That isn't true. It was one key factor, not the only factor. Like with Apple in the 1970s, there were certainly several precursors that eventually led to the big 1970s moment for San Francisco food. For the tech industry, society had the Industrial Revolution, the Model T, and Bill Hewlett and Dave Packard founding their namesake company back in 1939 in a Palo Alto garage.

There hasn't been much written about early San Francisco cuisine, which is a little surprising for a city that is hardly young (founded in 1776 as Yerba Buena, the same year the Declaration of Independence was signed on the opposite coast). However, maybe it isn't surprising because what little we know is the cuisine back in the city's youth was pretty simple and not exciting. The *San Francisco Chronicle*'s Peter Hartlaub wrote a fantastic article in 2015 about San Francisco's less-than-remarkable early restaurant history, looking back through the newspaper's archives. "San Francisco dining in the early years was a product of the city's economics," he wrote. "San Francisco had grown from 500 residents to 150,000 in less than 25 years. Most of those residents were male, broke, and with exceptionally low standards. The streets were unpaved. At places like Miners restaurant and What Cheer House, a layer of dust would settle on the tables, the patrons, and the 10-cent steaks."

Indeed, mid-1800s Gold Rush–era cuisine didn't seem to be lavish, though an oyster omelet called "hangtown fry" (see page 329) came out of it in the Sierra

Foothills-Gold Rush country town of Placerville. Speaking of that hangtown fry, as far as I know, the only restaurant that serves it in present-day San Francisco is Tadich Grill, which happened to open in 1849, the same year the California Gold Rush began (yes, that's why San Francisco's football team is the 49ers).

The author John Briscoe puts Tadich Grill's important role in San Francisco history in perfect perspective to open his outstanding book *Tadich Grill: The Story of San Francisco's Oldest Restaurant, with Recipes*: "Tadich Grill, San Francisco's oldest restaurant, has mirrored its city's history, from its founding in 1849, the year of San Francisco's real birth during the Gold Rush, to its survival of two catastrophic earthquakes. In a way, it has also projected the city's future. It has fed its future mayors when they were young and again years later when they were cutting, over sand dabs, the deals that would decide the city's ever-flamboyant future."

Sand dabs and hangtown fry? That doesn't sound quite like a culinary capital's cuisine. But that was just the beginning...and after all, they used mostly local ingredients like Chez Panisse would 120 years later.

Eighteen forty-nine is also the same year that a chocolate maker named Domingo Ghirardelli arrived in San Francisco from Italy via the Cape of Horn and Peru (there was no Panama Canal back then). Of course, the Ghirardelli brand became a giant in the global chocolate industry. Many fellow Italian immigrants like Ghirardelli also moved to California in the second half of the 1800s. The city founded its Fisherman's Wharf on the far north side of the city in 1900, where Italian, specifically Sicilian, immigrants had a huge role in establishing the fishing and restaurant businesses there. Nunzio Alioto, a Sicilian immigrant, founded Alioto's, a restaurant at Fisherman's Wharf, in 1925, after the city started rebounding from the destructive 7.9 magnitude earthquake in 1906. Alioto's sadly closed in 2022, but just a few miles away, near downtown San Francisco, Sam's Grill (founded in 1867) and John's Grill (debuted in 1908) continue to operate like Tadich Grill. All three share a somewhat common menu philosophy that shows a little of those early Gold Rush–era Italian immigration roots with dishes that are Italian American seafood-centric—cioppino, sand dabs, seafood pastas. Oh, and stiff martinis—and that's also a heated debate, whether the drink was created in Italy or San Francisco (or New York).

Fisherman's Wharf and North Beach, San Francisco's historic Italian neighborhood, border the city's Chinatown, which is the largest Chinatown district in North America. Like the aforementioned Italian immigration, many Chinese came to California during the Gold Rush era. The oldest still-serving Chinatown restaurant, Sam Wo, opened in 1908. Unfortunately, this Chinatown history provides a sad reminder of terrible government acts against the Chinese immigrants, including the Chinese Exclusion Act of 1882. According to a KQED (San Francisco's PBS affiliate) article, Chinatown only started to truly flourish after the 1906 earthquake, when city documents and immigration records were burned: "Many Chinese were able to claim citizenship, then send for their children and families in China. Legally, all children of US citizens were automatically citizens, regardless of their place of birth." So this, combined with the end of the aforementioned Act in 1943 and China being a US ally in World War II, helped to firmly establish Chinatown's prominence—and its subsequent dining scene—in San Francisco.

These main immigration currents through the second half of the nineteenth century and the first half of the twentieth century helped set the stage for that eventual 1971 post–Chez Panisse époque.

One other key influence was the opposite of sand dabs and steaks; it was the city's oh-so-glitzy twentieth-century special occasion restaurants. The *Chronicle*'s Peter Hartlaub wrote in that 2015 look-back article: "While the lower class ate with little discrimination in the decades after the Gold Rush, the rich got richer, and their overindulgent feasts looked like something out of a dysto-

pian future, or maybe a 'Monty Python' film." (Unfortunately, San Francisco of present day isn't completely unlike this.)

Julius' Castle opened in the 1920s, and the Carnelian Room opened in the 1950s. Both had posh food that, by all accounts, was great and plenty luxurious. However, both restaurants were ultimately best known for their settings and views—Julius's Castle being on Telegraph Hill and the Carnelian Room residing 52 stories high above the then-tallest skyscraper west of the Mississippi, located at 555 California Street. These were special occasion restaurants. Then, in 1959, The Mandarin was opened on Polk Street by legendary chef Cecilia Chiang, marking the beginning of San Francisco's definitive, ambitious Chinese cuisine restaurant—truly not Americanized food from China—which would be frequented by the city's Chinese and non-Chinese residents and visitors alike. It was a game changer.

So, all of this—the global cuisines, the high-quality cooking, the passion for dining out, the care for exceptional ingredients—was all there by the 1960s and then elevated to the highest heights with a pivotal nudge from San Francisco's peers on Shattuck Avenue in Berkeley in the early 1970s.

Everything from 1971 and before prepared the Bay Area for its After Chez Panisse era. Gayle Pirie and John Clark, the chefs and co-owners of Foreign Cinema in the Mission District, wrote about the burgeoning California cuisine in the Bay Area in their must-read *The Foreign Cinema Cookbook: Recipes and Stories under the Stars*: "Whether driving to Berkeley to dine at Chez Panisse or sitting at the bar at Stars in San Francisco, wherever we ventured, we brought something back to the line: flavors to remember, sensations to capture, and restaurant energy to synthesize and distill." It was a truly special time in a special place to be eating and cooking in San Francisco.

Together, all of this—not just one place but all of the decades of ingredients— set the stage for why we're sitting here today, over 50 years later, talking about San Francisco's magnificent food scene.

~~~~~~~~~~~~~

The best way to understand San Francisco's dining scene is to understand its neighborhoods. They are the fabric of what is ultimately a residential city made up of one or a few business districts in each of the 20 to 25 or so neighborhoods. And, each one has its own distinct personality, whether that's expressed in its architecture, cultural heritage, socioeconomic status, natural environment, or whatever. You know when you're in the Outer Richmond compared to Nob Hill compared to Potrero Hill compared to Downtown. It's in these neighborhoods that it is possible to unearth San Francisco's food identity: diverse, charming, generally small and family-run businesses with an emphasis on the best ingredients, preferably with most of them procured from the many nearby farms and ranches around the Bay Area and Central Valley.

Almost all San Francisco neighborhoods have a very distinct, can't-miss-it personality—some are bustling and hip, while others are relaxed and quiet, and most are uniquely in between.

Some neighborhoods specialize in one cuisine, while others have forty kinds of restaurant cuisines offered. Getting to know these neighborhoods is the way to peel the layers of the San Francisco onion. And, many of them also have excellent weekly farmers markets that are essentially equal parts amazing produce, excellent vendors serving breakfast and/or lunch, and a vast street party that is fun for all ages. San Francisco tourism does tend to be dominated by its world-renowned sights (Golden Gate Bridge! Lombard Street!), but its food scene is a much more intimate, small-scale, neighborhood-by-neighborhood affair.

It's a city where it's easy to have a short, delicious dining crawl, but it's also easy to go to a far corner of the city seeking out one elusive, specific dish.

It goes without saying that this city's eats have never been better. Obviously, the talent level of chefs has never been higher. The quality of cooking equipment and ingredients has never been better (what, they didn't have sous-vide cooking in 1849?). There's also the less tangible reason why things are so great for San Francisco diners nowadays: energy. The chefs are excited to be cooking here because this is the grand stage. This is the Olympics. For a restaurant-filled setting, San Francisco is everything Reno sings about in Cole Porter's "You're the Top" in the musical *Anything Goes*. There are restaurants from two of the great titans of the food television and restaurant empire world: Tyler Florence and Michael Mina (San Francisco is fickle about chains and celebrity chefs, but those two get a pass since they live here and made a name for themselves here). There are timeless classics, like Swan Oyster Depot and House of Prime Rib, where memories have been made for decades and millennials appreciate them just as much as their grandparents did in the 1970s.

It's important to book reservations far in advance because chefs here are revered like professional athletes or major movie stars elsewhere, even if the rest of the country might only pay attention to the likes of Thomas Keller and Alice Waters when it comes to Bay Area chefs (neither has ever cooked at a restaurant in San Francisco, by the way!). As this book will show you, these San Francisco chefs cook with immense talent, and they also cook with enormous heart. Kim Alter, Val Cantu, Harrison Cheney, Alexander Hong, and Mike Lanham are just a few of their many peers who continue to innovate the world of fine dining, blending impeccable craftsmanship with an elegance that isn't *too* over-the-top. Mister Jiu's and San Ho Won thrill diners at each service with Brandon Jew's modern California-influenced Chinese cuisine at the former and Corey Lee's contemporary California meets classic Korean cooking at the latter. Zuni Café and Nopa set the stage for the seasonal, local ingredients–focused style of cuisine with a delightful rustic edge that San Francisco is known for; yet peers like Octavia, Rich Table, and Pearl 6101 take that template and give it a bit of a more creative, globe-trotting spin.

In the mid-2010s, *Bon Appétit* magazine took San Francisco to the viral long-lines level by (deservedly) naming two boundary-pushing, ambitious, wonderful restaurants as their Best New Restaurant. State Bird Provisions and its compelling dim sum–style service won the award in 2012 and is still extremely difficult to get a reservation at. In 2015, Aaron London's AL's Place won with "snackles" like brine pickled fries and by putting meats as "sides" to emphasize the importance of the seasonal produce and local seafood on the menu. Both restaurants are rooted in Northern California, but they're not afraid to bring in influences from around the world. They cook food that is fresh, beautiful, captivating, and, here it is again, energetic. You feel the love and the excitement throughout a meal. Sadly, AL's Place closed in 2022, but its message of focusing on local ingredients, fun, and creativity will continue to live on in San Francisco restaurants.

Are you interested in trying different cuisines from within China or Japan? Specific regions of Mexico and India? Guam? Sri Lanka? A pop-up with amazing fish and chips and quite the name ("Cod Damn")? Stellar pho and pupusas? A definitive cioppino and Dungeness crab Louie? Beignets and muffulettas on par with the best in New Orleans? Bagels and pizza that match up with their peers in New York (it's true!)?

It's all here. There's no place like San Francisco, and there's nothing quite like eating your away around the City by the Bay.

GLOSSARY OF KEY PRESENT-DAY NAMES

Here's a handy guide to a few of the major current chefs and restaurants in San Francisco that definitely deserve to be mentioned in this book. Of course, we don't have space to write about everyone who is truly influential in this robust dining scene, but this group certainly should be considered very influential.

LORETTA KELLER

SoMa was hardly the marquee dining neighborhood in 1993, back when Keller opened Bizou, compared to how it is today. Bizou eventually transformed into Coco500, which closed in 2014, yet both exemplified the small, charming Californian-Italian-French bistro that is SF's signature restaurant style. Keller has also been a key figure in the prominent food programs at the Exploratorium and the California Academy of Sciences. She is now the culinary director of Uccello Lounge at the SF Conservatory of Music, where you can still try her signature meringue, coffee gelato, chocolate sauce, and candied almond "vacherin" dessert.

PATRICIA UNTERMAN

Most of us food writers tend to have very little overlap with working in restaurants. Unterman is the rare exception. The Stanford and UC Berkeley graduate cofounded Hayes Street Grill in 1979—the same year she also became the *San Francisco Chronicle* restaurant critic (and eventually became the critic for the *San Francisco Examiner* and author of the *San Francisco Food Lover's Guide*). Would a restaurant owner be allowed to be a major newspaper dining critic these days? Definitely not. But Unterman is one of SF's greatest food writers ever, and Hayes Street Grill is still a fantastic destination for sustainably caught fish and seafood and peak seasonal local produce.

TARTINE BAKERY

As much as classic sourdough gets all the San Francisco bread hype, this Mission District bakery's signature country bread (it's a sourdough but not the classic SF kind) by Chad Robertson is far and away the most famous bread in the city. In my copy of Tartine's book, the recipe spans 45 pages (!), but at least half of it is photos. It's a great checklist challenge for home bakers. But, if you're anything like me when it comes to patience, I just swing by the bakery at an off hour (3 p.m.!) and pick up a loaf and as many desserts as I can carry without a car. The bakery started in 2002 as a partnership between Robertson's breads and his wife, Elisabeth Prueitt, designing the pastries.

TRACI DES JARDINS

Originally from the Central Valley, Des Jardins became one of the most important chefs of modern times in San Francisco, thanks to the 21-year run of her California-French restaurant, Jardinière, one of the seminal city restaurants of any era with its fantastic cuisine, Pat Kuleto design, and joie de vivre vibe in the heart of it all by City Hall and the major concert houses. However, she was already a well-known chef before Jardinière, cooking at many esteemed places around the globe and being the opening chef at Rubicon. And after Jardinière, Des Jardins forged a great partnership with Bon Appétit Management Co., opening places like Arguello and The Commissary in the Presidio, plus concepts in the Ferry Building and Oracle Park. She is a chef but also an entrepreneur who is willing to take on a challenging concept or location, whether it's opening only on weeknights (School Night in Dogpatch) or being a culinary adviser for a revolutionary new food company (Impossible Foods). Along with restaurants and businesses, Des Jardins has been very active in community nonprofits and charities.

NANCY OAKES

There are few places that capture the magical potential of San Francisco better than Oakes's three-decade-old Embarcadero restaurant, Boulevard. With Bay Bridge views and an elegant-meets-whimsical belle époque setting envisioned by the city's two leading star architects (Pat Kuleto originally and Ken Fulk with the 2020 refresh), Boulevard is the definition of a beloved institution, yet its (often wood-fired) food continues to be fresh and exciting—the paragon of what makes

San Francisco such a special food city. Eat here and you'll know why this book exists. Oakes is also co-owner of Prospect (just off the Embarcadero, not far from Boulevard) and the historic North Beach bar-restaurant–party scene Tosca Cafe. Prior to Boulevard, she earned rave reviews as chef-owner of L'Avenue in the Richmond. It's also very important to note that Oakes has played an instrumental role for many years with the city's Meals on Wheels organization.

ACQUERELLO

This impeccable upscale restaurant between Polk Street and Van Ness is the answer for "What was San Francisco's perpetually most under-the-radar special occasion dining destination for the past thirty years?" Chef Suzette Gresham and cofounder Giancarlo Paterlini opened the restaurant in 1989, and it continues to be at the top of fine dining game, yet is not as showy and flashy as most of its peers. The cheese cart is epic and the entire traditional-meets-modern-Italian style of cooking is always a sincere pleasure. Acquerello is a consummate, proper restaurant for restaurant lovers that still feels exciting instead of dated.

NOPA

Which came first, the neighborhood or the restaurant? Nopa is the nickname for the North of the Panhandle neighborhood between Alamo Square and Golden Gate Park. Nopa is also a fantastic restaurant, opened in 2006 by partners Allyson Jossel, Laurence Jossel (who had in earlier years become a prominent chef in town at Chez Nous), and Jeff Hanak. It's on every must-visit list for its many signature dishes, including the Moroccan vegetable tagine, burger, and pork chop (the best in town). In many ways, it's the 2000s–2010s version of Stars and Zuni Café, as the stalwart California cuisine place in town that is fine for a quick drink or a lavish meal, and it seems to be bustling at later hours when most of the city is already closed up. Also, if you're like me and care about diligent geography, Nopa the restaurant is actually northeast of the Panhandle.

RON SIEGEL

Few chefs have the résumé or respect from fine dining peers that Siegel has. Nowadays, he's running his own Madcap restaurant in Marin County. However, he had a profound impact in the kitchen at many of the city's very best past and present restaurants, including Charles Nob Hill, Michael Mina, Masa's, and the Dining Room at the Ritz-Carlton. Outside of San Francisco, he's best known as the first American chef to win on *Iron Chef* in Japan back in 1998.

CHARLES PHAN

It's hard to imagine San Francisco without The Slanted Door, Phan's beloved contemporary Vietnamese restaurant. And yet, it still hasn't reopened over three years since the COVID-19 pandemic started. The restaurant started in the Mission, then eventually moved to the Ferry Building, where it's been the anchor fine dining tenant ever since. Hopefully the restaurant reopens soon, as Phan has opened various concepts in the Bay Area and beyond in the past decade, but it's the Ferry Building's Slanted Door that is truly his signature restaurant.

DOMINIQUE CRENN

I first met Crenn at the SF Chefs Festival on Union Square in 2010 when she was the executive chef of Luce at the InterContinental San Francisco and just starting to be known within city food circles. In the decade since then, she has opened her trio of Crenn restaurants (Atelier Crenn, Bar Crenn, and Petit Crenn) and become possibly the most recognizable San Francisco chef around the world, thanks to all of her awards and media appearances. It's remarkable to look back at this exceptional career growth. However, what's really remarkable is the food at each of her restaurants. Atelier Crenn is generally considered the most edgy of all the starry SF fine dining temples.

COREY LEE

Before opening his own restaurant in San Francisco, Lee was already well-known in the Bay Area as the head chef at The French Laundry. Since then, his first restaurant, Benu, opened in 2010 in SoMa and continues to be one of the city's definitive tasting menu experiences. His other two restaurants, Monsieur Benjamin and San Ho Won, are also citywide favorites, where the former in Hayes Valley is an excellent French bistro and the latter presents Korean-inspired charcoal BBQ and cuisine in the Mission.

CALIFORNIOS

Arguably *the* restaurant of the moment as I sit here writing in 2023, it's a truly unique and special contemporary Mexican restaurant in a spectacular, elegant modern setting, courtesy of Chef Val Cantú, designer Carolyn Cantú, and wine director Charlotte Randolph (Carolyn's sister/Val's sister-in-law).

GARY DANKO

One of the city's most well-known chefs—if for no other reason than he's one of the remaining few prominent chefs with a namesake restaurant. Even though Restaurant Gary Danko is right by Ghirardelli Square and Fisherman's Wharf, it's also not just for tourists. It's been one of the city's best splashy French-inspired places since opening in 1999 (before that, Danko was an acclaimed chef in SF at the Dining Room at the Ritz-Carlton before the aforementioned Ron Siegel took over there) and continues to not hold anything back when it comes to a special dining experience. It's neither modern nor tired. It's Gary Danko.

PIM TECHAMUANVIVIT

Chef Pim's pair of Thai restaurants, Kin Khao (Union Square) and the sleeker, more contemporary Nari (Japantown), are the city's gold standards for enjoying riveting Thai dishes and, honestly, two of the city's consistently best restaurants of any cuisine. The Bay Area has followed her career since long before she opened Kin

Khao, though. Chef Pim worked in Silicon Valley, then launched one of the most successful food blogs of all time (seriously, how many food blogs do people remember years later?) and a very popular small-batch jam brand. Scientist, writer, jam maker, acclaimed chef. Not a classic career path...but San Francisco diners are thrilled with Nari and Kin Khao as the most recent stops.

IKE'S LOVE & SANDWICHES

Ike Shehadeh's sandwich concept is now a borderline West Coast megachain, but it all started in the Castro in 2007. In 2010, Ike's Place became a sort of poster child in the perpetual SF landlords/grouchy neighbors against a small, popular restaurateur battles (eventually Ike's Place moved to a new space nearby). Luckily, Ike's Place has gone on to soar to very lofty heights of success. But, it's one of the most memorable of the (too) many real estate and endless rules/laws-focused battles that small food businesses constantly face in this ultrabureaucratic city.

BRUCE HILL

Hill is truly a chef's chef—not only did he create the Chef's Press (a cast-iron pressing tool for cooking), but he worked his way from esteemed 1980s and 1990s restaurants like Stars, Aqua, and Oritalia to being the chef for many cherished restaurants in the city like BIX, Zero Zero, and Fog City that were originally part of the powerful Real Restaurants group. Zero Zero closed in 2022 and Hill very recently stepped away from BIX in 2023, but his impact on San Francisco restaurants remains immense.

BELINDA LEONG

The former Manresa and Gary Danko pastry chef is the owner of b. Patisserie, a tremendous bakery-pastry shop–café near Lower Pac Heights that is best known for Leong's phenomenal kouign-amann pastries (imagine glazed and extremely buttery croissants). If every neighborhood had a b. patisserie, the world would be a better place.

RYAN SHELTON

Unlike, say, Barcelona or Los Angeles, San Francisco tends to gravitate more toward roast chicken and homemade pastas than flashy, pyrotechnics-evoking high-end modern cuisine. Shelton's oh-so-creative cooking at his Fillmore restaurant, Merchant Roots, is one rare exception. He changes the menu and literal menu concept every few weeks. Whether it's "Alice in Wonderland's Mad Tea Party" or "School," somehow Shelton always pulls it off without being gimmicky. This is the truly rare example of fun fine dining.

DEL POPOLO

It was a perfect storm of timing for pizzaiolo Jon Darsky—the surge of food trucks in the early 2010s and the rising interest in (and quality of) puffy, leopard-spotted Neapolitan pizzas. So, Darsky outfitted a truck with a glass-enclosed shipping container holding an actual wood-fired brick pizza oven imported from Naples that was a marvel to see roaming the streets of San Francisco. Now Del Popolo has a stationary restaurant in Lower Nob Hill, and, to me, it's safe to say it's the city's leading place for Neapolitan pizza.

SAN TUNG

Ask a hundred San Franciscans where to get wings, and all hundred of them will point you toward the dry-fried wings of this Inner Sunset Korean restaurant. It's without question one of the definitive dishes in SF.

THANH LONG

Dating back to 1971, the An family's Outer Sunset Vietnamese restaurant is best known for its iconic duo of garlic noodles (created by Chef Helene An) and roast crab, which has legions of devoted followers from nearby and all over the world.

ARNOLD ERIC WONG

Originally from San Francisco, Wong is one of SF's most prolific and overall immensely talented and accomplished chefs for both savory and pastry. He opened two of the most popular and influential restaurants of the 2010s that defined their city neighborhoods, which weren't particularly well-known for restaurants at the time (Bacar in SoMa and Eos in Cole Valley), while also cooking at some of the city's most notable restaurants before and after those restaurants (E&O Trading Co., Café Kati, Masa's). Nowadays, Wong is helping shape some of the most compelling food "at a bar" (with fellow excellent chef Phil West, who co-owned Range in the Mission for many years), where there's no doubt that The Treasury, Heartwood, and The Beehive are watering holes first, but the small and large plate creations are every bit as special as the drinks.

GERALD HIRIGOYEN

San Francisco diners are familiar with Basque cooking because of one restaurant: Piperade. Chef/owner Gerald Hirigoyen introduced many diners to his home region of Spain with dishes like garlic soup with rock shrimp, bacon, and egg, and a terrine with warm sheep's milk cheese and ham, drizzled with aged sherry. He also ran a great Basque tapas-centric restaurant called Bocadillos in the Jackson Square area for 13 years (that location is now the superb Maison Nico café-pastry shop–bakery). Hirigoyen announced that he will retire from Piperade in 2023.

SEÑOR SISIG

Of the dozens if not hundreds of clever food trucks to emerge after the 2008 recession, perhaps none has quite thrived in the subsequent decade like this Mexican-Filipino concept that still is a force on the food truck circuit but is also popular at its Mission and Ferry Building eateries.

BURMA SUPERSTAR

San Francisco is home to many cuisines, where oftentimes it's hard to pinpoint who really was the game changer for that cuisine in making city diners become knowledgeable. That isn't the case for Burmese dining. This Inner Richmond restaurant made its tea leaf salad and rainbow salad about as well-known as a Caesar salad in this town. It has subsequently expanded into various B Star and Burma Love locations.

OUTERLANDS

It takes a lot to convince San Franciscans to go to the far reaches of the Richmond or the Sunset to then wait in line for brunch. However, Outerlands (it's also the nickname for this stretch of the Outer Sunset near the beach) proved that the trek is worth it. It's a definitely homey yet modern Californian restaurant using all seasonal local ingredients for dinner, but also bringing that philosophy to weekend brunch and weekday lunch. The house-baked bread is among the very best in SF.

ZUNI CAFÉ

An alum of Stanford and Chez Panisse, the late Judy Rodgers may not have founded Zuni Café (it started as a Southwestern-Mexican cuisine restaurant in 1979), but she certainly made a monumental mark on the restaurant when she joined as the chef in 1987—and, in turn, had a tremendous impact on San Francisco dining history. Rodgers brought the Chez Panisse spirit to Zuni Café but also gave the urbane restaurant a unique California-meets-Mediterranean personality that has set the standard for what is usually considered San Francisco's definitive cuisine.

So, what's the next equivalent of Tadich Grill or Julius' Castle or The Mandarin or Chez Panisse? We'll see. In 2023, San Francisco is a city at a crossroads between struggling and thriving, where the COVID-19 pandemic shutdowns and expensive real estate market have made operating a restaurant in the city extraordinarily difficult. Downtown feels like a quiet suburb on Friday afternoons. Yet, it's easy to find restaurants filled with diners eating a $90 Wagyu steak or a $300 tasting menu on a random Tuesday night at 9 p.m.

That crossroads also refers to San Francisco dealing with its past and future. Rice-A-Roni might be the "San Francisco Treat," but that was definitely a thing of the post–World War II past. I live in San Francisco and have never even heard someone mention that "treat." Speaking of signature dessert treats, the beloved San Francisco ice cream sandwich IT'S-IT and Ghirardelli chocolate aren't even produced in San Francisco. With remote work, housing prices, and lack of building space, a lot of people and businesses simply can't or won't live or work in this city anymore. It's a problem, no matter how anyone tries to make it not look like one.

But, as we've seen time and time again, San Francisco is no stranger to facing challenges and adapting. We're a city that is familiar with climbing hills, whether by foot or cable car. Between all of those hills, the fog, the bay, the Pacific, and the diverse neighborhoods, there's that one part of the city that brings together its residents and visitors across centuries: food. It continues to be a city that loves to eat.

11 WAYS TO EAT LIKE A SAN FRANCISCAN

1. Not only do you know the listed farms/ranches/purveyors shown on the menu—you order dishes specifically because of the listed farms/ranches/purveyors.

2. You order soups and other cold-weather-style dishes more often in the summer than in the winter.

3. You make most of your reservations for dinner thirty days in advance—always when you literally have no idea if you will actually be free, and so you plan your activities and social life around those dinners.

4. You have no problem with standing in line for one to two hours to get a single food item because it's trendy or famous.

5. It isn't a baseball game without garlic fries. Hot dogs, peanuts, and Cracker Jack are skippable at a Giants game, but you couldn't possibly watch a game without Gilroy garlic fries.

6. Unless it's a Reuben, you almost aways order a sandwich on Dutch crunch.

7. The year is split in half—Dungeness crab season and not Dungeness crab season.

8. You expect every local restaurant to be farm to table these days, so it's almost shocking to hear a restaurant actually say that it is farm to table when it's usually just an assumed thing.

9. You have a favorite dim sum place and a go-to burrito spot. The city has many contenders for the "best" of those particular cuisine/dish niches. Ask fifty San Franciscans and you'll get about fifty different answers for both.

10. You think of the neighborhoods by restaurants...almost to the point that you forget which is which. Nopa is NoPa, Outerlands is the Outer Sunset, Zazie is Cole Valley, Piccino is Dogpatch, etc.

11. You're not in a hurry when dining out. You plan your days around eating. We celebrate our city's restaurants. The restaurants won't rush you, and you shouldn't rush the restaurant to get to your next stop. Stop, savor, and enjoy—it's the San Francisco way.

~~~~~~~~

HOW TO SOUND LIKE A LOCAL SAN FRANCISCO DINER

(Okay, before we get started, just never call the city "Frisco"! Frisco is a suburb of Dallas or a town near Breckenridge in Colorado's Rockies. Now, we can continue.)

BEAN TO BAR

This is the cacao-bean-to-chocolate equivalent of farm to table—a phrase that the Mission's Dandelion Chocolate loves to use.

CLAUDE THE CLAW

Are you skittish about seeing a fried chicken talon as you bite into lunch? One taste of this fried chicken sandwich at Birdbox (a pandemic pivot turned permanent by the elaborate tasting menu destination Birdsong) will change your mind.

CRAZY CRAB

The best food at Oracle Park and arguably the greatest Dungeness crab sandwich in SF! You'll find it in the centerfield area of the Giants' ballpark. It was also once upon a time in the 1980s the Giants' actual mascot for a very brief period.

CRUFFIN

Remember in the 2010s how croissant anything was the best way to go viral? Cronuts? San Francisco had the home of the cruffin (croissant-muffin), Mr. Holmes Bakehouse in Lower Nob Hill. It was seriously delicious. And then the wheels fell off, bankruptcy eventually ensued, and nobody even remembers cruffins anymore.

DOLORES PARK PICNIC

It means gather your friends; bring some halfway decent wine, your dog, and sandwiches or picnic provisions from a Mission purveyor; find a sunny spot in the Dolores Park (maybe something to...smoke...well, I won't comment on that); and enjoy the quintessential weekend staycation getaway within the city.

DORADO-STYLE BURRITO

The famous La Taqueria burrito in the Mission...except maybe even improved via this off-menu phrase requesting a griddled, extra-crunchy flour tortilla.

DUTCH CRUNCH

Forget about sourdough. San Franciscans usually ask for their sandwiches on the kind of giraffe-spotted roll that has just the right amount of fluff, crunchiness, and tanginess. It's sandwich bread perfection.

FOUR-DOLLAR TOAST

This was the phrase for the freshly baked bread by Josey Baker at The Mill on Divisadero that would be served as toast with excellent jam...and sold for $4! It became (unfairly) a symbol of all things gentrified and bougie. The cheapest toast now at The Mill is $5.50 (the cinnamon sugar one) and well worth it.

HOPR

Also known as the House of Prime Rib! But everyone really just calls it by its acronym, which means that a night of prime rib, martinis, and Yorkshire pudding revelry awaits.

HOT DOG BILL'S

It's...not actually a hot dog stand. Their specialty is a hot dog–shaped burger that golfers love at the prestigious Olympic Club in the far southwest corner of San Francisco. Most of us will never golf there, though, so we'll never eat the Burgerdog there. Luckily, there is now a Hot Dog Bill's stand at the Chase Center! So, you just have to pay $200 for a Warriors ticket instead to be able to enjoy what many San Franciscans think is the city's best burger in any shape.

IS THE GOLDEN GATE BAKERY OPEN?

Great question. I never know. The mythical egg tarts at this Chinatown bakery are truly magnificent—a delicate, melt-in-your-mouth, perfectly calibrated kind of sweet-creamy pastry treat. But the hours are resolutely unpredictable, so much so that there is a website/social media handle devoted to this entire question.

OLDEST DIM SUM IN AMERICA

That's the historic Hang Ah Tea Room, opened in 1920 and a must visit on any Chinatown eating and history tour.

RAVIOLO DI RICOTTA

This is decadent pasta heaven—a giant ravioli stuffed with ricotta and egg yolk, and the composition is then lightly coated in browned butter. It's the signature dish at Michael and Lindsay Tusk's wonderful Californian Italian spot in Jackson

Square, Cotogna, the less formal (not necessarily all that casual) next-door sibling to the couple's prominent fine dining powerhouse, Quince. The dish is probably best known as being the object of desire for every actual and wannabe Instagram influencer.

THE REBEL WITHIN

We all feel rebellious sometimes. This was essentially a rebellious muffin designed by pastry chef/baker William Werner, the founder of Craftsman and Wolves in the Mission. Muffins are usually kind of simple and dessert- or fruit-centric. This one is a soft-boiled egg–stuffed, sausage-and-cheese savory muffin that is basically breakfast all together in muffin form. It's absolutely delicious and, of course, popular with the food photography set.

SECRET BREAKFAST

When was the last time you put bourbon in your cornflakes? It's okay; no secrets here. We do it all the time in San Francisco...well, when it's bourbon–cornflakes ice cream, which is the signature flavor at Humphry Slocombe in the Mission (and now its other locations in the Bay Area).

Q&A, JOYCE GOLDSTEIN

COOKBOOK AUTHOR, FORMERLY CHEF/OWNER AT SQUARE ONE

From cooking at Chez Panisse during its early days to her own celebrated restaurant, Square One (located near the Embarcadero and Jackson Square by Sydney Walton Park), to spending decades visiting San Francisco's leading restaurants and markets, Joyce Goldstein is truly an authority on the city's dining scene and California cuisine. It was an honor to speak with Joyce in spring 2023 about her career and eating and cooking in the City by the Bay. (Note: This conversation has been edited for clarity and brevity.)

TF: You've had such a prolific career as a chef and cookbook author, so let's start at the beginning. How did you go that route and pursue a career in the culinary world and end up at Chez Panisse?

JG: Well, first, I have to explain that I grew up in Brooklyn with a very limited amount of ingredients used in my home cooking. And, then I got to live in Italy for a year and travel a lot in Europe, which completely changed my palate, changed my focus. And then, coming to San Francisco where we have a clientele that's pretty knowledgeable, where we have different farms and seasons—that sort of formed the direction where I was going. I was at Chez Panisse for three years running the café, and we got things delivered regularly every day from Greenleaf Produce, and they were connected to all the different farms. Obviously, the menu was very seasonal and very fresh because you got deliveries every day or every other day, so everything was in peak condition.

Then when I opened Square One, I did the same thing. I stayed with a lot of the same purveyors, but my menu was different because, at Chez Panisse, we did a little Italian and a lot of French. At Square One, we did Mediterranean, so we could have Greek food, Turkish food, French food, Italian food, Spanish food, all these things on the menu, and it made it more interesting for our customers because they were very regular. They came quite often during the week and you want to keep them engaged. So, you get a printout of what produce is available, you look at it, you order what you wanted, and then the stuff came in and you tasted it...and then you ran with it to see where you want to go.

TF: As you mentioned the different cuisines of the Mediterranean influencing the Square One menu and also studied in Italy, did you travel a lot around the Mediterranean?

JG: A lot. A lot of travel. And, also a lot of research. I'm a cookbook collector. I am an experimental diner. I'll try a restaurant if someone says it's good. I remember being in Spain one summer, where gazpacho was on every menu. And you tasted all of them until you got the one that you liked, and then you had something to measure toward when you were cooking at home. That was the flavor that you tried to reach. So, it just means paying attention to everything you put in your mouth and doing your homework.

TF: I'm just curious—there's so much folklore around Chez Panisse, and if I'm correct, Square One opened the same year that Stars did, in 1984—what was it like back then? Obviously, farm to table using peak, seasonal local produce is such a well-known, common thing now. But in San Francisco in 1984, was it kind of revolutionary? What was the dining scene like at that time?

JG: Well, there were two levels of diners. There were the really informed diners who went to farmers markets, who recognized the names of farmers, who were aware of seasons. And then there were the people who just went out to eat and wanted a good meal and a nice evening. But you had to cook one meal and you hoped that it would please the people who didn't know much about food, as well as please the ones that did. That was your goal—to make it so memorable that regulars knew what was on and the newcomers had their eyes opened.

TF: I'm sure you visit lots of restaurants in San Francisco now and read lots of cookbooks; how are things different now in San Francisco from the dozen-plus years that Square One was around?

JG: We have many, many more restaurants. We have less fusion food. We have points of view on a menu. We have chefs that are well-known and then places that are just popular. There's a greater variety for people. In the '80s, there were really so few restaurants. And now, there are hundreds and hundreds. So, you have to find your audience and the audience has to find you. You have to keep it interesting. You have to use good-quality ingredients. People in San Francisco know good ingredients, shop at the farmers markets, recognize farmers' names. They're knowledgeable, and they expect to be delighted and hopefully learn something new in eating something on the menu.

TF: Looking toward the future now, what restaurants excite you now? Who do you think is sort of leading the charge forward?

JG: Well, it isn't so much like that . . . I like to go where I like the flavors, the palate, the selection of recipes. I probably am fairly narrow-minded because there are certain things I like and certain things that don't interest me at all. I like eating at Nopa...love its food. I eat at Delfina. I eat at Perbacco. I eat at Yank Sing quite a bit. I eat at Kitchen Istanbul. You know, any place that has a menu with food that is interesting to me, then I'm a good supporter and I'm loyal.

TF: For people who might be new to San Francisco, what are some of the farmers markets they should really know about?

JG: I go to the Ferry Plaza Farmers Market. We [Joyce and her daughter-in-law] go on Saturdays, usually very early before the mobs come in, and there are some farms that I go to first to see what they have. I taste if I can or smell at least. There are some farms that you can consistently count on for having good stuff.

TF: I'm curious since I never had the opportunity to dine at Square One, did Square One have any signature dish or dishes?

JG: Square One changed its menu *every day* from top to bottom. The only things that repeated were oysters and Caesar salad. Everything else changed because our focus was Mediterranean, so you might have in one day a Turkish dish, two Italian ones, a Spanish one, a Greek one, depending on what produce was available and what it inspired us to make. We had a very varied menu. If people were coming in on a certain day of the week, they could call me up and I could put it on the menu because the menu changed so often—you want to make people happy.

We had a very loyal staff. Most of our people in the kitchen stayed ten years or longer, which makes life a lot easier.

TF: Wow, that doesn't seem to exist much these days in San Francisco, unfortunately.

JG: Yes, we had a very loyal staff and very loyal customers.

TF: Okay, last question. I have to ask because you mentioned the Caesar as a signature. What's the secret sauce to a great Caesar salad?

JG: Good anchovies (packed in good oil), good garlic—not rancid garlic. Excellent olive oil and fresh lemon juice. That's it. It's not a very complicated dish. Good lemons for tartness. Extra-virgin olive oil. The right amount of salt and pepper. And, beautiful, beautiful romaine.

MICHAEL BAUER

TF: When you arrived in San Francisco and started with the Chronicle in 1986, what do you remember were some of the signature restaurants of SF at the time? If my chronology seems correct, some of the eventual classics like Stars and Square One were quite new then, while longtime fine dining standards like Ernie's and Carnelian Room were just a couple years from closing?

MB: When I accepted the position of food editor at *The Chronicle* in 1986 I had only been to San Francisco once, to attend a conference. At that time the three restaurants I made a point of visiting were Stars, Square One, and Chez Panisse. Frankly I wasn't in love with San Francisco, based on my one visit, but from my time in Kansas City and Dallas I knew that the Bay Area was a food mecca not only for its restaurants but for its coffee, chocolate, bread, cheese, and wine. I came here because the area was ripe for coverage. I planned to stay only about five years, but the longer I was here I found more and more layers of the food scene to peel back.

TF: During your thirty-two years at the newspaper, it's remarkable to see how food media went from a niche part of the SF media landscape to the sensation it is now, with the internet and podcasts—everyone pretty much thinks they are a dining critic. Back in 1986, how did restaurants play a role in San Francisco society? Were they even close to as beloved and followed as they are today?

MB: San Franciscans have always loved food: that didn't start with the internet. In fact, I think our love of food can be traced back to the Gold Rush, after which San Francisco became a major financial and recreational hub. At that time there were houses of prostitution on just about every corner. In fact, one of the most popular restaurants in the 1870s and 1880s was Jack's, which closed several decades ago but goes back to 1864. Many people didn't realize that, when it opened, the restaurant was on the first floor and the girls were sequestered upstairs. Many of the houses began offering the "free lunch" where men would dine and then meet the girls. The food became the lure and since that time there's always been a link between food and carnal pleasure.

TF: Are there any major pre-1960s chefs or restaurants that you've learned about over the years who played a pivotal role in setting the stage for San Francisco to become the world-class restaurant city it is today? From my research, it seems

like there's the early Tadich-John's-Sam's-Swan Oyster Gold Rush and post-earthquake era, and then it seems to pick up again with the iconic 1960s and 1970s places like The Mandarin, Chez Panisse, and Ernie's?

MB: There have been shining stars in most decades. Victor Hertzler is considered one of the first celebrity chefs dating to when he took over the kitchens of the St. Francis Hotel after the 1906 earthquake. You still find his creation, Celery Victor, on some menus. Since the 1950s, San Francisco has been a center for Chinese cuisine, led by The Mandarin, which opened around 1960 and closed in 2006. Cecilia Chiang created an elegant Chinese restaurant with high-quality artwork, custom-made McGuire chairs, and many dishes she introduced to America including potstickers, minced squab, and beggar's chicken. Even today I'd be hard pressed to name a Chinese restaurant that met her standard. She was always resplendent in fashions she created herself. In fact, around 2015 Saks featured several dozen of her outfits in a special exhibit during Chinese New Year.

Also in the late 1950s, Alice Chan started Yank Sing, which is still considered one of the top dim sum houses in San Francisco. And we can't forget that the oldest dim sum house in the United States is Hang Ah Tea Room, which opened in 1920 and is still in business today.

I'd be remiss in not mentioning Vic Bergeron, who in 1934 opened Hinky Dink's in Oakland and became internationally famous when he moved across the Bay and opened Trader Vic's in 1951. It closed in 1994 and is now the home of Le Colonial. Bergeron is largely responsible for the popularity of tiki drinks (Mai Tai, etc.) in the 1950s and 1960s and for his fantastical blend of cultures, creating such menu items as crab rangoon. The Tonga Room in the Fairmont Hotel opened in 1945 and continues to carry on the tiki tradition.

The Asian trend was taken to new heights when China Moon opened in 1986 and Barbara Tropp gained an international reputation for her meticulous food. Charles Phan lifted Vietnamese food to new heights when he opened the original Slanted Door in 1995, along with Betelnut, which opened the same year.

TF: What cooking inspirations and SF restaurants do you think of when you hear the term "California cuisine" that we writers use all the time? Is it just farm to table as a different phrase?

MB: Of course, the freshness of the product is one thing that set "California cuisine" apart, but it also is in the blending of cultures and the fact that chefs replaced heavy sauces with vinaigrettes and salsas. In general it evokes the feeling of a lighter cuisine. That said, I think this style led to the small plate trend that started at such restaurant like Chez Nous, which opened in 2000 and closed in 2007 (now the home of SPQR).

TF: Before San Francisco, you lived and wrote in the Midwest and Texas. Were there any hints at a Chez Panisse–like farm-to-table movement in other parts of the country during the 1960s and 1970s, like we had in the Bay Area?

MB: I don't think there was in the 1970s when I was in Kansas City. When I moved to Dallas in 1982, places like Stephan Pyles's Routh Street Café sourced local products, but it wasn't called "farm to table." At that time Pyles and a group of other chefs were trying to define and refine a "new Southwestern cuisine."

TF: Back to SF, your 2016 article looking back at the 30 most important restaurants of your first 30 years as critic is a must-read for anyone interested in SF's food scene and why it is so prominent today. Are there any on that list that still really stand out to you or deserve to be more revered like how Stars and Chez Panisse still are?

MB: There are almost too many to mention. Many restaurants added to the dining scene. It was more incremental than revolutionary. The French Laundry is certainly a restaurant that deserves the accolades because of the way the restaurant made the Napa Valley an international dining destination.

In light of the current attack on transgender people, I'm struck as to how important AsiaSF really is. The restaurant, which opened in 1998, celebrated what at the time they called "gender illusionists." The food is an Asian mishmash and the entertainment has evolved over the years. Some performers are transexual or in the process of sex change but they work in a totally accepting environment that celebrates rather than denigrates.

TF: Now that you can dine out without a few newspaper review deadlines each week, what are the new and/or old places that you love going back to in SF? Which places are you really excited about and might go in a hypothetical 40 Restaurants of 40 Years list.

MB: In my thirty-plus years of dining out every night, I never got tired of the ritual. To me, restaurants, even those with mediocre food, are fun to go to. The positive side is that I don't have to continually chase the new restaurants and can enjoy time and again restaurants I enjoy.

On many weekends you can find me at Eliza's, where you can get a whole Peking duck for $24.85. I continue to love several Italian restaurants including Delfina, A16, and Cotogna. I appreciate the family ownership, pricing, and food at such classics as Original Joe's and House of Prime Rib. I'm happy that Annie Ho has opened her follow-up to the burned-out Hong Kong Lounge II with HK Lounge Bistro. I also love going to Boulevard, Gary Danko, and Trestle. Nopa and Rich Table remain among my favorites. I also plan to restart my tradition of going to The French Laundry around Christmastime.

If I was doing a story subsequent to the thirty-year piece I'd include Corey Lee's San Ho Won for his dynamic interpretation of Korean food. I'd also include Francis Ang and his take on Filipino food at Abacá. Then there's Val Cantu and his refined take on Mexican food at Californios. I also was very impressed by the Indian food masterminded by Sri Gopinathan at Copra.

And there's SingleThread Farm in Healdsburg where Kyle and Katina Connaughton rightfully deserve their three Michelin stars.

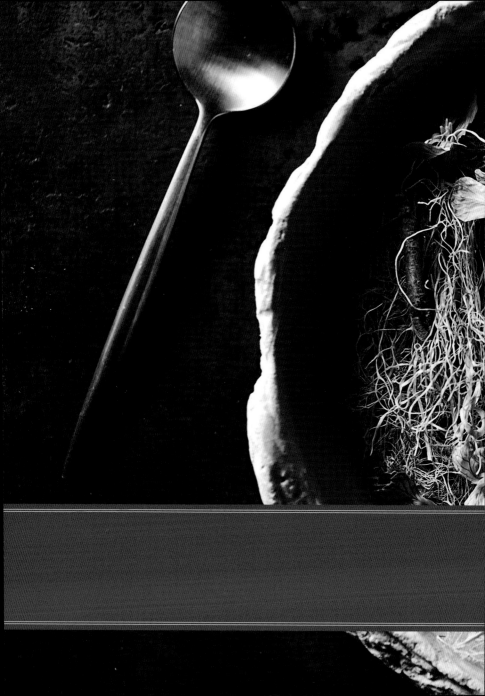

APPETIZERS AND
SMALL PLATES

KOMBU-CURED SHIMA AJI WITH SMOKED BUTTERMILK SAUCE AND RADISH

NIGHTBIRD, KIM ALTER

An evening at Nightbird is just as mesmerizing as *The Nutcracker* or the symphony at the nearby War Memorial Opera House and Davies Symphony Hall. Chef Kim Alter's tasting menu is consistently thoughtful, innovative, and distinctly seasonal—pushing the envelope without feeling like it's trying too hard to be ultramodernist or flashy. Each of the riveting courses is honest, delicious food, except that you probably can't make it at home. Except, you can! Here's your chance with a dish that perfectly represents the kind of early course a diner at Nightbird would enjoy. Alter kindly cut each part of the dish into a very specific, organized order.

YIELD: Allot 2 oz. fish per person; servings will vary

SHIMA AJI

1 FILLET SHIMA AJI, SKIN ON

1 SHEET KOMBU

FRESH LEMON JUICE, TO TASTE

KOSHER SALT, TO TASTE

1. Break down the shima aji. Place the kombu on top of the flesh and cure the fish for 12 to 24 hours in the refrigerator.

2. Remove the kombu (use it to make the dashi, below). Remove the skin and slice the aji thinly for presentation.

3. Right before serving, sprinkle a few drops of lemon juice on the flesh and season with salt.

ESPELETTE OIL

1 CUP CHOPPED ESPELETTE PEPPERS

1 CUP OLIVE OIL

KOSHER SALT, TO TASTE

1. Toast the peppers in a dry skillet over low heat for 2 to 3 minutes. Cover them with the oil and remove the pan from heat.

2. Let the oil cool, season with salt, and strain.

continued...

DASHI

800 G FILTERED WATER   **20 G KOMBU**

1. In a small pot over low to medium heat, combine the water and kombu. Do not boil. Barely simmer until flavor is present. Strain.

- Alter does not add bonito for this recipe, but you can if you want more depth of flavor or to use the dashi for a soup or broth later.

BUTTERMILK SAUCE

200 G BUTTERMILK   **15 G LIQUID SHIO KOJI**
30 G DASHI (SEE ABOVE)   **KOSHER SALT, TO TASTE**
10 G FRESH LEMON JUICE

1. Cold smoke the buttermilk, using applewood chips. Add the dashi, lemon juice, and shio koji and season to taste with salt.

BLACK VINEGAR GELEE

400 G DASHI   **1.5% SHEET GELATIN BY WEIGHT**
19 G SHIO KOJI   **½ SHALLOT**
20 G BLACK VINEGAR

1. In a small pot, combine the dashi, shio koji, black vinegar, and shallot. Bring to a boil.

2. Add the gelatin, then strain and place in the refrigerator.

3. Once solidified, break the gelee into small pieces to cover the fish.

CHIVE OIL

4 BUNCHES FRESH CHIVES

KOSHER SALT, TO TASTE

1 CUP OLIVE OIL

1. Blanch the chives in lightly salted boiling water, then transfer to an ice bath. Remove from the ice bath, squeeze all excess water out, and chop.

2. Transfer the chives to a blender, season with salt, and blend. Add ice cubes if needed, to help break up the chives and keep them cold.

3. Slowly drizzle the olive oil into the blender while it is running. Strain the chive oil through a filter.

PLATING AND GARNISH

1 BUNCH RED RADISHES

MICROGREENS LIKE SHISO
AND KOHLRABI

BABY RADISHES AND RADISH
FLOWERS

1. Chill the plates. Clean the radishes and julienne. Place the radish on one side of the plate.

2. Lay the seasoned and sliced fish on top. Spoon the black vinegar gelee over the fish.

3. Garnish with the microgreens, baby radishes and radish flowers. Pool the buttermilk sauce and oils on the side.

MICHAEL MINA'S TUNA TARTARE

MICHAEL MINA, VARIOUS RESTAURANTS
PAST AND PRESENT, INCLUDING AQUA

San Francisco has its Mount Rushmore of historical dishes (cioppino, crab Louie, hangtown fry, etc.). This signature dish from one of the city's most iconic present-day chefs would certainly go in the modern equivalent of that collection. Tuna tartare has become a bit of a cliché starter on menus throughout the country, but this Mina version with the pivotal trio of pine nuts, chilies/jalapeños, and Asian pear remains the genre's gold standard.

Michael Mina arrived in San Francisco the day before the 1989 Loma Prieta earthquake to help open Aqua as the chef de cuisine with celebrated chef George Morrone, and he persevered from that inauspicious start to eventually work at Aqua for over a decade and become one of the city's most legendary chefs. This tuna tartare was created by him at Aqua in 1991 and has pretty much followed him everywhere throughout his career.

YIELD: 1 to 2 servings

HABANERO SESAME OIL

1 CUP TOASTED SESAME OIL **¼ HABANERO CHILI**

1. Place the oil in a small pot with the habanero and heat until about 120°F/49°C.

2. Remove from the heat and let cool to room temperature.

3. Strain and store.

continued...

TUNA TARTARE

4 OZ. AHI TUNA (SUSHI GRADE), CUT INTO SMALL DICE

PINCH FRESH MINT CHIFFONADE

⅛ TEASPOON MINCED GARLIC

2 TEASPOONS TOASTED PINE NUTS

½ TEASPOON EQUAL PARTS FINELY MINCED JALAPEÑO, FRESNO, AND HABANERO CHILIES

2 TABLESPOONS SMALL-DICED PEELED ASIAN PEAR

⅛ TEASPOON ANCHO CHILE POWDER

½ TEASPOON HABANERO SESAME OIL (SEE PAGE 51)

⅛ TEASPOON MALDON SALT

¼ TEASPOON KOSHER SALT (MORE OR LESS, IF DESIRED)

1 QUAIL EGG YOLK

2 SLICES PULLMAN/WHITE BREAD, TOASTED, CRUST REMOVED AND CUT IN HALF CORNER TO CORNER

1. Combine all the ingredients, except the bread, in a mixing bowl. Toss to combine well.

2. Transfer the mixture to a chilled bowl. Refrigerate until ready to serve.

3. Shingle the toast with the tuna mixture. If you like, you can have fun and shape the tuna mixture into a heart shape or with a ring mold. Serve immediately.

CAVIAR SOBA

GOZU, MARC ZIMMERMAN

After several years as executive chef of Alexander's Steakhouse, one of the city's best and glitziest steak palaces, Marc Zimmerman set off on his own with a fantastic, intimate restaurant near the Embarcadero serving intricate tasting menus that incorporate Wagyu beef into every dish. Sometimes it's subtle (like in this spectacular soba-evoking dish), and other times it's ultra-high-quality Wagyu beef kissed by the flame of the restaurant's centerpiece robata grill.

The caviar course is the first course following canapés. It sets the tone for the menu to come. Buckwheat is lightly toasted over the fire and infused into soy milk that is then made into a silken "tofu." Flavors of cold soba (chive, shiso, wasabi, lemon) accompany and caviar allows the other flavors to play just as much a role in the dish as the caviar itself. Beef is fermented with koji, water, and salt to create a Wagyu shoyu that is then made into a sauce that ties everything together. We often speak in the restaurant about the nuance of Wagyu. This Wagyu kaeshi sauce defines that nuance. Beef is certainly present but is playing a much different role than it traditionally does. This speaks to much of our cuisine at Gozu.

—Chef Zimmerman

YIELD: 4 servings

continued...

Caviar Soba
See page 53

WAGYU GARUM KAESHI

KAESHI BASE

225 G SAKE

300 G MIRIN

320 G BEEF GARUM TEA

30 G GRANULATED SUGAR

30 G BONITO, SHAVED

20 G RAUSU KOMBU

1. In a rondeau, reduce the sake by half. (Weigh the sake and pot before heating and after reduced.)

2. Add the mirin and bring to a simmer.

3. Add the beef garum tea and sugar. Stir to dissolve the sugar.

4. Pour into a container. Add the bonito shavings and kombu to infuse.

5. The kaeshi can stay like this with the bonito and kombu. In fact, it will age well like this.

KAESHI FOAM

500 G KAESHI BASE

200 G WAGYU DASHI

18 G VERSAWHIP

1.2 G XANTHAN GUM

15 G ULTRATEX 8

1. Blend all the ingredients using an immersion blender with the blending attachment. Set aside.

BUCKWHEAT SILKEN TOFU
(MAKES 10 SERVINGS)

TOFU BASE

500 G BUCKWHEAT GROATS

1 GALLON HODO SOY MILK (THICK VERSION FOR TOFU MAKING)

1. Roast the buckwheat at 330°F/165°C, fan 4, 100% humidity, for 15 minutes.

2. Meanwhile, pour the soy milk into a 6- or 8-quart Cambro (reserve the jug for storage).

3. Once the buckwheat is golden brown, add to the soy milk straight out of the oven while still hot. Blend with an immersion blender for about 90 seconds.

4. Pass through a fine-mesh fabric bag.

5. Pour the liquid back into the gallon jug.

TO SET TOFU:

360 G TOFU BASE

28.8 G KAPPA CARRAGEENAN

18 G BALEINE SEA SALT

1. Heat the tofu base in a pot to 158°F/70°C.

2. Add the salt and kappa. Whisk.

3. Pass through a strainer.

5. Quickly portion 36 g into each of 10 cups or serving dishes of choice.

6. Let the tofu set at room temperature, then refrigerate.

continued...

FROZEN MEYER LEMON CELLS

MEYER LEMON SEGMENTS, SEEDED

LIQUID NITROGEN

WOODEN MALLET OR HAMMER

1. Arrange the lemon segments in a single layer in a half hotel pan. Do not place this directly on a counter! Pad with wood or towels to protect the counter surface.

2. Slowly and carefully pour liquid nitrogen over the lemon cells.

3. Give the lemon cells time to freeze.

4. Smash the frozen segments with the mallet.

5. Place in a container and store in the freezer until ready to use.

PLATING
(PER PORTION)

PINCH THINLY SLICED FRESH CHIVES

½ TASTING SPOON FROZEN MEYER LEMON CELLS

BUCKWHEAT SILKEN TOFU (SEE PAGE 57)

KAESHI FOAM (SEE PAGE 56)

8 G KALUGA CAVIAR

3 DROPS WASABI OIL

3 SHISO FLOWERS AND LEAVES

1. Arrange the chives and frozen Meyer lemon cells on the tofu.

2. Spoon enough of the foam over to cover.

3. Add the caviar.

4. Finish with the drops of wasabi oil and the shiso flowers and leaves.

SWEETBREADS WITH BLACK CURRY

NISEI, DAVID YOSHIMURA

Before you hesitate at the idea of sweetbreads, give this outstanding dish a try. David Yoshimura started Nisei as a pop-up (after the chef cooked at Californios and several of the greatest fine dining spots in the world), and it has subsequently evolved to be a powerhouse brick-and-mortar tasting menu destination on bustling Polk Street at the base of Russian Hill. Yoshimura is one of the city's great young culinary stars, receiving a Michelin star a year after opening in 2021. Nisei's menu weaves together his Japanese American heritage in a beautiful series of courses, and this Japanese black curry is undoubtedly one of the riveting headliners.

The cuisine at Nisei can be described as contemporary Japanese American cuisine, highlighting the best ingredients of California; and no dish represents my personal style as well as the Japanese Black Curry. Japanese curry in itself is a Japanese dish adopted from different cultures and is very popular amongst Asian Americans. Nisei takes this humble dish and elevates it by making a complex curry recipe from scratch, adding earthy sweetbreads to match the rich sauce, and finally complementing the dish with local chanterelle mushrooms and fermented Napa cabbage. Everything we source for the dish comes to Nisei from the bounty of California: sweetbreads, mushrooms, and all produce used for the curry. The hakusai (fermented Napa cabbage) is a very traditional Japanese pickle, which is made in-house to cleanse the palate while enjoying the curry.

—Chef Yoshimura

continued...

BLACK CURRY

300 G YELLOW ONION, SLICED	1 G CLOVES
100 G CARROT, SLICED	2 CARDAMOM PODS
50 G CELERY, SLICED	1 CINNAMON STICK
50 G FRESH GINGER, CHOPPED	4 G SHIO KOMBU
200 G BANANA	1 BAY LEAF
600 G GREEN APPLE, CORED AND CHOPPED	1 TABLESPOON HONEY
100 ML GRAPESEED OIL	70 ML SAKE
SALT, TO TASTE	2,500 ML CHICKEN STOCK
6 G CUMIN	100 ML KOIKUCHI SOY SAUCE
12 G CORIANDER	100 ML MIRIN
2 G TURMERIC	1 TABLESPOON SQUID INK
4 G FENNEL	4 TABLESPOONS BUTTER, SOFTENED
1 G CAYENNE PEPPER	

1. Robot-coupe all the vegetables and fruit.

2. Place the grapeseed oil in a rondeau and warm it over medium-high heat. Transfer the puree to the rondeau. Season with salt and add all the herbs and spices. Stir in the honey.

4. Deglaze with the sake, then the stock.

5. Simmer for 1 hour.

6. Blend and pass through a strainer.

7. Season with the koikuchi, mirin, and salt. Stir in the squid ink.

8. Finish with the butter right before serving.

SWEETBREADS

5 LBS. BEEF SWEETBREADS, CLEANED

SALT, TO TASTE

MIREPOIX (2 ONIONS, 1 CARROT, 1 STALK CELERY, 1 CLOVE GARLIC)

BUTTERMILK, AS NEEDED

DREDGE OF EQUAL PARTS ALL-PURPOSE FLOUR AND CORNMEAL

RICE BRAN OIL, FOR FRYING

1. Brine the sweetbreads overnight in a solution that is 1% salt, then drain.

2. Heat 12 quarts water to 180°F/82°C. Add salt, the sweetbreads, and mirepoix and poach for 1 hour, maintaining the temperature.

3. Drain and peel the outer membrane from the sweetbreads.

4. Portion the sweetbreads and cover with buttermilk.

5. Drain the sweetbreads and dredge in the flour/cornmeal mixture.

6. Heat the oil to 350°F/177°C. Fry the sweetbreads.

7. Dip the sweetbreads in the black curry, plate, and serve.

STEAK TARTARE

MILLER & LUX, WAYFARE TAVERN, TYLER FLORENCE

There's no doubt that Tyler Florence knows how to cook beef (one of SF's finest burgers is found in his original restaurant, Wayfare Tavern)—or, in the case of steak tartare, to not cook but beautifully season it. His Mission Bay restaurant, Miller & Lux, is an absolute marvel of posh, clubby steak house design (leather booths that can fit a party of eight), but this tartare might just be as special as the setting and the bay view. Beef tartare and basketball. What a natural pairing! Serve the tartare cold with warm potato chips or sourdough crostini.

YIELD: 1 serving

---

4 OZ. CHILLED RAW BEEF FILET, FINELY MINCED

1 TABLESPOON CHOPPED CAPERS

1 TABLESPOON MINCED SHALLOT

1½ TEASPOONS MAYONNAISE

1 TEASPOON DIJON MUSTARD

2 TEASPOONS MINCED FRESH CHIVES

2 TO 3 DASHES HOT SAUCE (TYLER LIKES TABASCO)

2 TEASPOONS EXTRA-VIRGIN OLIVE OIL, PLUS MORE TO FINISH

JUICE OF ¼ LEMON

¾ TEASPOON KOSHER SALT

½ TEASPOON FRESHLY CRACKED BLACK PEPPER

1 EGG YOLK

5 OR 6 LEAVES FRISÉE LETTUCE

1 RADISH, THINLY SHAVED

3 TO 5 FRESH PARSLEY LEAVES

1. Place the beef, capers, shallot, mayonnaise, mustard, chives, hot sauce, olive oil, lemon juice, salt, and pepper in a small bowl and fold together until it is mixed evenly.

continued...

2. Pack the beef mixture into a 4-inch ring mold in the center of a 9-inch salad plate. Press evenly into the mold, leaving a small indent in the center of the mold.

3. Remove the ring mold and place the egg yolk in the indent.

4. Garnish the top of the tartare, around the egg yolk, with the frisée lettuce, shaved radish, and parsley leaves.

5. Drizzle the top with a little olive oil to finish.

Q&A, VIRGINIA MILLER

ACADEMY CHAIR, WEST NORTH AMERICA, THE WORLD'S 50 BEST
RESTAURANTS; DINING CRITIC, *THE BOLD ITALIC*

TF: Before we go down the endless road of talking about SF dining history and trends, let's hear what everyone wants to know, since very few, if any, people dine at more new restaurants in San Francisco than you. When you aren't checking out the constant stream of new places, where do you return to again and again?

VM: I always say I don't have the luxury of being a regular anywhere, not only with my constant dining everywhere in SF and the Bay Area for 22 years, but traveling half of every month elsewhere internationally for the same. So, if I visit a place two or three times in a year, it means it's one of my most beloved. To name just a spare few I can't get enough of over the years: Cafe Jacqueline, Tony's Pizza Napoletana, State Bird Provisions, Capo's, Rich Table, Anchor Oyster Bar, Breadbelly, b. Patisserie, True Laurel, Mandalay (Burmese), Kin Khao, Swan Oyster Depot, La Taqueria, Sorrel, Palette Tea House, Flour + Water, Lazy Bear, Sasa Japanese, Aedan Koji Kitchen, Chili House, Lily (Vietnamese), Helmand Palace (Afghani), and on and on.

TF: Of the thousands of restaurants across San Francisco, is there a particular theme or style of cooking that you'd describe as the city's signature culinary hallmark and what sets us apart from New York, Paris, LA, etc.?

VM: There are a few key signatures SF excels in, from the nation's only longtime (since the 1980s) rich Burmese restaurant culture, to our historic SF-style seafood houses (e.g., crab Louie and cioppino both have their roots in SF), to robust Filipino and Mexican restaurants from vibrant populations since the 1800s, to the nation's first and oldest Chinatown and Japantown and all the food cultures that has sparked over a century, just to name a few. But to focus in, one area we excel at is fine dining that is distinctly Californian, meaning a bold, innovative, pioneering mash-up of cultures showcasing our best-in-the-world ingredients and soil—and with farm to table launched as a trend in the Bay Area since the 1970s, long before anywhere else, local and seasonal are in SF's roots and standard at most places, not a trend.

As fabulous as L.A. is, and I partly grew up there and just outside NYC, fine dining has never been L.A.'s strong suit, even as it slowly improves in that area. SF has excelled at this for decades with visionary restaurants that combine the best of the rich diversity of California, which holds the US's biggest populations of most Asian countries, heavy populations of Europeans and Latin Americans and, of course, our roots in Mexico and (by far) the largest US Mexican population.

We have also long been the baking capital of the nation. Back in the 1800s when we put sourdough on the map and were lined with Filipino bakeries, etc. When Acme changed the artisanal baking game in 1970s Berkeley. [Since 2002] when Tartine sparked a global pastry and bread renaissance as Chad Robertson and Elisabeth Prueitt's example schooled bakers the world over. The wealth of world-class bakeries (b. Patisserie, Neighbor Bakehouse, et al.), and award-winning bakers (Belinda Leong, Josey Baker, William Werner, etc.) and one-of-a-kind bakeries (Breadbelly, Juniper, etc.), as well as all the superb breads that have long been standard in-house from SF's fine dining to midrange restaurants.

TF: You've been writing about San Francisco restaurants for decades now. How has the city changed when it comes to the dining experience—both in terms of what's on the plate and atmosphere?

VM: Twenty-two years here, I've spent my adult life studying food and drink everywhere in the Bay Area, with NYC and LA area roots and constant US global travels (I've "researched" at over 13,000 restaurants and counting!). SF was and remains one of the best dining cities anywhere, a place that schooled me ever since I arrived and accelerated my passion for food and drink into expertise. The quality-per-capita level is so much higher here than any city I've been to in over 40 countries and 42 states. The sheer volume of world-class offerings in a small city space was overwhelming then and remains so now. If anything, it is more sophisticated now. When I first moved here in 2001, spots like Bacar and Chris Cosentino's ahead-of-its-time Incanto were game changers with "whole package" offerings in food and drink, Foreign Cinema was barely two years old, Slanted Door was still in its original Mission location, and I was smitten with all of the above. Patricia Unterman's great *Food Lover's Guide* was my bible. I visited every single place in her books my initial years, as I did every single restaurant in the Zagat and TimeOut restaurant books, and well beyond getting to know SF's small, intimate neighborhoods.

While rightly revered classics like Zuni Café, BIX, and Boulevard still reigned at the time, we lost some greats over the years that expressed their own unique take on Bay Area cuisine, like Bar Tartine (how I still miss chef Nick Balla's still unparalleled anywhere, cutting-edge Hungarian-meets-Japanese cooking!), Anthony Myint and Karen Leibowitz's truly cutting-edge Mission Street Food (which eventually led to Mission Chinese), Jason Fox's killer (Michelin-starred) Commonwealth, innovative AQ, Chris Cosentino's unparalleled Italian Incanto, Jeff Banker and Lori Baker's Baker & Banker, modern Japanese at Bushi-Tei, modern Vietnamese great Bong Su, and so many others. But for every one of those, there are hundreds of treasures that are still going strong, whether for decades (Acquerello, Anchor Oyster Bar, etc.) or the past decade plus (Aziza, Flour + Water, Delfina, Atelier Crenn, State Bird Provisions, Rich Table, SPQR, Sons & Daughters, etc.). And there are so many more newcomers even just in the last two years pushing innovation and deliciousness rarely seen in many cities, like Nisei, Osito, Aphotic, Copra, etc.

TF: Most SF diners don't think of the city's food history much beyond the opening of Chez Panisse (in Berkeley) and then the farm-to-table movement afterward. But the city truly did have a robust food history for decades preceding the 1970s, right?

VM: Absolutely. Whether cocktails/cocktail bars being born as the world knows them now mainly in SF, NYC, and New Orleans, SF's cocktail world of the 1850s on was insane when Jerry Thomas ran bars here and pisco first came to North America. So was SF's deep roots pioneering craft coffee in numerous movements since the 1800s (read the fascinating *Bay Area Coffee: A Stimulating History* by Monika Trobits).

Since the 1800s on, many movements and dishes grew out of SF, from the nation's bread and chocolate renaissance since Boudin Bakery started the sourdough craze in 1849 and Ghirardelli launched artisanal chocolate in 1852, to SF being THE city that mainstreamed Chinese food in America with its deep 1800s Chinese population and by popularizing the "gateway" of Americanized Chinese food that took the nation by storm in the 1950s, from chop suey to egg foo yung, dishes created by Chinese in SF. Also, iconic dishes from cioppino to crab Louie all have their roots here. [The] earliest and densest Filipino, Japanese, Chinese, etc., neighborhoods, restaurants, and bakeries [have been] part of SF's fabric since the 1800s.

TF: Who are some of the restaurants/chefs/personalities that you think of when considering the key influencers for setting the stage for San Francisco to become the world-class food city it is today?

VM: Of course, we have wonderful representatives who showcase what we do globally, like the amazing Dominique Crenn and Kyle and Katina Connaughton at SingleThread in Healdsburg. And pioneers like the great Suzette Gresham of two-Michelin-starred Acquerello since 1989, who is a shining example for chefs everywhere. But there are many who continue to create some of the best food in the nation and launch amazing chefs.

Just a few: Stuart Brioza and Nicole Krasinski of State Bird Provisions, The Progress, and The Anchovy Bar, with current chef, [the] great Gaby Maeda. Evan and Sarah Rich of Rich Table, which launched the career of Brandon Rice, who went on to open the delightful Ernest, and currently Rich Table's talented Gizela Ho. For over twenty years, Mourad Lahlou (Aziza and Mourad) [has been] crafting modern Moroccan food like nowhere in the US. Same with Pim Techamuanvivit's Thai cuisine at Kin Khao and Nari. There is no fine dining restaurant quite like David Barzelay's two-Michelin Lazy Bear. Or neighborhood gem Sorrel from Alex Hong. There is the ever-great restaurant duo of Angler and Saison. And some of the best Italian fine dining and pasta anywhere at Flour + Water (Thomas McNaughton and Ryan Pollnow), Quince (Michael Tusk), SPQR and Mattina (Matthew Accarrino), and Acquerello (Suzette Gresham). Gifted Mexican chefs abound in SF, like longtime great Gonzalo Guzmán of Nopalito. There is nowhere in the nation serving modern Filipino food quite like what Francis Ang does at Abacá. Or modern Guamanian food like Shawn Naputi and Shawn Camacho do at Prubechu. The list goes on, but chefs like these are the fabric of our city and draw and hone so much talent around them.

TF: And who are some of the current chefs you think are defining San Francisco cuisine of the 2020s?

VM: As mentioned, chefs Gaby Maeda (State Bird) and Gizela Ho (Rich Table) are two of our most gifted young female chefs I could see opening their own spots at some point. There is no menu quite like the cured fish and Champagne/White Burgundy collection at Robbie Wilson's fab Le Fantastique. Chef Anya El-Wattar of Birch & Rye is crafting modern Russian cuisine with heart like nowhere else in the nation.

New chefs making big waves and innovating (some earning Michelin stars right out of the gate) are David Yoshimura of Nisei, Osito's Seth Stowaway, Aphotic's Peter Hemsley, and Copra's longtime Indian chef, [the] great Srijith "Sri" Gopinathan (previously of the only two-Michelin Indian restaurant in the nation, Campton Place in SF). Since 2018, chef Alex Hong of Sorrel and Rodney Wages of Avery are also among our boundary-pushing best showcasing SF. So are the exciting modern Korean restaurants and chefs, like SSAL, San Ho Won, Suragan, and Bansang.

TF: One of the unique attributes of San Francisco dining is the mix of quiet neighborhood spots and then nearby are the most elaborate of tasting menu spots in the country. How does the city pull off this huge spectrum of dining destinations?

VM: It really is an unparalleled feat for a city this small mileagewise with such global excellence at all levels. It's in huge part to the unique beauty and unparalleled ingredients of SF and the surrounding regions (not to mention being the epicenter of drink, from wine countries to the United States' most vibrant, pioneering craft distillers since the early 1980s). But it's also due to SF's since-infancy history of pushing boundaries, being open to all manner of people and creative movements, and the city's cutting-edge, leading-the-way innovation in everything from food and the arts to the environment and tech.

TF: Finally, San Francisco has so many excellent off-the-tourist-beaten-path neighborhoods and restaurants. Where should readers visit that they might not read about (except in your articles!)?

VM: I've mentioned so many gems already, but I'd encourage visitors to spend their time in our neighborhoods as our tiny, wildly changing and diverse neighborhoods are the soul of San Francisco. Explore the Richmond (north) and Sunset and Parkside Districts (south) on either side of Golden Gate Park, encompassing almost half the city leading to the ocean. Not only will you find endless Chinese populations and superb regional Chinese food (even rare Old Mandarin Islamic food) but dense populations—and thus authentic food—of Vietnamese, Thai, Burmese, Russian, and Irish, to name a few. There are hundreds of affordable, excellent treasures packed within blocks.

Explore our first-in-the-nation, unparalleled Japantown. The Mexican and Latin population that has long made the Mission District great, down to street-side carts selling late-night bacon-wrapped hot dogs, Tijuana style, or roadside fruit carts. The cafés and supermarkets of SF's densely [populated] Asian and Mexican Excelsior neighborhood. The lost-in-time 1970s vibes of chill West Portal. Sleepy but action-packed food greats in Dogpatch. Laid-back vibes and killer downtown views in Potrero Hill. Of course, hip Hayes Valley, the best Chinatown ever, and unparalleled North Beach, which is so Italian, so Beat poet, and so very SF.

SUPPLI

CHE FICO, DAVID NAYFELD

Executive chef/co-owner David Nayfeld's contemporary-leaning Italian menu is constantly filled with all kinds of delights, from outstanding home-made pastas to some of the city's greatest pizzas (yes, give the "Ananas" pie with pineapple a try!). Since opening in 2018, the pitch-perfect suppli (pomo-doro risotto, breaded and filled with Fontina, dill, and pecorino) have been a staple of the Che Fico experience, as a bit of a traditional way to start dinner before the real pyrotechnics begin.

YIELD: 50 pieces

---

5 CUPS CANNED TOMATO JUICE

1½ CUPS WATER

2 TABLESPOONS OLIVE OIL

7 TABLESPOONS BUTTER

2 YELLOW ONIONS, CUT INTO SMALL DICE

1½ TABLESPOONS SALT, PLUS MORE AS NEEDED

3 CUPS ARBORIO RICE

1 CUP WHITE WINE

½ CUP TOMATO PASTE

8 OZ. GRATED PARMIGIANO REGGIANO CHEESE

4 OZ. FONTINA CHEESE, CUT INTO 2 x ½ x ½–INCH RECTANGLES

ALL-PURPOSE FLOUR, AS NEEDED

4 TO 6 EGGS, BEATEN

BREAD CRUMBS, AS NEEDED

CANOLA OIL, FOR FRYING

3 CUPS GRATED PECORINO ROMANO CHEESE

1 CUP CHOPPED FRESH DILL

1. Heat the tomato juice and water in a small pot.

2. Heat the olive oil and 5 tablespoons of the butter in a small rondeau, until the butter has melted.

continued...

---

3. Add the onions and salt. Sweat over low heat until the onions are fully cooked and translucent.

4. Add the rice and toast lightly, until most of the fat appears to be soaked up.

5. Add the wine and cook until it has evaporated.

6. Slowly add the tomato water, about 1½ cups at a time, and stir constantly until it is mostly absorbed.

7. Keep adding the tomato water in this way, until it's all used up and the risotto is thickened and cooked.

8. Take off the heat and add the tomato paste, parmigiano, and remaining 2 tablespoons butter.

9. Pour the risotto onto a parchment paper–lined sheet tray, let cool slightly, then refrigerate.

10. Once chilled, scoop even amounts onto a clean tray lined with parchment.

11. Stuff each ball with a piece of the fontina, shaping the rice around the cheese in an oblong quenelle shape.

12. Set up a breading station: flour, beaten eggs, and bread crumbs in separate containers.

13. Using one hand for dry and one for wet, dredge the risotto quenelles in the flour, coating them evenly and shaking off any excess.

14. Roll the flour-coated quenelles in the eggs using the wet hand, drain off the excess, then place in the bread crumbs, coating evenly.

15. Wash your hands and reshape the suppli as needed. Refrigerate until ready to fry.

16. Heat the canola oil to 350°F/177°C in a deep fryer or saucepan. Gently drop the suppli in the oil in batches and cook until golden brown on the outside and hot in the center, about 4 minutes.

17. Drain on a rack and season with salt. Repeat until all the suppli are cooked.

18. Generously sprinkle with the pecorino and dill.

AVOCADO "TOAST"

HILDA AND JESSE, KRISTINA LIEDAGS COMPTON

Is there a bigger, more tired cliché in San Francisco food these days than avocado toast? Probably not. Luckily, the innovative cooking of North Beach's contemporary brunch specialist takes the avocado toast concept and shapes it into a fascinating new dimension. It's pretty representative of Hilda and Jesse's penchant for being creative and exciting—serving a clever brunch for dinner and being a bright, chic setting with beautiful art touches surrounded by cafés with the typical throwback, classic aesthetic of North Beach.

YIELD: 2 servings

SOUR CREAM AND ONION DILL DIP

1 ONION, CUT INTO SMALL DICE

2 TABLESPOONS OLIVE OIL

1 CUP SOUR CREAM

1 CUP MAYONNAISE

1 BUNCH FRESH DILL, FINELY MINCED

SALT, TO TASTE

FRESH LEMON JUICE, TO TASTE

1. Cook the onion in the olive oil until tender and sweet. Remove from the heat and let cool.

2. In a bowl, mix the onion with the sour cream, mayonnaise, and dill. Season with salt and lemon juice to taste.

continued...

TEMPURA BATTER

300 ML COLD CLUB SODA

6 G SALT

1.5 G XANTHAN GUM

120 G THAI RICE FLOUR

1. Combine the club soda, salt, and xanthan gum in a bowl. Add the rice flour and blend.

TO FINISH AND ASSEMBLE

RICE BRAN OIL,
FOR FRYING

3 SWEET POTATOES,
SLICED ¼ INCH THICK

SALT, TO TASTE

1 AVOCADO, SLICED AND SEASONED
WITH LEMON JUICE AND SALT

DILL FRONDS

GRATED, PEELED FRESH
HORSERADISH ROOT

1. Heat the oil to 350°F/177°C.

2. Coat the sweet potato slices in the tempura batter and fry until crisp.

3. Drain on paper towels and immediately season with salt.

4. Arrange the fried sweet potato slices on serving plates and top with the sour cream and onion dill dip, sliced avocado, dill fronds, and grated horseradish.

PAN-FRIED SAND DABS

TADICH GRILL

For a city that is surrounded by water on three sides (hence, why the Bay Area region directly south of San Francisco is called "The Peninsula"), it's always surprising how we often don't discuss local fish with the same reverence as all the local produce and the grapes from our prolific vineyards.

Dungeness crab? Yes, we enjoy that all that time when it's in season. However, halibut, black cod, salmon, and many more fish in the sea (and bay) don't get the same special treatment (like prix-fixe menus focused specifically on them) like the local tomatoes, Brentwood corn, and Dungeness crab do.

If there's one local fish that San Francisco is truly known for, it's sand dabs. Yes, humble, low-key sand dabs. Unfortunately, it doesn't have the greatest reputation for tender texture or pristine flavor (you'll never see the French Laundry serve the fish), but when it's fresh and prepared correctly, it's a simple yet special experience. Go to the legendary Tadich Grill to sample their recipe or try it at home, and you'll surely become a fan of sand dabs.

YIELD: 4 servings

---

1 EGG

¼ CUP MILK

3½ TO 4 LBS. SAND DAB FILLETS, SKIN REMOVED

FLOUR SEASONED WITH SALT AND PEPPER, OR FINE CRACKER MEAL

2 TABLESPOONS OLIVE OIL, PLUS MORE AS NEEDED

FRESH PARSLEY, FOR GARNISH

1 LEMON, CUT INTO WEDGES, FOR SERVING

continued...

---

1. Combine the egg and milk in a shallow bowl and beat until well mixed. Dip each fillet into the egg mixture, then dredge them thoroughly in the seasoned flour, shaking off any excess.

2. Place a large nonstick sauté pan over medium heat. When hot, add the olive oil. When the oil is hot, add the fillets in a single layer (you will have to work in batches, adding more oil as necessary), and cook for 4 minutes, or until second side is golden brown. Transfer to a warmed platter and keep warm in a low oven as the remaining fillets are completed.

3. Transfer the fillets to individual plates, garnish with the parsley, and serve immediately with the lemon wedges.

OYSTERS ROCKEFELLER

In the aforementioned Tadich Grill book, Briscoe notes that this iconic baked oysters dish comes from our dear friends in a fellow smaller big city with an outsized reputation for excellent cuisine: Antoine's restaurant in New Orleans.

Antoine's opened in 1840, nine whole years before Tadich Grill debuted in that mighty mid-nineteenth century decade that most of us here in the 2020s had no idea was such an important decade for American culinary history.

We certainly love oysters here in the Bay Area, yet we don't really have a signature recipe for enjoying them other than to slurp them on the half shell and wash them down with a crisp white wine or rosé from Sonoma County (and there's nothing wrong with that!). So, let's send our gratitude to the Big Easy via Tadich Grill for this great, timeless way to enjoy oysters.

YIELD: 6 Servings

36 LARGE OYSTERS

4 CUPS ROCK SALT

1 ½ CUPS FIRMLY PACKED FRESH SPINACH

¾ CUP FRESH PARSLEY LEAVES

¾ CUP CHOPPED GREEN ONION, WHITE AND GREEN PARTS

6 SHALLOTS, COARSELY CHOPPED

3 TABLESPOONS CHOPPED FRESH

FENNEL FRONDS

¾ CUP UNSALTED BUTTER

2 TABLESPOONS ANCHOVY PASTE

TABASCO SAUCE, TO TASTE

1 CUP FRESH BREAD CRUMBS

¼ CUP PERNOD OR RICARD

SALT AND FRESHLY GROUND BLACK PEPPER, TO TASTE

continued...

1. Preheat the oven to 450ºF/232.2ºC. Shuck the oysters, straining and reserving the liquid. Scrub and dry the deep halves of the shells, discarding the shallow halves. Pour the rock salt into large baking dishes and arrange the shells on top. Place 1 oyster in each shell.

2. Combine the spinach, parsley, green onion, shallots and fennel in a food processor and blitz until uniformly chopped. Place a sauté pan over low heat. When warm, add the butter. When the butter has melted, add the vegetable mixture and sauté for 5 minutes, until tender.

3. Stir in the anchovy paste, several dashes of Tabasco, and the bread crumbs. Cook, stirring, for 2 to 3 minutes, until well mixed and thick. Add the reserved oyster liquid or more bread crumbs to adjust the consistency as desired. Add the Pernod, season with salt and pepper (and more Tabasco sauce, if preferred), and stir well. Spoon the sauce onto the oysters and bake for about 5 minutes, until the oysters are plump and the sauce is heated through. Remove from the oven and serve at once.

Q&A, GAYLE PIRIE

EXECUTIVE CHEF/RESTAURATEUR, FOREIGN CINEMA

TF: There's truly no place like Foreign Cinema. What is it like owning a restaurant with such a magical setting?

GP: Curating the environment that is known as Foreign Cinema is one of the greatest professional joys we have had the honor to be a part of, and taps every artistic inclination we possess. The psychology of a restaurant must be a healthy, evolving balancing act that maintains the harmony and joy of service.

Once the original lease was procured, a unification of all the four quirky spaces began to unfold, though construction, reduction, and a grand vision. The outdoor courtyard back wall became a focal general muse, and the idea of cinema projected against that great wall revealed itself to the initial team during construction.

TF: Foreign Cinema will turn 25(!) in just a few months in 2024. What has this incredible ride been like for you and John (since joining the restaurant early on), for the restaurant, and for its constantly changing Mission District home?

GP: Foreign Cinema turning 25 next year is powerfully symbolic to us, and to the family of Foreign Cinema. Being a part of the growth and evolution of an inspired yet improbable concept is beyond prideful, it's simply outrageous. Coming to work amongst this great team is fun and exciting to this day. We want that joy to exude to our guests, who may be long-term regulars or brand-new arrivals to San Francisco. The Mission District, our home base, remains a vital, thriving neighborhood, in the throes of constant change. Like the city itself, there is a resilience felt on the streets and in the immediate community of excitement and vibrance. While the area knows both sides of the current issues, like affordability, the New Mission Theater, our neighbor, was built in 1919, and is a symbol of recovery and renaissance, called the "new" mission theater, way back then. That says a lot.

TF: How would you personally describe Foreign Cinema's cuisine style?

GP: Describing the cuisine of Foreign Cinema is at once Californian in flavor and sensibility: local, sustainable, seasonal farm-to-table style, with a great trattoriaesque sensibility, as diners experience an array of choices in menu offerings, from small bites to larger main courses, and our oyster/shellfish menu, evoking a European style, enveloping a classic Parisian style to palazzo–al fresco feel. The menu is everything John and I crave and wish to eat each day.

The menu is written each day, reflecting the mood of the day: weather, incoming farm deliveries, and the kitchen's imagination. Signature dishes pepper the menu with a fluidity that matches those other informing conditions. Our guests expect changes, and are eager participants whether we run Chef Josh's porchetta or our beloved brined heritage pork chops.

TF: I've always been curious, since this is Foreign Cinema, after all—what are your favorite classic films? Are there any films that work particularly well with a special occasion dinner like a birthday celebration at Foreign Cinema?

GP: Films? Oh my, where do we start? Some of our favorite films include *La Belle et la Bete*, *Lawrence of Arabia*, *Chitty Chitty Bang Bang*, *Klute*, *Kelly's Heroes*, *Grand Prix*, *Duel*, *Bullitt*. We find that the best films to screen these days, especially since the pandemic, are films with spectacular kinds of imagery and meaning that evoke childlike enthusiasm and recognition amongst the guests. These can be from their childhoods, or iconic SF-shot cinema like *Vertigo*; other films that elicit overwhelming adoration are Kurosawa's

Kagemusha, Billy Wilder films, *Amélie*, *The Wizard of Oz*, *Big Trouble in Little China*, *Butch Cassidy and the Sundance Kid*, to name just a few.

TF: Finally, where do you and John like to dine in the city when you have a rare free day or night?

GP: We love to eat out when we are able, and some of our spots in the city include: Hayes Street Grill, Zuni Café, Tommaso's, Prospect, Rich Table, Rintaro, and Cotogna, among so many others; San Francisco remains a truly great dining out town.

SPANISH TORTILLA

BELLOTA, GONZALO TECUAQUE

Combine San Francisco's top Spanish restaurant and one of Spain's most iconic tapas and...here you go! The Absinthe Group's ode to Spanish cuisine with California's farm-to-table influences at the border of the Design District and SoMa is a terrific choice for a grand paella dinner or a series of smaller tapas with some gin and tonics and sherry. Either way, you'll surely be starting with one of the all-time classic tapas: a tortilla.

YIELD: 2 servings

1¼ LBS. POTATOES
(3 OR 4 MEDIUM-SIZE)

1 MEDIUM ONION

1 CUP OLIVE OIL

SALT AND FRESHLY GROUND
BLACK PEPPER, TO TASTE

6 EXTRA-LARGE OR JUMBO EGGS

1. Peel and thinly slice the potatoes and onion; it's easiest if you use a mandoline.

2. In an 8- or 10-inch nonstick skillet over medium heat, heat the oil. After 3 or 4 minutes, drop in a potato slice. When tiny bubbles appear around its edges, add the rest of the potatoes, the onion, a good pinch of salt, and a liberal sprinkling of pepper. Gently turn the mixture in the oil with a wooden spoon, and adjust the heat so the oil bubbles lazily.

3. Cook, turning the potatoes gently every few minutes, until they are tender when pierced with a small knife. Adjust the heat so they do not brown. If the potatoes begin to break, they are overdone; stop cooking immediately.

4. As the vegetables cook, beat the eggs with some salt and pepper in a large bowl.

5. Drain the potatoes in a colander, reserving the oil.

6. Wipe out the skillet, and heat over medium for 1 minute. Add 2 tablespoons of the reserved oil.

7. Gently mix the warm potatoes with the eggs, and add to the skillet. As soon as the edges firm up, after 1 minute or so, reduce the heat to medium-low. Cook for 5 minutes.

8. Insert a rubber spatula all around the edge of the tortilla to make sure it will slide from the pan. The top will still be runny. Carefully slide out onto a plate. Cover with another plate and, holding the plates tightly, invert them.

9. Add another tablespoon of reserved oil to the skillet and use the spatula to coax the tortilla back in. Cook for 5 minutes, then slide from the skillet onto a clean plate. Serve warm (not hot) or at room temperature.

SCALLOP TIRADITO

KAIYŌ

The Japanese Peruvian cuisine known as Nikkei might continue to be hard to find in San Francisco, but there's certainly a huge following for its exciting genre-blending specialties. With an original location on Union Street in Cow Hollow and a twelfth-floor rooftop bar-restaurant in SoMa (bundle up, it's rarely not windy there!), Kaiyō is *the* place to try Nikkei (in addition to classic Peruvian dishes), accompanied by a pisco sour, of course.

YIELD: 2 servings

PASSION FRUIT LECHE DE TIGRE

1½ CUPS FRESH LIME JUICE

2 TEASPOONS GINGER JUICE

½ TEASPOON SALT

2 TABLESPOONS
PASSION FRUIT PUREE

4 SPRIGS FRESH CILANTRO

3 TABLESPOONS FISH STOCK

½ TABLESPOON ROCOTO PUREE

1. Place all the ingredients in a blender, puree, and strain.

ASSEMBLY

PASSION FRUIT LECHE DE TIGRE
(SEE ABOVE)

5 TO 6 OZ. HOKKAIDO SCALLOPS,
SLICED ACROSS AS THINLY
AS POSSIBLE

SALT, TO TASTE

2 TABLESPOONS SMOKY YAM PUREE

2 TABLESPOONS PICKLED RED ONION, CUT INTO BRUNOISE

1 TABLESPOON CHIA SEEDS, SOAKED IN WATER TO COVER 5 MINUTES RIGHT BEFORE PLATING, DRAINED

2 TABLESPOONS CILANTRO OIL

1 TABLESPOON MICRO CILANTRO LEAVES

1. For each serving, pour a pool of the Leche de Tigre on the plate and arrange the scallop slices one next to the other.

2. Sprinkle a pinch of salt over the scallop slices.

3. Place a dot of the yam puree and a bit of the pickled red onion on each scallop slice.

4. Pour the chia seeds over the leche de tigre and around the scallops.

5. Garnish with the cilantro oil and micro cilantro leaves as you see fit.

Q&A, UMBERTO GIBIN

GENERAL MANAGER AND CO-OWNER, PERBACCO

TF: After growing up in Venice and Piemonte, what led you to pursue a career in hospitality? Were you always interested in restaurants?

UG: I had no idea that I would end up in the hospitality industry. Nobody in my family is a restaurateur. After high school, like everyone else, I was supposed to choose what to do with my education. I knew I was not a very studious individual. One of my teachers suggested that I enroll in the hotel and restaurant school in Torino. She said that it would be the best way for me to learn a trade and do what I like to do the most, which is traveling and learning foreign languages. I chose the hotel side. I wanted to become a hotel general manager. In those days hotels' GMs were considered personalities. During the summer break, hotels and restaurants from Italy and other nations in Europe would come to recruit students as apprentices. I chose to go to Germany at the Schlosshotel outside Frankfurt. I was fifteen. The hotel was a castle that at one time housed Frederick I. It was a very luxurious place. When I entered the dining room wearing a tailcoat suit, I was hooked. Although I graduated in hotel management, I used my degree very little. To further my knowledge in the industry, I took a final course at the prestigious Hotel and Restaurant School in Lausanne. The rest is history.

TF: What brought you to San Francisco? What was the dining scene like here in the late 1970s/early 1980s?

UG: After graduating, I worked at several amazing places all over Europe. Le Caprice and Annabel's in London, Taillevent in Paris, Villa d'Este in Como, and the Palace Hotel in St. Moritz, to name a few. Then came time to serve in the military (mandatory) service. After the army I decided to experience working on a cruise ship. I had the time of my life. On one of the cruises I met a young lady. She lived in San Francisco. In November 1978, I came to visit her. The city was decorated for the holidays. I fell in love with San Francisco. Together with a friend, we went back to Italy, packed, and came back. The young lady is long gone but I am still here. My first job in the city was at the venerable Ernie's. In those days there were many Italian and French restaurants serving mediocre food. And then we had all the fancy places like Ernie's, Le Trianon, La Bourgogne, Doros, L'Etoile, etc. It was like being back in Europe. While working at Ernie's in the evening, my now dear friend and mentor Larry Mindel was opening what became a groundbreaking Italian restaurant called Ciao. It was a sleek restaurant that reminded me of the hot new restaurants in Milano. No one had ever seen making pasta in front of you. I was offered a lunchtime job. The volume was incredible.

Soon after, the Donatello Hotel and Donatello Restaurant opened. My friend Giancarlo Paterlini of Acquerello fame was in charge of the dining room. He asked me if I wanted to join him. I did. I left Ernie's and Ciao. Donatello was a spectacular restaurant. We wanted to be the San Domenico of Imola in San Francisco.

TF: Can you tell us a little more about three of the San Francisco icons from around that period that you worked at—Ernie's, Masa's, and Ciao? Those are restaurants that we hear about all the time, even now, three or more decades later.

UG: Ernie's was where all the celebrities and San Francisco society came to eat. At that time Jackie Roberts was the chef. He and Roland Passot were responsible for bringing nouvelle cuisine to San Francisco. Ciao revolutionized casual Italian restaurants. Everyone wanted to be seated in the elevated area in front of the bar so they could be seen. Prominent attorneys like Melvin Belli were there regularly. Masa's was unique also. The tragic passing of Chef Masa opened the door for young chefs like Julian Serrano and Ron Siegel. What these two chefs created was art. Masa's was the hottest ticket in town for many years.

TF: What led you to open Perbacco? What are some of the dishes that you think really represent the signature personality of the restaurant and your home region of Piemonte?

UG: My wife, Leslie, and many of my friends encouraged me to open my own restaurant. I looked at many spaces but always got cold feet. What if I failed? After leaving the Kimpton Group, these very friends pushed even harder. It is then that I decided that it was time. I had the concept. I had the name but I did not have a chef. There were many talented chefs out there but none that I really wanted to be associated with. Until I thought of Staffan Terje. At that time he was the executive chef at Scala's. Although we never worked at the same restaurant, I had the pleasure to work side by side with him at numerous hotels and restaurants opening with the Kimpton Group. He was a great cook and a true encyclopedia when it came down to food. And he knew how to control costs. I called him up. We met a couple of times at the Campton Place (near Scala's), and Perbacco was born. We signed the lease in 2005, and we opened in October 2006. The dishes that became unmovable from the menu are the Vitello Tonnato, Agnolotti dal Plin, Tajarin with 5-Hour Pork Sugo and Pappardelle. A true testimony that we were on the right track was when renowned Italian food critic Edoardo Raspelli reviewed Perbacco for Torino's daily newspaper *La Stampa*. He said that not even in the Langhe were these dishes so good.

TF: You've spent so much of your life in hospitality and are one of San Francisco's greatest examples of a restaurateur/host who is so gracious and wants to make sure guests have a truly special experience during each visit to your restaurants. What are some of the keys to success for a restaurant to have friendly, sharp, smooth service like at Perbacco and Barbacco?

UG: This business is hard. If you don't do it right, you just waste energy and time. The fact that I am there twelve-plus hours every day is one of the key factors of the success that both restaurants are enjoying. I am the face of the restaurants. I know what my guests like. I know the tables that they like to sit at. I saw families grow. But I couldn't do it without the help of some of my most trusted employees. They are the ones that make me look good. At the end of the day, I always tell them that we are only as good as the last dish of pasta served. Always aim at giving 120 percent. Never lower your standards. Stay true to your concept. Don't try to be everything to everybody.

RESERVE CAVIAR AND COASTAL SUCCULENTS

SAISON, RICHARD LEE

If you've had the great pleasure of dining at the brilliant Saison, you'll surely remember that outrageously wonderful blast of seaweed butter accompanying hearth-kissed caviar that makes all other caviar jealous. Here's a special look behind the literal culinary magic.

It is a course that represents what we do at Saison so perfectly. It is a course that combines beautiful locally sourced products like caviar from Wilton, California, that is cured in our smoked salt; coastal spinach that has a beautiful brininess that complements the caviar; a broth made from smoked fish; and the freshest market leeks, all brought together by various preparations of seaweed from the Mendocino coast. The caviar is warmed by our hearth after being wrapped in giant kelp. It is a course that I fell in love with when I first got to Saison. It brings together fire-cooking techniques with pristine local products that are handled in the best way possible with elegance and finesse. All this [is] presented tableside, giving us an opportunity to bring the kitchen to the guests at the tables. This course represents the ethos of Saison and the story we are trying to tell perfectly.

—**Chef Lee**

YIELD: 1 serving

KELP PACKET

1 (10-INCH-SQUARE) DRIED KELP SHEET, REHYDRATED AND WASHED

6 (2-CM-SQUARE) PIECES BRAISED CALIFORNIA SEA MUSTARD

40 G SAISON RESERVE CAVIAR

1 SPRAY TUNA GARUM

1 OZ. CLARIFIED SEAWEED BUTTER (SEE PAGE 96)

1 (1 X 30–CM) KELP RIBBON

continued...

1. Flatten out the kelp sheet.

2. Place some of the braised sea mustard in the center of the kelp sheet, making a 3 x 2–inch rectangle.

3. Spread the caviar in the same space and top with a spray of the tuna garum.

4. Place the remaining sea mustard on top of the caviar.

5. Pour the seaweed butter over the entire contents.

6. Fold the bottom of the packet upward, then the top third down.

7. Trim the excess kelp to keep it neat, fold the side to make a perfect rectangle, and use the kelp ribbon to tie it all together and appear gift wrapped.

8. When ready, gently warm the packet over a bed of soft embers, allowing the rehydrated kelp to steam internally and warm the caviar through; this should take around 1 to 2 minutes.

LEEK BROTH

300 ML KELP WATER

1 G ALMOND WOOD–SMOKED SALT

25 G SHAVED HONKAREBUSHI

100 G LEEK WHITES, CUT INTO 0.5-CM PIECES

1. Warm the kelp water until you see small bubbles form at the bottom of the pot, before the liquid comes to a simmer.

2. Add the salt and honkarebushi and allow it to steep for 5 minutes, while gently raising the heat.

3. Once you begin to see a slight production of steam, add the leeks and let them steep for 1 to 2 minutes. You want to make sure you're capturing all the aroma and heat from the leeks without extracting the sugar, as you do not want the broth to be sweet.

4. Quickly strain.

continued…

CLARIFIED SEAWEED BUTTER

1 LB. CULTURED BUTTER (UNPASTEURIZED AND AGED 60 DAYS), CUBED

30 G DRIED CALIFORNIA KELP, JULIENNED

10 G DRIED CALIFORNIA SEA MUSTARD

10 G DRIED CALIFORNIA SEA LETTUCE

1. In a small pot over medium heat, warm the butter.

2. Add the kelp and sea mustard and stir as you allow the fat to separate from the butter.

3. Slowly skim off the milk solids until the butter is fully clarified.

4. While the butter is still warm, add the sea lettuce and allow it to warm for 30 minutes on low heat.

5. Blend all the contents together and allow the clarified butter to rest with all the sediment at a minimum of another hour. (The longer the contents stay in the butter, the stronger the aroma and flavor.)

6. Strain the clarified butter before using.

POACHED COASTAL SUCCULENTS

CLARIFIED SEAWEED BUTTER

2 SPRIGS AGRETTI

10 G BLOOMSDALE SPINACH

3 SAMPHIRE

2 SPRIGS PURSLANE

3 BUNCHES NEW ZEALAND SPINACH

1. When the kelp packets come off the fire, warm the seaweed butter in a copper pot until it is 185°F/85°C. Gently poach the succulents in the seaweed butter, starting with the agretti for 20 seconds, then add the Bloomsdale spinach for 30 seconds.

2. Lastly add the samphire, purslane, and New Zealand spinach and allow everything to poach together for 20 seconds.

3. Remove everything from the butter together.

ASSEMBLY

1. Make a bed in a serving bowl using the Bloomsdale spinach and agretti, then gently place all the succulents on top.

2. Pour 1 tablespoon of the seaweed butter on top, along with ¼ cup of the leek broth.

3. Tableside, open the kelp packet, allowing all the aromas to escape in front of the guest.

4. Scoop the caviar from the packet, place it on the succulents, and serve immediately.

Shrimp Vennai Roast
See page 100

SHRIMP VENNAI ROAST

COPRA, SRIJITH GOPINATHAN

After earning a Michelin star for his contemporary Indian cooking at the iconic Campton Place, Chef Srijith Gopinathan switched gears for his next San Francisco project with a menu that is largely inspired by his youth on the Kerala Coast of India. There are already countless signature dishes at his gorgeous Fillmore–Lower Pacific Heights dining destination, Copra, but make sure to include this terrific shrimp preparation on your table.

YIELD: 2 servings (chutney yields for much more than that)

CHUTNEY

½ CUP GINGELLY OIL

10 CURRY LEAVES

1 OZ. FINELY CHOPPED FRESH GINGER

1 TABLESPOON BLACK LENTILS

1 TABLESPOON LENTILS

2½ OZ. GARLIC CLOVES, PEELED

2 OZ. STEMMED KASHMIRI CHILIES

4 OZ. DICED RED ONION

¾ CUP DICED TOMATOES WITH SKINS AND SEEDS

2 OZ. SLICED HABANERO CHILI

2½ OZ. TAMARIND PUREE

3 TABLESPOONS DESICCATED COCONUT

2 TABLESPOONS TOMATO PASTE

SALT, TO TASTE (OPTIONAL)

SUGAR, TO TASTE (OPTIONAL)

1. Heat the oil in a heavy-bottomed sauté pan until it begins to smoke. Add the curry leaves, ginger, lentils, garlic, Kashmiri chilies, and onion. Cook until the lentils turn light brown and the onion is slightly roasted.

2. Add the tomatoes, habanero, tamarind, coconut, and tomato paste and cook, partially covered, over medium heat, stirring occasionaly until it comes together as a thick mass, about 10 minutes. Do not let the mixture burn.

3. Taste and adjust the flavor with salt and sugar, if you like. Blend the mixture into a thick, coarse puree. Store in the refrigerator until ready to use; it will keep in the refrigerator for 3 days and in the freezer for a month.

SHRIMP MARINADE

JUICE OF ½ LIME

1 TABLESPOON CHOPPED FRESH CILANTRO

1 TABLESPOON GINGER GARLIC PASTE

1 TEASPOON TURMERIC

SALT, TO TASTE

12 LARGE (16/20 COUNT) SHRIMP, SHELLED AND DEVEINED

1. In a small bowl, mix the lime juice, cilantro, ginger garlic paste, turmeric, and salt together. Add the shrimp and toss to coat well. Let marinate in the refrigerator for 15 to 20 minutes.

BROWN BUTTER

4 OZ. UNSALTED BUTTER, CUT INTO CUBES

1. In a heavy-bottomed saucepan over medium heat, melt the butter. As it begins to melt, it will start to froth. Once the frothing starts to slow, the milk solids in the butter should begin to turn brown. Watch carefully. When you see this happening, immediately pull the pan off the heat. You can place the pan in an ice bath to avoid burning.

continued...

FINAL COOKING AND ASSEMBLY

1 TABLESPOON SHREDDED CURRY LEAVES

1 LIME WEDGE

SHREDDED CUCUMBERS, FOR GARNISH

1. In a hot pan over high heat, cook the shrimp 1 minute per side; the goal is to get them 60 to 70 percent done.

2. Remove the pan from the heat. In a bowl, combine 1½ tablespoons of the chutney, 1 tablespoon of the brown butter, and the shredded curry leaves. Add the shrimp and toss to coat.

3. Return the shrimp back to the skillet with an additional ½ to 1 tablespoon of brown butter and cook over medium heat for about 2 more minutes, until the shrimp are done. Add more brown butter if needed. The surface of the shrimp should be well roasted so that the natural sugars in the chutney get caramelized well.

4. Serve as an appetizer with a wedge of lime and shredded cucumbers for garnish.

Q&A, PAOLO LUCCHESI

EDITORIAL DIRECTOR, RESY; FORMER FOOD AND WINE EDITOR OF THE *SAN FRANCISCO CHRONICLE*; FOUNDING EDITOR OF *EATER SF*

TF: First off, I know you're a huge Giants fan. What's your go-to order at Oracle Park?

PL: At the ballpark, I usually stick to the overpriced beer and maybe a hot dog if I'm feeling particularly *Field of Dreams*y. If I'm with my kids, odds are that we'll find a Ghirardelli sundae in the mix too. But when possible, I try to bring in a sandwich from one of my favorite spots—Submarine Center in West Portal, Palm City in the Outer Sunset, Roxie Food Center by Balboa, Lucca Delicatessen on Chestnut. Big, crusty deli sandwiches are something that I remember from my childhood going to Candlestick Park, especially day games, and it still feels right. Pregame, though, the move is Red's Java House.

TF: Switching to restaurants, you're our city's leading voice (in my humble opinion) for highlighting venerable, longtime San Francisco restaurants and often unheralded restaurants, specifically in the quieter residential areas of the city. What do you think is the special magic that these often small, family-owned restaurant stalwarts and the quieter neighborhoods have that is so unique to San Francisco?

PL: The most successful restaurants—regardless of how we define "successful"—are able to forge a connection with their diners and, by extension, a community. This is even more true when it comes to those stalwarts that have stood the test of time and somehow keep producing great experiences for their guests, whether it's a regular who goes there weekly or a newcomer who just moved to town. I think of places like Old Mandarin Islamic and New Taraval Cafe, Tommy's Mexican and Tommy's Joynt—restaurants that have been around for decades, but when you go there, you see so many different generations and communities, all unified by the shared experience of a meal there. And you see staffers and owners who have been there through those same generations. Restaurants are about humans and human connections. That's where the magic is. In the people.

TF: Which new and old restaurants do you find yourself returning to again and again?

PL: Some of my haunts have evolved as my life has evolved—new family, new neighborhood, and such—but there have been a few eternals. Joe's of Westlake is a place that's been in my life since high school. It's the epitome of a community hub, and that kind of midcentury Italian American food sparks a lot of family memories.

I've had a special relationship with SPQR throughout my adult life—it opened on my first day at *Eater* (my first real restaurant writing gig), and I've watched it evolve under Matthew Accarrino into the restaurant it is today. It's where my wife and I had our first date, and where we went after we got engaged; we still go there every autumn.

I wrote Flour + Water's cookbook, so I have a connection to the magic that Tom and the team have created there, and it's the kind of food I crave—seasonal to the extreme, rooted in tradition, and always creative. I learn something new every time I go there, whether it's a technique, an ingredient, or a history.

And I mentioned Old Mandarin already, but it's an incredibly special place and one I'm in constant awe and appreciation [of]. It's perfect.

TF: It's kind of an impossible question to answer, but I'll ask anyway, since it's a book all about SF food . . . Is there a way to describe in a nutshell what it is that makes San Francisco's dining scene and culture so special, compared to our peers in New York, LA, Paris, etc.?

PL: I think every city has a secret sauce that makes its dining scene special and unique. Here in San Francisco, so much revolves around our access to the world's best ingredients. It's a cliché, but Northern California's farms are truly incredible, and it's all in our backyard. So much starts there, both in the city's overall culture and certainly with the chefs. From there, I think you can see how our current restaurant scene has grown over the decades from its time and place. We have great Chinese food: our Chinatown is one of the oldest and largest in North America, and the city's Chinese restaurants are more spectacular than ever these days, whether you're looking for regional specialties or modern cooking or dumpling shops. We have great Mexican food: the Mexican community has always been strong here, especially in the Mission District, and taquerias and taco trucks are as essential to San Francisco (and the larger Bay Area) as slice shops are to New York and patisseries are to Paris.

We have great casual restaurants that serve fine dining–level food: due to cost and zoning constraints, more smaller restaurants popped up, and San Francisco really pushed forward the way that neighborhood restaurants can become destination restaurants in their own right, from Delfina to State Bird to Rich Table to Kin Khao. And I guess the last thing that really defines our current dining culture is the fine dining scene, and the way that tasting menus have exploded here in the last ten years or so. Certainly tech money is a big part of that boom—both on the consumer and the investor fronts—but also there's a willingness from diners to be swept away by a restaurant as entertainment or a night out, in the same way that you might go to a Broadway show or sporting event in another city.

TF: Since you started your journalism career, you've surely seen lots of changes in the SF dining world. What have been some positive changes or trends over the years?

PL: For the restaurant industry overall, the big one has been the push coming out of the #MeToo movement and the pandemic for a more compassionate and professional working environment. When combined with the ongoing staff shortage, I think more owners and operators understand that team culture, a living wage, and benefits should be priorities within the industry.

On the journalism front, there's been a huge—and exciting—shift in food media in the last decade. When I started, the vast majority of food media was focused on white-owned restaurants, and particularly those of a certain price point or lineage. Due to a number of factors, especially a new generation of writers and editors with more diverse backgrounds, that's steadily changed to be more inclusive. In turn, you're seeing more opportunity for entrepreneurs and chefs to share their own cultures through food in a wider range of possibilities, whether it's a fine dining restaurant, a café, a food truck, or a catering company.

TF: Speaking of journalism, you have a rare perspective on the SF dining world, having worked with *Eater*, the *Chronicle*, and now at Resy. How have those different experiences shaped your view of dining out in San Francisco? And, how do you think those outlets have had an impact on the SF dining scene? When I started my career, which was roughly around the same time as *Eater* launched, restaurants were still a little bit of a niche subject. Now, they're a key part of pop culture—as popular as music and sports in the Bay Area!

PL: As much as I'd like to think it was simply those outlets that have changed the game, I think they were part of a larger perfect storm that led to this incredible restaurant boom in the first two decades of the twenty-first century and especially the 2010s. The Bay Area was a central part of this, but it was something that was happening globally, and certainly in America. Like you said, restaurants became pop culture. If the spark was the success of the Food Network and Bourdain's *Kitchen Confidential*, then the explosion came with the rise of the internet, which connected restaurants and chefs to other restaurants and chefs. It became so much easier for a chef in San Francisco to see what, say, René Redzepi and David Chang were doing in their cities. Suddenly you didn't have to make the pilgrimage to El Bulli or The French Laundry, like you did in the '90s, to see avant-garde cuisine. Ideas spread, opportunity spread.

And connected to that, of course, is the rise of social media, wherein every single diner becomes a reviewer, a photographer, and/or an advertisement. Dinner became theater in more ways than one, as we're sharing where we are eating, what new restaurant is opening, and what dish is the must order. Suddenly, the general public didn't just interact with food media on a weekly basis when the food section was published, or on the first of the month, when *Bon Appétit* landed in your mailbox. It was something you always had in your phone in your pocket.

TF: One more SF dining journalism question—longtime SF readers certainly remember GraceAnn Walden, the original Inside Scoop writer for the *Chronicle* in the 1990s. For those who didn't have the chance to read her articles for the paper, can you say a little bit about her career and enormous impact on how San Francisco became fascinated by restaurant news?

PL: GraceAnn was one of a kind. She was the original Inside Scoop columnist at the *Chronicle*, and she took the tradition of classic newspaper columnist—the Herb Caen model, if you will—and brought it to the food world. It was informative, fun, gossipy. She had her heroes and her villains. I never worked with her, but the thing I learned most from reading through her archives—and also what I learned from a lot of veteran journalists—was the value of a reporter doing the work and being an insider. You can't report on a community from your desk. You have to meet people, you have to experience the beat, you have to earn respect and the trust that you'll be fair and accurate.

TF: Finally, as a student of San Francisco history, is there one restaurant from San Francisco of Days Past that you've always wished you had the chance to dine at?

PL: Stars is an obvious answer here. It was before my time, so I never got to experience its grandiosity. I walked in the space decades after its closure, and it felt like a mausoleum. I would've loved to have seen it alive and at the peak of its popularity. I think a lot about the physical grandeur of the restaurants of the second half of the twentieth century, and I think that's the thing I'd be most curious to experience. It'd be really cool to experience so many landmark restaurants during the peak of their popularity, to see [those] buzzing, see-and-be-seen rooms.

But there are also those one-of-a-kind spots—unicorns, if you will—that I wish I could visit. The original location of Sam Wo, for example, during its heyday. (I only went there during its final months, though the new location is still lovely!) Doggie Diner. Hippo Burger.

TODAY'S RICOTTA

FLOUR + WATER, THOMAS MCNAUGHTON AND RYAN POLLNOW

If pasta were as simple as just flour and water, we'd all be outrageously terrific pasta chefs like Thomas McNaughton and Ryan Pollnow, right? Ok, it's not that easy. There's also technique, impeccable ingredients, years and years of practice... on and on to get to the point of serving captivating, consistently excellent traditional and pretty innovative pastas to a packed house nightly like Flour + Water does in the Mission. I'll admit that I have visited Flour + Water for dinner more often than any other restaurant since it opened in 2010. That's largely because no two visits are ever the same, in a great way. The pastas change so frequently and there is always some combination that is mind-blowing and ultrasatisfying. And, contrary to what some diners might believe, there's much more at this superb restaurant besides pasta. The ricotta starter is also a mainstay of the menu with a rotating cast of subtle accoutrements like Sicilian olive oil and honeycomb. It's the perfect prelude to a dinner of some of SF's best pasta and pizza.

YIELD: about 2 cups

---

8 CUPS WHOLE MILK	1 TABLESPOON KOSHER SALT
1 CUP HEAVY CREAM	¼ CUP FRESH LEMON JUICE

1. Line a colander with cheesecloth and place it inside a larger bowl. Set aside.

2. In a heavy, 6-quart pot, combine the milk, cream, and salt and bring to a simmer over medium-low heat, stirring occasionally. This will take about 15 minutes.

3. When the milk just begins to simmer, add the lemon juice. Stir constantly until the mixture starts to curdle, approximately 4 minutes.

4. Remove the pot from heat to ensure the milk does not continue to simmer. Continuing to simmer the milk after the curds begin to separate will result in a dense and dry ricotta. Allow the curds to rest for 10 minutes.

5. Pour the milk mixture into your prepared colander to strain the curds from the whey by-product. The milk will have formed hard curds—your ricotta cheese. You can use it after 5 minutes because not much more moisture will be extracted by further draining. If desired, reserve the whey liquid by-product for another use. At Flour + Water, the cooks use the whey for braising meat, for pasta pan sauces, and in vinaigrettes.

SOUPS, SALADS, BREADS, VEGETABLES, SIDES, AND SAUCES

HOG ISLAND CLAM CHOWDER

HOG ISLAND OYSTER CO.

There are few greater pleasures in San Francisco dining than sipping a glass of rosé and slurping Tomales Bay (near the Marin coast) oysters at that oyster farm's restaurant in the Ferry Building. I'm smiling just thinking about this as I type it. Hog Island, though, is so much more than just an oyster bar. There are ceviches, crudos, seafood stew, and, curiously, SF's finest grilled cheese sandwich. But on a cool, foggy late morning or midafternoon when the wind picks up, nothing is more satisfying than a bowl of clam-forward (and flour-free!) clam chowder featuring the Manila clams grown by Hog Island. "Where I grew up, nobody puts flour in the chowder," says cofounder John Finger.

YIELD: 8 servings

---

6 LBS. SMALL HOG ISLAND MANILA CLAMS IN THE SHELL

8 TO 10 MEDIUM-SIZE YUKON GOLD POTATOES, PEELED AND CUT INTO BITE-SIZE CUBES

2 TABLESPOONS BUTTER

3 SPRIGS FRESH THYME

8 OZ. HIGH-QUALITY BACON, DICED

½ SMALL STALK CELERY, THINLY SLICED

2 LARGE LEEKS, WHITE PART ONLY, THINLY SLICED ON THE DIAGONAL

1 LARGE CARROT, PEELED AND THINLY SLICED

1 QUART HEAVY CREAM

FRESHLY GROUND BLACK PEPPER, FOR GARNISH

FRESH PARSLEY, CHOPPED, FOR GARNISH

continued...

---

1. Place the clams in a colander in the kitchen sink and rinse thoroughly under running water. Pick through and discard any with broken or open shells that will not close when you flick at them with your finger. Allow the clams to drain in the sink while you prepare the chowder base.

2. In a large stockpot, bring 5 to 6 cups of water to a boil (no salt) and cook the potatoes until they are al dente, just shy of fork-tender. Drain the potatoes, reserving the cooking water.

3. While the potatoes are boiling, in a large, heavy-bottomed pot over low heat, melt the butter with the thyme. Add the bacon and render it.

4. Add the celery and leeks and cook until the vegetables are translucent.

5. Add the carrot and cook until you can bend a slice without breaking it.

6. Add the potatoes and 4 cups of the reserved potato water.

7. Portion your clams out per single or double servings (about 12 oz. per serving). Working in batches, place the serving(s) of clams in a heavy-bottomed sauté pan over medium heat. Ladle 1 cup of the chowder base on top, cover the pan, and simmer for about 5 minutes, until the majority of the clams open.

8. Skim through and pick out any clams that have not opened. (Don't skip this step—unopened clams may spoil the chowder.)

9. Add in ½ cup cream per serving and bring the chowder to a simmer (1 to 2 minutes). If it is too thick, add some more of the reserved potato water.

10. When the chowder is bubbling in the middle, it is ready to serve. Pour individual servings into warm soup bowls and add the clams.

11. Garnish with cracked pepper and chopped parsley and serve with warm, crusty French bread to soak up the broth. Place extra empty bowls on the table for discarding clamshells. Enjoy!

DUNGENESS CRAB LOUIE

SWAN OYSTER DEPOT

The go-to at the "Swan," of course, is Dungeness crab when it's in season, and it's arguably best enjoyed with on a bed of lettuce with plenty of Louie dressing on the side. Make sure to have some sourdough as well, and you'll swear that you can hear Tony Bennett singing in the background.

YIELD: 4 servings

4 LBS. LIVE DUNGENESS CRABS

SALT, TO TASTE

LETTUCE, AS NEEDED

3 CUPS BEST FOODS OR OTHER QUALITY MAYONNAISE

½ CUP COCKTAIL SAUCE OR KETCHUP (IF USING KETCHUP, ADD

A TINY BIT OF WATER AND WHISK TO MAKE IT LESS VISCOUS)

½ CUP CHOPPED BLACK OLIVES

½ CUP DICED SWEET GREEN RELISH

½ CUP HARD-BOILED EGG, MASHED OR DICED

1. The crabs should be alive until they are dropped in water. Dead crabs are no good. Dungeness crabs are vicious, so keep your fingers away from their claws and grab from the rear.

2. Handling with care, place crabs in boiling salted water and let the water return to a boil. Once the water is boiling again, cook the crabs for 20 minutes.

3. Drain the crabs, crack them, and shell them. Arrange lettuce leaves on the plates and top them with the crab.

4. Place all of the remaining ingredients in a mixing bowl, whisk to combine, and dress the salads with it. You should have some leftover dressing, which can be served on the side.

HOUSE-MADE LOUIE DRESSING

ORIGINAL JOE'S

To me, outside of sourdough, Louie is the marquee San Francisco–invented offering to the greater culinary world. Sorry, cioppino doesn't really count, because it's not all that easy to replicate in a lot of places. But Louie is one of the key salad dressings around the globe. So, I wanted to see a contrast between two San Francisco institutions. Original Joe's has been a part of San Francisco since it started out as a 14-seat counter with a sawdust floor in 1937; it is now the pinnacle of time-travel sophistication—all the best of the modern 2020s and all the best of midcentury gravitas and charm. They don't make 'em like this anymore.

YIELD: 1½ cups

¾ CUP MAYONNAISE

6 TABLESPOONS CHILI SAUCE

2 OZ. SCALLIONS, MINCED

2 OZ. PITTED GREEN OLIVES, MINCED

1 TEASPOON WORCESTERSHIRE SAUCE

1 TEASPOON PREPARED HORSERADISH SAUCE

SALT AND PEPPER, TO TASTE

1. Combine the mayonnaise, chili sauce, scallions, olives, Worcestershire, and horseradish in a medium bowl, using a whisk.

2. Add salt and pepper to taste.

GREEN GODDESS DRESSING

PALACE HOTEL

The history, the mesmerizing glass dome—everyone freezes the moment that they first step into the Palace Hotel's grand, opulent Garden Court. It's a breathtaking spot that has so many captivating stories from the past, just like the hotel itself. After all, it was the inventor of *two* pivotal dishes (more on the second one later!). Green goddess dressing was first conjured up here, and now you'll find it all over the country. But remember, it was first served on New Montgomery Street! But, is it called the green goddess just because of the chives and parsley?

Green goddess dressing was created at the Palace Hotel in 1923 by Executive Chef Philip Roemer. Chef Roemer created the dressing for a banquet held at the Palace. The event was honoring actor George Arliss, who was the lead in William Archer's hit play The Green Goddess.

—**Palace Hotel**

YIELD: about 2 generous cups

---

1 CUP MAYONNAISE

½ CUP SOUR CREAM

¼ CUP SNIPPED FRESH CHIVES OR MINCED SCALLIONS

¼ CUP MINCED FRESH PARSLEY

1 TABLESPOON FRESH LEMON JUICE

1 TABLESPOON WHITE WINE VINEGAR

3 ANCHOVY FILLETS, RINSED, PATTED DRY, AND MINCED

SALT AND FRESHLY GROUND PEPPER, TO TASTE

1. Stir all the ingredients together in a small bowl until well blended. Taste and adjust the seasonings. Use immediately or cover and refrigerate.

THE PALACE GREEN GODDESS TODAY

PALACE HOTEL

Now it's time to compare and contrast from 1923 to 2023!

YIELD: 1 gallon

2 BUNCHES FLAT-LEAF PARSLEY, ROUGHLY CHOPPED

2 BUNCHES FRESH CHERVIL, ROUGHLY CHOPPED

2 BUNCHES FRESH TARRAGON, ROUGHLY CHOPPED

5 CUPS FRESH SPINACH

½ BOTTLE CAPERS, CHOPPED

¼ BOTTLE WORCESTERSHIRE SAUCE

½ CUP CHOPPED GARLIC

¼ CUP CHOPPED SHALLOTS

1 TABLESPOON SUGAR

6 ANCHOVY FILLETS, RINSED, PATTED DRY, AND MINCED

3 CUPS TARRAGON VINEGAR

½ CUP DIJON MUSTARD

3 EGG YOLKS

6 CUPS CORN OIL

SALT AND PEPPER, TO TASTE

1. Place everything, except the oil, salt, and pepper, in a blender or in a container and use an immersion blender. Blend on high until smooth.

2. With the blender running, slowly pour in the oil.

3. Season with salt and pepper to taste.

4. This can be stored in the refrigerator in an airtight container for up to 10 days.

Q&A, ALEXANDRE VIRIOT

EXECUTIVE CHEF, LA SOCIÉTÉ BAR AND CAFÉ

TF: How have these opening months of La Société been? If I'm correct, this is your first professional experience in SF? What's it like compared to other markets?

AV: It's been great! When I worked abroad, we had to import so many of our products to get the highest quality. Here in San Francisco, you are surrounded by it!

TF: You've literally cooked all over the world. How do you quickly adapt to cooking in an entirely new climate and, oftentimes, a new continent?

AV: I've moved around my entire life. In fact, I think the maximum amount of time I've lived anywhere has been five years! As a result, I am quite comfortable adapting to new places. When you cook in different countries, you learn that palates can be quite different and adjust your technique based on this. For instance, what we consider perfectly seasoned in America is considered too concentrated in some parts of Asia, so when I used to make stock, I would roast the bones for less time to mellow out the flavor. They are often small cooking adjustments, but they make a big difference as far as keeping your guests happy.

TF: What was it like cooking at restaurants of Guy Savoy, Alain Ducasse, and Joël Robuchon? That's a Mt. Rushmore of chefs right there. I'm intimidated just saying their names, let alone working for them!

AV: First of all, my goal in my culinary career was to cook and learn from the top chefs in my field, and I feel so fortunate that I got an opportunity to work with Savoy, Ducasse, and Robuchon. Each of them has a different style, from their technique to how they plate. However, they all aligned on their main focus, find the best product possible and showcase it.

TF: Can you tell us a bit about your menus and cooking style at La Société? How does the Bay Area affect your cuisine there?

AV: It's French and farm to table. Being in San Francisco, it is all about seasonal cooking. I have spent a lot of time learning about the growing seasons, which are very different here in the Bay Area. I spend a lot of time at the market meeting different farmers.

TF: I have to ask, as a big fan of duck à l'orange and escargot dishes (which are both sadly rare to find in SF), what are the keys to success for those two bistro cuisine stalwarts?

AV: The idea behind our restaurant was to feature traditional French dishes with a modern twist. For the duck, we add a reduction of orange juice to the sauce. With the escargot, we use a garlic parsley butter, but we add chartreuse to ours to add an herbaceousness. We also incorporate a house-made tomato jam that cuts the fat and adds texture.

CORN SOUP PANNA COTTA AND CRAB SALAD

LA FOLIE, ROLAND PASSOT

Just days before the COVID-19 pandemic began in earnest, Chef Roland Passot's beloved La Folie restaurant in Russian Hill took its final bow to a series of standing ovation dinners after a stellar 32-year run. By the 2010s, it was undoubtedly San Francisco's primary example of spectacular haute French cuisine. Every dinner was an event—decadent, celebratory, thrilling—long after that trend had faded away elsewhere. And, amidst all of the (mostly great) modernity in SF fine dining nowadays, I wanted to make sure that La Folie continued to live on, so it's a tremendous honor that Chef Passot kindly shared this wonderful dish with us.

YIELD: 6 servings

3 EARS FRESH CORN, KERNELS REMOVED FROM THE COBS, COBS RESERVED (YOU SHOULD HAVE ABOUT 1 CUP OF KERNELS)

SALT AND PEPPER, TO TASTE

6 FRESH BASIL LEAVES

3 TABLESPOONS BUTTER

½ SWEET ONION, DICED OR 1 LB. SLICED ONIONS

4 OZ. DRY VERMOUTH

6 OZ. HEAVY CREAM

4 SHEETS OF GELATIN

1 OZ. FRESH LEMON JUICE

½ CUP OLIVE OIL

⅛ TEASPOON PIMENT D'ESPELETTE

1 LB. FRESH DUNGENESS CRAB, COOKED AND CLEANED

1 BUNCH CHIVES, CHOPPED, TOPS RESERVED FOR GARNISH

MICRO GREENS, FOR GARNISH

PEA SHOOTS, FOR GARNISH

MUSTARD GREENS, FOR GARNISH

ANCHO CRESS, FOR GARNISH

RADISH SHOOTS, FOR GARNISH

continued...

1. In a pot, cover the cobs with water. Season with salt and simmer for 25 to 30 minutes. Add the basil leaves to the stock, strain, and set it aside.

2. Place the butter in a large skillet and melt it over medium heat. Add the onion and sweat until translucent. Add the corn kernels and sweat for another 5 minutes, stirring often. Add the dry vermouth and bring to a boil. Reduce by one-quarter, add the cream, and bring to a boil. Reduce the heat and let it simmer for 5 minutes. Add the corn stock and cook until the corn is tender. Puree the soup, strain it, season it with salt and pepper, and set it aside.

3. Place the gelatin leaves in water and let them bloom until soft. Remove the gelatin from the water and squeeze it to remove excess water.

4. Take 4 cups of the soup and dissolve the gelatin in the mixture. Add the remaining soup and mix thoroughly.

5. Pour about 1 inch of the mixture into small soup bowls. Refrigerate for about 2 hours, until the panna cottas are set.

6. Combine the olive oil and lemon juice. Add the piment d'espelette.

7. Add the vinaigrette to the cleaned crab, stir in the chives, and season with salt and pepper.

8. To serve, place a small scoop of crab on top of the panna cottas, in the middle of the bowl. Garnish with the remaining ingredients and enjoy.

Q&A, LETICIA LANDA

EXECUTIVE DIRECTOR, LA COCINA

TF: Let's start with how you learned about La Cocina. You were studying anthropology at Harvard and read about the organization?!

LL: Hi! I had actually just graduated from college when I read an article in *The New York Times* about La Cocina, entitled "For Women, a Recipe to Create a Successful Business." I knew I was moving to San Francisco, because I had gotten a fellowship at an organization called Hispanics in Philanthropy (HIP), but I hadn't yet made the road trip across the country. When I arrived, I made a point of visiting the La Cocina booth at the Ferry Plaza Farmers Market. I can remember buying CMBSweets jam and just really admiring everything about the organization. I met Valeria Perez Ferreiro at the HIP holiday party that year, and shortly after that she hired me!

TF: Were you always interested in the food industry and/or helping out small businesses?

LL: I have always loved to cook and have always loved the way that food transmits culture. I loved cooking with my mom and making recipes that my grandmothers in Mexico had given to her. I also always loved discovering new foods from different parts of the world. I've always loved reading cookbooks and trying new spices, new techniques, and ways of approaching ingredients differently by different cultures. That's certainly part of what drew me to San Francisco, and then to La Cocina—the opportunity to try foods from so many different parts of the world through all the immigrants who have made their home here. Through the small food businesses they have started here. I (like so many other people) had worked in restaurants while I was in college, but I definitely knew a lot less about the business side of things when I began at La Cocina. Which in a lot of ways mirrors the experience of so many of our entrepreneurs who are cooks who then learn how to be accountants, marketers, managers, etc.

TF: La Cocina is truly one of the most important and unique programs of any kind in San Francisco, with how it has helped launch the careers of dozens of chefs, largely immigrants and people of color. Can you tell us a bit about the incubator and how it helps these chefs fulfill their goals?

LL: La Cocina's program focuses on talented low-income women of color and immigrant women, because they often work in the food industry but experience significant barriers to the economic freedom business ownership can bring. All participants launch with less than $5,000. The tremendous talent that resourcing these entrepreneurs unlocks is evidenced by the fact that since 2005, La Cocina has incubated 130+ businesses, some are grossing up to $2 million annually. Sixty percent of La Cocina entrepreneurs are parents, and twelve businesses are run by entrepreneurs and their adult children, demonstrating the power that business assets have for families and communities.

Since 2005, La Cocina has focused on small-business incubation with a vision to reduce barriers to business ownership for women of color and immigrant women. La Cocina is both the space (a modern building and commercial kitchen) and the program (an innovative business incubator), which together provide talented entrepreneurs the necessary tools to launch their businesses, achieve financial independence, and claim their place in a more inclusive economic landscape.

While many incubators prioritize curriculum completion and business launch, La Cocina takes the long road to ensure true economic sustainability. Entrepreneurs can be active in our program for six years and can receive around a hundred hours of annual technical assistance. Although our program has found efficiencies with a cohort model, it is also very much tailored to the individual needs of each entrepreneur. All aspects of curriculum, how we advocate for opportunities, and how we cultivate the power of these women are rooted in a deep understanding of their individual talent and the belief that they are powerful advocates for themselves, their families, and their communities.

TF: How do chefs get connected with La Cocina and pitch their ideas? And how do you eventually help them find a permanent location for their food concepts?

LL: At this point it's mostly word of mouth—chefs hear about us from someone in their community who has heard about our program. We also do a lot of outreach through our network of partner organizations to do recruitment. We have orientations every other month and host drop-in markets where people who are interested in the program can come sell their food and get feedback from our staff and volunteers. We have an application process, so interested chefs submit a business plan and answer questions, and then we do an in-person interview where we also try their food. Once a business has gone through our preincubation program and has shifted from the growth phase of incubation to focusing on exit, staff works closely with the entrepreneur to figure out how they are going to leave our shared-use kitchen.

This looks different for each person. A chocolate maker may be looking for a copacker or for a different shared-use kitchen space. Someone wanting a restaurant will be looking for either locations to build out or turnkey restaurant spaces they can purchase the lease of. We have an amazing network of volunteers who, in addition to our staff, support entrepreneurs in reviewing leases, thinking about their kitchen design, and what operations in a new space will look like.

TF: Can you talk a little about the La Cocina Municipal Marketplace? I know it's been a long time in the works and is both trying to elevate the neighborhood and the program participants who are vendors there.

LL: La Cocina Municipal Marketplace offers economic opportunity for seven working-class women of color and immigrant women entrepreneurs, an inclusive and accessible space with delicious and affordable food for Tenderloin residents, and an innovative model for conscious, community-led development in inner cities. Much like La Cocina's incubator kitchen, the marketplace offers a path for low-income entrepreneurs that lowers the barriers to entry, mitigates risk via a shared cost of maintenance, increases equity in business ownership, and creates more assets for the owners, enabling them to pass on lower costs to consumers and make cities more livable.

TF: Last question—it's a big-picture San Francisco dining scene question. What do you think are the key ingredients that make our city's dining scene so exciting and unique?

LL: The combination of people from all over the world who have made the Bay Area their home, using ingredients that are grown/caught/raised nearby....the incredible quality and proximity of the raw materials, and then the way that those ingredients get translated and adapted by so many different cultures that have made their home here feels like the most special thing to me. Migration, food, and our incredible weather are the perfect formula for making the Bay Area's dining scene so magical.

RADICCHIO SALAD

ANGLER, PAUL CHUNG

Along with pristine preparations of raw fish and seafood and hearth-grilled fish, as the name alludes to, the Saison Hospitality Group's Embarcadero restaurant is known for all kinds of specialties and atmosphere traits—the incomparable salted caramel on soft serve; the taxidermy in the back room; the superb cocktails in impeccable glassware; the Bay Bridge views. And then there's the reason that everyone is wearing a bib: this wondrous, oh-so-delightful (and at times messy) crimson-colored salad. This is a salad that is the main event, not just a plate of lettuce.

The radicchio shares the ethos of Saison Hospitality. We use a singular ingredient and transcend it with the use of smoke and fire. The XO adds great depth and texture to the dish and is made with by-product, keeping it sustainable and zero-waste. Both the XO and dressing are smoked; this allows you to taste the beauty of our hearth even in cold preparations like our salad. **—Chef Chung**

YIELD: 10 servings

---

1. Peel back the outer layers of the radicchio and save for later.

2. Core out the center root of the radicchio and gently begin pulling the leaves apart. Be sure not to rip the leaves, as you will be rebuilding the heads after they are washed.

3. Keep each grouping of leaves together, so that the rebuilding of each head is aligned. Rinse the leaves in ice water to keep the leaves crisp.

4. Before rebuilding the head, pat dry each leaf to make sure they are dry and ready for the dressing when needed.

continued...

RADICCHIO XO

2 QUARTS EXTRA LEAVES
NOT USED FOR THE SALAD

EXTRA-VIRGIN OLIVE OIL,
AS NEEDED

GRAPESEED OIL, AS NEEDED

2 CUPS ELEPHANT GARLIC, SLICED
PAPER-THIN LENGTHWISE
ON A MANDOLINE

2 CUPS DICED SHALLOTS

1. Paint the extra leaves with olive oil.

2. Flatten them over a wire grate and hang them over embers, in a place that is about 115°F/46°C (at Angler, they do this in their hearth) for 5 to 6 hours, slowly drying them. The goal is to dehydrate the leaves to get them crispy, as well as to imbue them with smoke.

3. Soak the sliced garlic, changing the water three times at 1-hour intervals to remove the residual bitterness. Pat the garlic dry to remove all the moisture.

4. Start the garlic in cold grapeseed oil, making sure to add enough oil that the garlic will float and not touch the bottom of the pot. This might be as much as a gallon of grapeseed oil. Allow the heat to rise to 300°F/149°C and cook for 10 to 15 minutes. You do not want the garlic to color and get bitter.

5. After frying the garlic, remove it from the heat. Hold it in the smoker, and it will get crispy as it cools down.

6. Using the same oil, fry the shallots at 325°F/163°C until they develop an exterior shell, about 5 minutes, and then lower the temperature to 275°F/135°C and slowly allow the shallots to cook through and develop a crispy texture.

7. Fold the radicchio, garlic, and shallots together, making sure not to crumble everything. Add 2 cups of the frying oil.

BEET DRESSING

2 QUARTS BEET JUICE

2 QUARTS TAMARI

2 CUPS RAW SUGAR

SHERRY VINEGAR, TO TASTE

FRESH LEMON JUICE, TO TASTE

1. In a medium pot over high heat, rapidly reduce the beet juice by half; it should have a syrupy consistency. You want this stage to be done at a boil so the color sets.

2. In another medium pot, combine the tamari and raw sugar and reduce in the same way.

3. Once they are both reduced, place the pots in the smoker and smoke at 250°F/121°C for 1 to 2 hours, reducing the dressing more and making it the consistency of molasses.

4. Combine both the tamari and beet reductions once fully reduced and let cool.

5. Season with sherry vinegar and lemon juice to taste.

ASSEMBLY

1. Take the washed head of radicchio and lay it on a tray in individual layers.

2. Paint each leaf with the beet dressing, add a tablespoon of the XO, and drizzle with more sherry and lemon juice.

3. Rebuild the layers together to resemble the whole radicchio head and paint the outside of the salad as well. Drizzle more XO around the sides and the top of the salad.

4. Serve right away, while the XO remains crispy.

KALE SALAD

Kale salad at one of the world's greatest, most inventive cocktail bars? I mean, how does this make sense? Well, that's the Trick Dog kale salad for you. It has it all—it's crunchy, creamy, umami, craveworthy. And maybe kind of healthy. When San Franciscans mention "the kale salad," this is what they're referring to. If you pair it with Trick Dog fries, it's definitely an atypical vegetarian dinner, but surely a wonderful one. Note: Banyuls vinegar can be found at Whole Foods or any high-end grocery store. If unavailable, use champagne vinegar or red wine vinegar instead.

YIELD: 1 (very large) salad that serves 2 as an entree or 4 as a side salad; 2½ quarts dressing

DRESSING

8 EGG YOLKS	BANYULS VINEGAR, AS NEEDED
⅛ TEASPOON CAYENNE PEPPER	1½ QUARTS EXTRA-VIRGIN OLIVE OIL
1 TEASPOON SALT, PLUS MORE TO TASTE	WATER, AS NEEDED

1. In a food processor or blender, add the egg yolks, cayenne, salt, and ¼ cup Banyuls vinegar. Start the machine and slowly drizzle in the olive oil until a thick, almost mayo-like consistency forms. Begin to thin it out with more vinegar, a couple spoonfuls or drops at a time.

2. Continue to add the olive oil and repeat the process by adding more vinegar, olive oil, vinegar, etc. Make sure to add a little bit of water (like you would the vinegar) to thin out the dressing. You want the dressing to be quite thick, almost

continued...

like the consistency of a thinner mayo, and it it should be quite tangy from the vinegar, while still retaining the flavor of the egg. You want to fill up the food processor or blender completely.

3. Taste and add more salt or vinegar if needed. Refrigerate until ready to use.

SALAD

5 BUNCHES CURLY KALE

½ AVOCADO, SMASHED

JUICE OF ½ LEMON

½ CUP TOASTED UNSALTED
PUMPKIN SEEDS, DIVIDED

¼ CUP FRESHLY GRATED
PARMESAN CHEESE, DIVIDED

1 TEASPOON KOSHER SALT,
PLUS MORE TO TASTE

1 TEASPOON FRESHLY GROUND
BLACK PEPPER

1 CUP DRESSING (SEE PAGE 131),
OR TO TASTE

1. Remove the stems from the kale, then wash and dry it. Using the julienne blade of your food processor, push the kale through to cut/shred it. Place in a large bowl.

2. Add the avocado, lemon juice, half of the toasted pumpkin seeds, half of the Parmesan, and the salt and pepper.

3. Begin with 1 cup of dressing and mix everything together. Don't be afraid to work the avocado into the salad, as it adds a nice creamy texture. Add more dressing if needed and taste for salt.

4. Pile onto a plate or in a bowl and top with the remaining pumpkin seeds and Parmesan.

Q&A, REBECCA FINEMAN AND CHRIS GAITHER

MASTER SOMMELIERS AND CO-OWNERS, UNGRAFTED AND GLUGLU

TF: This is a book all about San Francisco food past and present...and, of course, wine and food go together in San Francisco like clam chowder and a sourdough bowl. Since we're surrounded by vineyards all around the bay, the city has a bit of a unique relationship with wine—both local and from regions afar. What do you think stands out in San Francisco diners' preferences and connections with wine, given this interesting dynamic? Do we tend to be open-minded or just want our reliable Sonoma and Napa wines?

CG: There's a little bit of both. San Franciscans love to travel, and when they return home, they want to consume things they tasted when they were on vacation. But they also head to wine country quite a bit and develop their loyalties to certain wineries.

TF: Both of you have worked at some of the city's top fine dining restaurants—Gary Danko, Spruce, Octavia, Sociale, and more. And we can count that under-the-radar Yountville place called The French Laundry as sort of San Francisco too. What was the relationship like between the wine programs and the kitchens at those kinds of places?

RF: At finer dining restaurants, there is an option to order a prix fixe menu with full wine pairings. The food menu might change every few days, which means we, as sommeliers, are always coming up with new food pairings. In an ideal world, we would get an opportunity to taste the dish and try a few different wines with it. But, in reality, we often don't get to taste the dish until it's plated for the staff, right before service. As trained sommeliers, we can still manage, though. We know enough about cooking and enough about wine to come up with theoretical pairings. Occasionally we will switch it out at the last moment, once we taste the dish, but generally the pairings we think are going to work do.

Some chefs are more willing to work with the sommeliers to make sure the new dish is tasted, and the pairing is confirmed before menus are printed. Others are less accommodating. This has more to do with the personality of the chef versus the restaurant itself. We've worked at places for long enough to see different people take the lead in the kitchen, with varying results for our relationship. Some chefs don't treat sommeliers with respect, which is a shame, because we make a lot of money for the restaurants.

TF: You are two of the very small number of master sommeliers in the country. And, maybe the only master sommelier couple? What was it like going through the rigorous studying and exams process together? Has that process helped shape your two restaurants?

CG: It was hard doing it together. It's a very stressful thing, and not a good idea to bring that sort of stress into a relationship. That being said, it was easier for us to know what we needed to do to support the other person. Rebecca passed the master sommelier before me. It made me realize that I hadn't given her enough credit, and I had been too focused on myself. When it came time for me to buckle down and get it done, she was there for me in a way I hadn't been for her.

RF: The exams were stressful, but opening a restaurant is a stressful thing too. I also wouldn't recommend bringing that sort of stress into a relationship. When we go home, we still discuss work. It's very hard to separate our work life and our home life, and it drives our oldest daughter crazy. However, we wouldn't have it any other way.

TF: Speaking of those two restaurants, Ungrafted and GluGlu, can you tell us a bit about both and how you work on the wine side with Chef David Aviles?

RF: Ungrafted was our first business. It is a restaurant and a bottle shop, and just a very cool space, filled with murals and art by local artists. It's in a historic building in the Dogpatch, a neighborhood which, until very recently, even native San Franciscans didn't know about. That is changing, and we are proud to be helping to lead that change.

GluGlu, on the other hand, is a wine bar. We only recently opened it at Thrive City, which is the name for the businesses surrounding Chase Center. It's also a very cool space, but much newer and more open, with a large patio and floor-to-ceiling windows.

At Ungrafted our focus is showcasing delicious wines from all around the world and also helping people learn in the process. We offer blind tasting flights, lots of wine classes, and a very complete and international wine list.

At GluGlu the goal is more simple: these are the types of wines we find ourselves drinking on our days off. They are highly quaffable wines that you keep wanting more of. The same goes with our food program. Our chef, David, went to culinary school and worked in the fine dining sphere for most of his career. Most recently he was running the ship at Acadia, a two-Michelin–starred restaurant in Chicago. However, his parents immigrated to the US from Mexico before he was born. They worked their butts off, and after sending all their kids to school, they decided to open a classic American diner. David has both of these experiences in his worldview. The food at GluGlu is the style of food David wants to eat— not a tasting menu, not expensive, but seasonal, colorful, highly shareable. It might look simple but is more complicated than you think. This is what we offer at GluGlu.

TF: What are the signature dishes at the restaurants?

RF: At Ungrafted we make a pull-apart bread that is very similar to kubaneh. We fill ours with za'atar and it is served warm, with a side of labneh for dipping. Another signature item is a fried chicken dish that was developed by Chef David. It is meant for two or three people, and we only offer it on the weekend: fried chicken topped with caviar, served on a bed of truffled polenta. It sells out every weekend.

GluGlu hasn't really been open long enough to have a signature dish, but I predict that our pan con tomate with mussels will soon be a classic. The mussels are cooked in our Rational oven, which steams them perfectly. It's an item that almost every single table orders.

TF: Both restaurants helped elevate their respective neighborhoods' dining profiles (Mission Bay and Dogpatch). What's it like being a part of creating a small neighborhood's restaurant personality, as opposed to just being part of a firmly established destination area, à la North Beach, Mission District, Divisadero?

CG: It's been exciting. We love helping to build the community, and, in turn, we become a fabric of that community. It does require some patience, though, which is often hard to exercise. But, at the end of the day, our regulars are very loyal, in a way that I sometimes think is missing in the more established neighborhoods.

TF: Ok, now to everyone's favorite topic with sommeliers...pairings! Let's think about San Francisco classics for a second. What am I pairing with that aforementioned clam chowder in a sourdough bowl? And, how about a Dungeness crab Louie salad? Cioppino? A Mission-style carne asada burrito? A dim sum lunch?

CG: Fun! Clam chowder is creamy, buttery, and rich. Let's pair it with an acidic grape like chardonnay, either oaked or unoaked: 1er cru Chablis or Chassagne-Montrachet.

RF: Now it's my turn. I love to pair a dry Riesling with crab Louie. There's a sweetness to crab, but it's not sweet enough to need a sweet wine. The acid from the Riesling cuts through the fat in the dish.

CG: Rebecca and I drink a lot of champagne with dim sum. It's not always a perfect pairing, but we love it. Dim sum is fun and champagne is fun.

RF: Carne asada goes well with Syrah or Rioja; the wines like to be paired with smoky, meaty foods. These are both wines that also pair perfectly with Korean barbecue.

TF: What are some of your other favorite pairings, whether tried-and-true classics or ones that we diners tend to not think about?

CG: Champagne and French fries.

RF: Rosé champagne and pizza or burgers.

SERENA CHOW-FISHER

Partners in business and in life, Serena Chow-Fisher and David Fisher split the responsibilities of the prixe fixe menu at their delightful Bernal Heights restaurant, Marlena, between Serena's desserts and this exceptional bread and David's savory dishes. Everything the pair created there was just wonderful—elegant, smartly composed, and exciting. No wonder they received a Michelin star in what seems like record time in 2021, when the restaurant was just a year old. With this recipe, now you have the chance to bake at home like one of the country's leading bakers/pastry chefs. In 2023, the couple departed Marlena, and they now plan to open a restaurant, called 7 Adams, in the Fillmore District. Fortunately for all, this bread is in their plans for the menu.

YIELD: 18 rolls

---

1 CUP WHOLE MILK

6 TABLESPOONS (80 G) SUGAR

1 PACKET (7 G) ACTIVE DRY YEAST

6 OZ. (170 G) ROOM TEMPERATURE BUTTER

3½ CUPS (440 G) BREAD FLOUR

1½ TEASPOONS (4.5 G) PLUS ¼ TEASPOON KOSHER SALT (DIAMOND CRYSTAL WAS USED IN TESTING)

1 WHOLE EGG

150 G HEAVY CREAM

MELTED BUTTER, TO BRUSH OVER BREAD

FLAKY SALT, FOR GARNISH (THEY USE MALDON)

1. In a small pot over low heat, warm the milk to 110°F/43°C. Stir in the sugar and yeast. Let the yeast bloom for 10 to 15 minutes.

continued...

2. In a stand mixer fitted with the dough hook, combine the butter, milk mixture, flour, and kosher salt. The dough is ready when it is homogeneous in texture and the side of the bowl is almost entirely clean.

3. Transfer the dough to a bowl and cover with plastic wrap. Let it sit in a warm place for about 1 hour. Once it's doubled in size, punch the dough down.

4. Roll the dough into little balls, each one weighing about 50 g. Again, let the dough sit in a warm place for about 1 hour.

5. Preheat the oven to 350°F/177°C.

6. To make an egg wash, whisk together the egg, cream, and remaining ¼ teaspoon salt, then run the mixture through a sieve to strain out any bits of egg.

7. Brush the balls of dough with the egg wash and bake for 7 minutes. Rotate the pan and bake for another 4 minutes, until the tops are golden brown.

8. Once removed from the oven, brush with melted butter and sprinkle with flaky salt.

Q&A, RAVI KAPUR

CHEF/OWNER, LIHOLIHO YACHT CLUB AND GOOD GOOD CULTURE CLUB

TF: What inspired you to completely change your professional route from business communications to cooking? That's quite the U-turn!

RK: I went to college without much of a long-term career plan. After two years it was obvious that I needed to make a change, and that's what led me to cooking. While a formal education wasn't achieved, there were some pretty valuable life experiences gained during that time—I was a lead singer in a punk/ska band and worked in a pizza shop cooking and washing dishes; without those experiences I wouldn't be where I am today. In 1998 I headed to SF to start at the CCA.

TF: How does your youth growing up in Hawai'i and experience in several notable SF fine dining restaurants (Boulevard, Prospect, Redwood Park, and more) shape your cooking style today?

RK: Regarding teaching style, family values are at the forefront. In Hawai'i, you always bring something to the table. You teach and lead with Aloha. To Aloha means to be intentional, have kindness, calmness, compassion, and meet people where they're at—proving crucial to me as I came up from cook to chef.

Regarding food, I grew up with a multicultural pantry due to my multiethnic heritage. When you grow up eating, learning, and later cooking from your personal story/pantry, it is the fiber of your being. I love that we are moving away from words like "fusion," "Asian inspired," etc. Those who grew up with multiethnic backgrounds understand that you can be 100 percent of each part of yourself. It's why we refer to our restaurants as "heritage driven."

TF: Back in the early 2010s, Liholiho Yacht Club was one of the early truly influential pop-ups in San Francisco...back when "pop-up" was just starting to be a term in the restaurant world. What were those days like?

RK: In part, powerful and inspirational. Finding the courage to cook food from my heritage and see people enjoy and appreciate it was a building block I hadn't experienced. A jumping-off point to feel confident to explore in ways I never realized. The pop-ups unlocked so many doors. In other ways, it was brutal. My wife and I were broke and had just had a baby. We were maxing out our credit cards and working on our pop-ups around the clock. We depended on friends for staffing. Reservations would no-show, and we sometimes had so much food left over. After a long day/night, we'd be left driving around trying to place incredible ingredients with restaurants we knew would appreciate it. Our pop-up days were exhilarating and exhausting.

While the support from the dining community was key to our success, none of it would be possible without my chef friends who were willing to host us in their restaurants. Initially, we had our first pop-ups at Citizen's Band (now closed) and had a long run at State Bird, and we would prep out of Perbacco. It was pretty wild, but again, without the restaurant community's support, I'm not sure Liho would be here today. That generosity will always be remembered, and now I make it a point to open up space for emerging pop-ups and help chefs starting their pop-ups.

TF: Of course, Liholiho Yacht Club has been a citywide favorite for seven plus years for the food and drink. But it's also beloved because it's just such a happy, fun place. How do you achieve this balance of excellent, high-level dining with such a cheery vibe?

RK: To me, restaurants are about the vibe, it's gotta be fun. It's the ability to craft an environment so when people walk in, they just feel like they're ready to have a great time. Yes, the food, drink, and service need to be on point, but the lights, music, energy, all those things are just as important. We have a unique hiring process. We do not accept résumés. We prefer to know where people are presently and where they want to see themselves rather than where they once were. You get a vibrant and cheerful space when you hire kind, caring people. And, of course, the giant picture of my mom whimsically greeting guests as they enter our space sets a pretty clear vibe.

TF: How would you describe the difference, menuwise, between Liholiho Yacht Club and Good Good Culture Club?

RK: Liho is pulling inspiration from the cultures that have made their way to Hawai'i in the last hundred years. The immigrants from the Asian diaspora that add to the depth and layers of what has shaped Hawai'i into what it is today. Our chef Kevin at Good Good grew up in San Diego and is pulling inspiration from his Laotian culture. Our goal is to cook delicious food; we are not recreating traditional dishes, but [are] aware that they inspire how we cook. When we pull from our shared cultures, we strive to honor those origins and understand the roots of our influences. Both restaurants are rooted in the same values, and it was important that they each had their own unique identity and vibe.

We often hear people say they like one or the other more—our motto in life: there is no need for "either-or" when there is plenty of room for both.

TF: You, Jeff [Hanak], and April [Ravi's wife] have been very eloquent in describing how you want the restaurant industry to be a healthier, kinder space for employees. You're truly making an impact on the city's restaurant scene. Can you tell us a bit about what your restaurants do to achieve this and how the industry at large can try to get to a better place?

RK: Core values.

During the shutdown, we faced the question, for years, we've griped about how broken our industry was. If, instead, we identified the things that could fix it? What would they be? We then determined our core values and rebuilt our model immersed in these ethos. Our values are Empowerment, Care, Growth Mindset, and Diversity. Identifying and leading with our values changed how we hire, pay, the hours we operate, and our decision to remove gratuity. We found that things fell into place once we identified our value system. Similar to a filter, we could run every decision through [it]. For example, departing from the archaic system of inequities, where the guest would decide which team members should benefit financially, was essential as it did not align with our values.

TF: Finally, where do you like to dine in the city when you have free time?

RK: We eat mostly at home, but when dining out we lean toward family- and chef-owned restaurants. We try to explore different spots each time we dine out. We have had fun exposing our son, Makoa, who is now twelve, to our vibrant SF dining scene throughout the years. A few favorites are Loló, Rintaro, Che Fico, Delfina, Rich Table, Gao, and the State Bird family.

Summer Squash Blossom
See page 146

SUMMER SQUASH BLOSSOM

SORREL, ALEXANDER HONG

Sorrel is one of the truly great 2010s stories of San Francisco dining. Alexander Hong ran the popular pop-up for several years before going permanent in a truly lovely Presidio Heights space with a skylight. Hong's cooking is a phenomenal example of upscale Californian with strong influence from Italy (Hong previously worked at Quince and Frasca in Boulder, two of the great Italian fine dining restaurants in the United States)—as in, impeccable technique, clean and exciting flavors, the very best ingredients, and cuisine that is elegant but never fussy. This squash composition showcases what Sorrel is all about and does better than just about anyone.

I made this dish last year in the heat of summer, and it was an instant hit. This dish symbolizes summer by utilizing the short season of baby flowering summer squash. The squash is stuffed with bulgur, miso, currants, and curry oil and grilled over charcoal. The squash is then painted with an acidic spiced oil and accompanied with curried yogurt. You can only get these baby flowering summer squash at your local farmers market. This dish is packed full of flavor and delicious served hot or cold.

—**Chef Hong**

YIELD: 4 servings

EGGPLANT FARCE

600 G PEELED EGGPLANT

45 ML EXTRA-VIRGIN OLIVE OIL

130 G MISO PASTE

200 G BULGUR (175 G BULGUR COOKED IN 400 G DASHI)

60 G ONION, SWEATED

16 G SESAME SEEDS

3 G CARDAMOM

6 ML CURRY OIL

50 G CURRANTS, HYDRATED

IN WHITE VERJUS

6 ML FRESH LEMON JUICE

3 G SALT

1. Prepare a gas or charcoal grill for high heat. Preheat a smoker to 200ºF/93ºC. Massage the eggplant with the olive oil and 100 g of miso, place it on the grill, and cook, turning it as necessary, until it is charred all over.

2. Transfer the eggplant to the smoker and smoke until it is extremely tender.

3. Place the eggplant and the remaining ingredients, including the remaining miso, in a bowl and stir to combine.

4. Transfer the farce to a piping bag.

CURRIED YOGURT

350 G GREEK YOGURT

350 G CRÈME FRAÎCHE

15 G MADRAS CURRY POWDER

1. Combine all of the ingredients in a blender on high.

2. Strain.

CURRIED OIL

250 ML EXTRA-VIRGIN OLIVE OIL
(HONG USES ASARO)

50 G MADRAS CURRY POWDER

1. In a small pot, combine the olive oil and curry powder. Bring to a simmer.

2. Remove from the heat. Cover and let steep for 30 minutes.

3. Strain.

continued...

ASSEMBLY

25 SUMMER SQUASH FLOWERS (STUFFED WITH EGGPLANT FARCE)

1. Steam the squash flowers for 7 minutes at 194°F/90°C, full steam.

2. Coat the flowers in the curried oil and grill until blackened.

3. Place a dollop of the curried yogurt on the plate with the grilled blossom on top.

CRISPY MAITAKES WITH SOUR CREAM 'N' ALLIUMS DIP

TRUE LAUREL, DAVID BARZELAY

Nicolas Torres's captivating cocktails at Lazy Bear's sibling bar are reason alone to visit this corner of the Mission District. However, it's just so hard *not* to eat there, because the food is hardly just the cocktails' supporting cast. The patty melt has its own following, and there are always a few seasonal treats. Along with the patty melt, these outrageously excellent crispy maitake mushrooms have been a menu mainstay since day one in 2017.

YIELD: 8 servings

ALLIUM POWDER

20 G GARLIC POWDER

20 G ONION POWDER

20 G SCALLION POWDER (MADE BY GRINDING DRIED SCALLIONS IN A SPICE GRINDER)

20 G CARAMELIZED ONION POWDER (MADE BY DEHYDRATING CARAMELIZED ONIONS, THEN GRINDING THEM IN A SPICE GRINDER)

60 G MUSHROOM SEASONING (BARZELAY USES IMPERIAL TASTE, A VIETNAMESE BRAND AVAILABLE ON AMAZON, BUT THE MCCORMICK BRAND UMAMI SEASONING MAY BE EASIER TO FIND, THOUGH IT IS SALTIER)

1. Mix all the ingredients together.

continued...

SOUR CREAM 'N' ALLIUM DIP

18 G ALLIUM POWDER
(SEE PAGE 149)

6 G SALT

500 G CRÈME FRAÎCHE

20 ML FRESH LEMON JUICE

10 G FINELY SLICED FRESH CHIVES

1. In a bowl, stir the allium powder and salt into the crème fraîche.

2. Refrigerate for at least 1 hour to let the allium powder rehydrate.

3. Add the lemon juice, then whip to soft peaks.

4. Fold in the chives. Refrigerate until ready to serve.

CRISPY MAITAKES

900 G MAITAKE MUSHROOMS

100 G ALL-PURPOSE FLOUR

100 G RICE FLOUR

200 G CORNSTARCH

132 G CRISP COAT OR EVERCRISP
(OPTIONAL; SEE NOTE ON
OPPOSITE PAGE)

16 G SALT, PLUS MORE
FOR FINAL SALTING

600 ML BEER, PREFERABLY STEAM
BEER, LAGER, OR PILSNER

PEANUT OIL, FOR FRYING

ALLIUM POWDER, FOR DUSTING

SOUR CREAM 'N' ALLIUM DIP
(SEE ABOVE), FOR SERVING

1. Tear apart larger maitake clusters into chunks reasonably sized to eat in one (or maybe two) bites, no longer than about 2½ inches.

2. Combine the dry ingredients in a bowl or pan and mix well. Stir in the beer until no dry clumps remain.

3. Heat oil for frying to 375°F/190°C.

4. Add the mushroom pieces to the batter a couple of handfuls at a time. Pull them out and drop them directly into the hot oil. Fry for 3 to 4 minutes, until golden brown and crispy.

5. Drain on a wire rack, salt to taste, and dust with a bit of allium powder.

6. Serve with the dip.

Note: You can leave out the Crisp Coat or EverCrisp (reduce the amount of beer accordingly). The mushrooms will still be very tasty but not quite as crispy and won't stay crispy nearly as long.

Q&A, LAUREN SARIA

EDITOR, *EATER* SF

TF: As *Eater* SF's editor, you're in a really unique position where you essentially have to know everything about everything when it comes to eating and drinking in SF. New restaurants, old restaurants, pop-up restaurants, cafés, bars... everything. How do you do it?

LS: As I like to say: it's a lifestyle! On average, I dine out between three and five nights a week, sometimes more and sometimes less, depending on what's going on. Typically, I prioritize getting to new restaurants, which I consider to be anything that's opened in the last six months, and I keep a running list of classic or older spots I haven't tried yet. I knock those out as I can. But a lot of the job is chatting with everyone you can—chefs, bartenders, servers, owners, and anyone who loves to eat! It's impossible to know everything, but it's totally possible to know people who pretty much do. The value of tips and recommendations from industry people and readers can't be understated. I also have a lot of help from the rest of the *Eater* SF team, including deputy editor Dianne de Guzman, who spearheads our coverage of the East Bay, so I don't have to crisscross the bridge all the time.

TF: In your opinion, what are some of the game-changing restaurants right now in the city?

LS: I continually point people to Nisei in Russian Hill, where Chef David Yoshimura hopes to reframe the way diners understand Japanese fine dining, specifically by drawing the focus away from sushi, ramen, and other more familiar foods. Each meal I've had there introduced me to new ingredients and dishes, from turtle soup to American unagi. The restaurant's beverage program also pushes the limits with a full sake pairing that [has] deepened my understanding of everything sake can be. I also love how Handroll Project in the Mission takes the technique and thought behind Michelin-starred Ju-Ni and applies it to a more casual and affordable concept, and, through its early days, Chef Srijith Gopinathan's Copra stands to expand San Francisco's Indian restaurant scene in a thrilling direction.

TF: What are some current trends that you're thrilled to see? And any that you wish would just go away?

LS: It might not be a "trend" exactly, but San Francisco's pastry scene continues to impress me at every turn. In a city with a long history of sourdough bread and world-class croissants, I never cease to be floored by the sheer number of excellent bakeries that seem to pop up every season. Right now, in terms of newcomers, I'm thinking about Maison Nico, Juniper, and Loquat—not to mention older standbys like b. patisserie and Breadbelly. This city's commitment to carbs is truly unrivaled.

As for trends I'm over, at the risk of sounding like a snob, can we chill out with the caviar? Or at least, please stop making me do "bumps."

TF: Switching from new San Francisco to the timeless places...when you think "Classic San Francisco," what places and dishes do you think of?

LS: I love the fact that every meal at House of Prime Rib feels like a special occasion, and there's nothing that transports you back in time quite like grabbing a drink and perching on the second floor of Vesuvio, where you can peer down at the bar below over the flickering candlelit chandeliers. Follow it up with a burger at Sam's and you've got yourself a foolproof night out. A few other classic spots I love: Zuni Café, The Buena Vista (I'll never, ever forget my first Irish coffee there), and Red's Java House, with those up-close Bay Bridge views.

TF: What do you think the key ingredient(s) is (are) that makes SF such a world-class dining city, even though it's a fraction of the size of places like LA, New York, and Tokyo?

LS: The accessibility of fresh, high-quality ingredients can't be ignored. One trip to the Ferry Plaza Farmers Market during peak season should be enough to convince you that San Francisco claims some of the most pristine produce in the country. But beyond that, I think this is a city that simply loves to eat. There's a reason the San Francisco Bay Area boasts the highest concentration of Michelin-starred restaurants of any city in the United States, and in my opinion, it's because there's a contingent of people here who love not just food but *dining*—and are willing to spend buckets of money to fuel that passion. I think that's what gives San Francisco's dining scene outsize depth and breadth in terms of its geographic size. California's diverse population also helps! I can point you to great places for Burmese, Thai, or Malaysian food, plus vegan Russian, Filipino-Mexican fusion, and halal Chinese, all within the 7x7.

TF: Finally, if you're allowed to say, which restaurants in SF do you return to again and again when you're not visiting places for work assignments?

LS: For comfort food, WesBurger 'N' More for a smash burger and tots; for dinner in my neighborhood, Beit Rima for hummus, baked halloumi, and delicata squash; and for special occasions (or just anytime I get it together enough to snag a reservation), Rintaro for silky house-made tofu and kurobuta tonkatsu. I also love brunch at Aziza and cocktails (ok, and a patty melt) at True Laurel.

MISO EGGPLANT (NASU DENGAKU)

IZAKAYA SOZAI

zakayas can be found in many corners of San Francisco these days, but Sozai was one of the first (and quickly one of the best) of the recent set of them that propelled this exciting growth for the genre of casual Japanese bars/restaurants with a variety of superb eats. Husband-and-wife team Ritsu and Suemee Osuka created an Inner Sunset destination for which diners happily Uber across town, put their name down, then wait an hour on a rainy Tuesday for. Everything is just so good—yakitori to tofu to ramen and far beyond. Regardless of what protein route you take, make sure to try the eggplant, which is fried but not battered and served with an incredible miso sauce.

YIELD: 2 servings

SAIKYO MISO SAUCE

½ CUP SAKE

½ CUP MIRIN

1 LB. SAIKYO MISO

5 TABLESPOONS SUGAR

1 TABLESPOON YUZU LIQUID

1. In a medium pot, bring the sake and mirin to a boil.

2. Add the miso, sugar, and yuzu liquid. Mix well.

continued...

EGGPLANT

NEUTRAL OIL, FOR FRYING

2 EGGPLANTS, CUT INTO
1½ INCH CUBES

SAIKYO MISO SAUCE
(SEE PAGE 155)

BONITO FLAKES, FOR GARNISH

CHOPPED SCALLIONS, FOR GARNISH

SESAME SEEDS, FOR GARNISH

1. Heat the oil to 350°F/177°C.

2. Flash fry the eggplant.

3. Sauté until the middle of the eggplant is softened.

4. Mix with the miso sauce.

5. Top with bonito flakes, scallions, and sesame seeds and serve.

Q&A, KRIS TOLIAO AND YUKA IOROI

CO-OWNERS, CASSAVA

TF: Kris, what led you to pursue a career in cooking after growing up in LA? How did LA and your parents' native Philippines shape your culinary voice?

KT: I didn't grow up with my parents. I lived with my sister and was emancipated at age sixteen. There were many hardships growing up and, because of them, I don't have much of a Filipino culinary background. It was only when considering what to do after high school that I thought of cooking. College wasn't an option for financial reasons, so it seemed like the only avenues available were military or culinary careers. I found information on Le Cordon Bleu and the idea of moving from Orange County to Pasadena sounded nice, so I decided to pursue a cooking career with my best friend.

TF: You've worked in both very traditional and contemporary kitchens, like Atelier Crenn for the latter. Can you tell us a bit about both of those influences for you?

KT: What I really appreciate about my experience in traditional kitchens is that I got to learn how to cook using classic tools and a good old-fashioned oven. I am also grateful to have spent much time in contemporary settings too. Being encouraged to go beyond an oven with sous vide, Rational, and all the other technologies that are now available was so valuable. Innovation has furthered my techniques, and I've been inspired by the borderless cuisines coming out of modern kitchens.

TF: The two of you started Cassava as a pop-up right after the recession, when pop-ups weren't really a thing yet. How did that go? And then, Cassava opened in the Outer Richmond...one of the quieter dining neighborhoods in the city when it comes to refined dining. Stepping back now and looking at those early days, it's amazing how Cassava was such a game changer not once but twice, right?

YI: That's so kind of you to say. The pop-up idea was brought to us by a friend who wanted to try it out. It was great fun! We actually just connected with a guest at our North Beach location who attended our very first dinner event at our apartment. They had been following us on Instagram this entire time and finally came into our restaurant! The North Beach location is our absolute dream. This very space is the first San Francisco restaurant that we dined at together during an overnight trip while we were still dating and living in L.A. This is a very huge, full-circle moment for us.

TF: How does the dynamic of a husband-and-wife-run restaurant work for both of you?

KT: The dynamic is perfect, and we wouldn't have it any other way. We met working in a restaurant. I was the sous chef and Yuka was the manager and working the bar. The clear separation of our duties has been very natural, and we have complete trust in each other's work. It may be different from other couples who are both chefs or operators.

TF: How are things different/similar for you two and Cassava in general with the new North Beach location? What are some of the signature dishes that are new and carryovers from the Richmond?

KT: The biggest difference in the culinary side of things is the kitchen and the storage. More is possible here at North Beach. On Balboa, we only had an electric oven and induction burners. We're not nearly as limited. A burger has always been something I've wanted to do, and we were finally able to add it to the menu. The pork chop we're serving now is definitely a step above what we had in the old location because of our new grill. Slow-braised meats, however, including lamb belly, duck confit, and beef cheeks, have always been my favorite things to cook, and they are still the star of our three-course prix fixe menu.

TF: And now that original location is an exciting wine bar! Can you tell us a bit about that and how it's striving to be a neighborhood fixture much like Cassava was?

YI: We are so happy to be catching up with our old neighbors and welcoming them in! I think what we are bringing back to that area is a classy wine-drinking experience with nice stemware, which we are very passionate about. There are spots that offer more casual or natural wines in simpler cups or smaller wine glasses, but no one is serving wine like we do. We're also offering fun but elevated bar snacks, like the short rib croquette with herb chimichurri. It's something that you wouldn't make at home, but small enough to enjoy with our fine wines. I think our wine bar is giving the strip an approachable sense of "nice things."

TF: Both of you have been some of the most eloquent voices about the myriad issues that restaurants face in San Francisco—wage fairness, a cooking style that doesn't need to adhere to one particular cuisine or niche, how expensive SF is, making the restaurant industry a safer and healthier one for employees...I could go on. And, I distinctly remember that Cassava was *ahead* of the health department when it came to COVID-19 rules and protections in those difficult early days of the pandemic. It's really wonderful and inspiring to hear about a restaurant that cares about so many important topics in the community! What's led both of you to talk about so much more than just delicious food and great experiences at Cassava?

KT: The biggest reason we do things the way we do things, and a lot of it is Yuka's lead, is because we work at our restaurant every day. We want to work in a safe environment, and we want to provide a safe environment for our staff. It's a different situation from other operators who might not work in service every day. Yuka was listening to what was happening in East Asia and Europe at the start of the pandemic, and it was scary! We didn't want to die working in our restaurant, so we did what we thought was right.

The misogynistic locker-room talk and the racial divide that I've encountered in other kitchens have always made me very uncomfortable. I completely backed Yuka's decision to create a system that eradicates toxic masculinity and racial inequity from our business. We're avoiding problems on a myriad of levels, and it's working. We have a wonderful staff with great retention, and we keep receiving résumés from others who want to be part of our healthy, safe, and supportive work environment.

TAPIOCA KEDGEREE (SABUDANA KHICHDI)

BESHARAM, HEENA PATEL

The cuisine of the Gujarat region (where chef/owner Heena Patel's parents grew up) is the driving force behind her cheery, energetic Dogpatch restaurant. *Besharam* essentially means "shameless" and Heena is certainly one of the most determined, exciting chefs in town. Originally from Mumbai, she is an alum of the La Cocina program and today one of SF's most important chefs, with an enormous following dining at her restaurant each week.

YIELD: 10 servings

TAPIOCA

2 CUPS PEARL TAPIOCA (AVAILABLE AT INDIAN GROCERY STORES)

2½ CUPS COLD WATER

3 TABLESPOONS MINCED SERRANO CHILIES

3 TABLESPOONS GINGER JUICE

1 TABLESPOON SALT, PLUS MORE TO TASTE

½ CUP CANOLA OR PEANUT OIL

1 TEASPOON COARSELY CRUSHED BLACK PEPPERCORNS

1 TABLESPOON FRESH LIME JUICE

1 CUP FINELY CHOPPED FRESH CILANTRO

1. Soak the tapioca in the cold water for up to 2 hours, stirring every few minutes. To test if they have soaked enough, you should be able to squeeze them easily between your fingers. Drain the tapioca through a sieve.

2. Transfer the soaked tapioca to baking trays. Toss and coat evenly with the chilies, ginger juice, salt, and oil. Sprinkle a touch of water on top.

3. Cover with aluminum foil and bake at 325°F/163°C until it appears translucent, about 45 minutes, stirring occasionally.

4. Remove from the oven. Sprinkle with pepper, lime juice, cilantro, and salt to taste.

GARNET SWEET POTATOES AND PURPLE POTATOES

1 QUART DICED GARNET
SWEET POTATOES

1 QUART DICED PURPLE POTATOES

3 TABLESPOONS MINCED
SERRANO CHILIES

3 TABLESPOONS GINGER JUICE

1 TABLESPOON SEA SALT,
PLUS MORE TO TASTE

6 TABLESPOONS CANOLA OIL,
OR AS NEEDED

2 TEASPOONS COARSELY CRUSHED
BLACK PEPPERCORNS

1 CUP FINELY CHOPPED
FRESH CILANTRO

1½ TABLESPOONS
FRESH LIME JUICE

1. Arrange the diced sweet potatoes and purple potatoes in a single layer on baking sheets. Toss and coat evenly with the chilies, ginger juice, salt, and oil. Sprinkle with water.

2. Cover with aluminum foil and bake at 325°F/163°C until fork-tender, 45 minutes to 1 hour, stirring occasionally.

3. Remove from the oven and sprinkle with the pepper, cilantro, lime juice, and salt to taste.

MASALA PEANUTS

3 TABLESPOONS CANOLA OIL,
FOR FRYING

6 TABLESPOONS RAW
SKINLESS PEANUTS

SALT, TO TASTE

KASHMIRI CHILI, TO TASTE

PINCH SUGAR

continued...

1. Heat the oil to 100ºF/38ºC.

2. Add the peanuts to the oil and fry until the skin starts to brown and the peanuts sound crispy.

3. Place the fried peanuts in a bowl and toss with salt, Kashmiri chili, and sugar.

ASSEMBLY

¼ CUP TOASTED SESAME SEEDS

1. Combine the tapioca, sweet potatoes, and purple potatoes and mix gently with your hands.

2. Top all with the toasted sesame seeds and masala peanuts. Serve hot.

SALT AND PEPPER CAULIFLOWER

TENDERHEART, JOE HOU

San Francisco diners first got to know Joe Hou because of his superb work as a pastry chef at Saison and Le Fantastique. And he sure knows his way around baking milk bread and creating wonderful desserts. Now he's running his own show at the LINE Hotel near Union Square, and has become the executive chef for its flagship restaurant, Tenderheart. He draws on his Chinese American heritage growing up in New Jersey for much of the menu, but this particular dish is actually a nod to a San Francisco Chinatown landmark—the salt and pepper wings at Capital Restaurant—except he makes it a fried vegan preparation and runs with it.

YIELD: 2 servings

CASHEW CREAM

2¼ CUPS CASHEWS

2¼ CUPS WATER

FRESH LEMON JUICE, TO TASTE

SALT, TO TASTE

1. In a container, combine the cashews and water and let soak overnight.

2. Transfer to a blender and blend until smooth.

3. Add lemon juice and salt to taste. If you want to be fancy, put the mix in an iSi canister and load with a N_2O charger.

continued...

PICKLED JALAPEÑO

1 JALAPEÑO CHILI

¾ CUP RICE WINE VINEGAR

¼ CUP SUGAR

PINCH SALT

1. Fillet the jalapeño and remove the inner white portion. Cut into strips.

2. In a small pot, combine with the vinegar, sugar, and salt. Bring to a boil.

3. Remove from the heat, cover, and let sit until cooled.

SALT AND PEPPER MIX

1½ TABLESPOONS BLACK
PEPPERCORNS

1½ TABLESPOONS WHITE
PEPPERCORNS

½ CUP SALT

1. Toast the black and white peppercorns separately until aromatic.

2. Grind until fine, then mix with the salt.

BRINED CAULIFLOWER

1 HEAD WHITE CAULIFLOWER (OR
WHATEVER COLOR YOU CAN GET)

2 CUPS PLUS 2 TABLESPOONS
WATER

2 TABLESPOONS SALT

1. Cut the cauliflower into florets. You want even-size pieces, about 1 inch or bite size.

2. In a medium bowl, combine the water and salt until the salt is dissolved.

3. Add the florets to the brine and let soak for 15 minutes, then drain.

continued...

BATTER

3¾ CUPS ALL-PURPOSE FLOUR

1¾ CUPS CORNSTARCH

1¼ TEASPOONS BAKING POWDER

SELTZER WATER, AS NEEDED

1. In a large bowl, combine the dry ingredients.

2. Add seltzer water until you have a thin batter. The thinner the batter, the lighter the fried coating will taste.

FRYING AND ASSEMBLY

CANOLA OIL, FOR FRYING

1. In a pot, heat the oil to 375°F/190°C.

2. Dip the cauliflower in the batter and immediately drop it into the oil. Agitate the cauliflower pieces so they do not stick, and cook evenly until golden brown.

3. Drain the cauliflower and immediately season with the salt and pepper mix.

4. Mount the cashew cream on the bottom of the plate, make an artistic pile of the cauliflower on top, and artfully place pickled jalapeño pieces all over for garnish with tweezers, chopsticks, or your hands, depending on how many times you've watched *Chef's Table*.

Q&A, FERNAY McPHERSON

OWNER AND CHEF, MINNIE BELL'S SOUL MOVEMENT

TF: When we last spoke (for KQED Bay Area Bites), Minnie Bell's had just opened in Emeryville. Now, a few years later, it's clear that your rosemary fried chicken and mac and cheese have an enormous following on both sides of the bay (including former *Chronicle* critic Soleil Ho). How has this journey been at the Public Market?

FM: Overall, it's been great, but the last five years at Public Market have been a roller-coaster as my team and I navigated the pandemic. We get to serve a variety of people throughout the Bay Area and have some incredibly loyal customers that dine with us weekly. Opening in the Public Market has also developed me as an entrepreneur, as it has given me the tools and experience to have my homecoming in San Francisco.

TF: Prior to opening the Emeryville location, you spent some time in the La Cocina program. Can you tell us about that experience?

FM: My experience with La Cocina has been amazing. I just went into the restaurant industry with a love for cooking, and they have helped me refine my cooking skills and strengthened me as an entrepreneur. They've also helped me to understand how important telling my story is for the industry and my community as a Black female business owner and chef. Lastly, La Cocina has also provided me with an amazing community of female chefs and business owners that I call family. I'm still very connected with La Cocina. I've served on La Cocina's board for the last three years, representing the entrepreneurs in the program and interviewing the businesses that are joining the new cohorts.

TF: Growing up in San Francisco, did you always want to be a chef? Any particularly special food memories from those years?

FM: I had no idea I was going to be a chef. My mom has an old picture of me at two years old with an apron and a spoon, so I guess it was my destiny. My love for cooking was always inside of me, but I didn't realize until my late twenties that I wanted to make a career out of it.

My era of growing up in San Francisco was a lot different than my parents' era, as there were a lot fewer Black businesses, so I held onto that culture with all that I could. I'll never forget the first time I had fried chicken from Powell's Place in Hayes Valley on Hayes Street. My mom brought it home in a paper bag, and it was the most delicious thing I ever tasted. I also frequented Jewel's on Presidio—their food was true soul food.

TF: What inspired you to start Minnie Bell's Soul Movement and serve this delicious homestyle food?

FM: I always knew I wanted to serve the food that I grew up eating and cooking with my family, but I also knew I wanted to put my own spin on it in a way that still resonated with my community. You'll see my personal touches throughout my menu with the addition of rosemary to my fried chicken and the brown butter in my cornbread.

The biggest inspiration for starting Minnie Bell's was my Aunt Minnie and Grandma Bell, hence the name. They were incredible home cooks and made me the chef that I am today. They would cook frequently for the whole family and put out the most beautiful and delicious displays of food. Also, every summer my Grandma Bell would take me and the cousins out to Patterson [Central Valley] and we would pick fresh fruits and vegetables (green beans, snap peas, black-eyed peas, green tomatoes). She taught me the importance of knowing where your food comes from, and that's something I'll always be grateful for.

TF: You grew up in the Fillmore District, which a few decades ago was considered the "Harlem of the West." It's been very sad to see how there are fewer and fewer Black-owned restaurants in that neighborhood and San Francisco in general over the years. How can we reverse that trend? What's your experience been like as a business owner and chef in SF and the East Bay? How do we get expensive, competitive San Francisco to a better, more sustainable place?

FM: I think the trend is slowly reversing now. It's about awareness and helping people understand the history of what happened to San Francisco's Black community and businesses. The city can continue to reverse this trend by giving Black business owners access to capital with more resources like the Fillmore Collective and Dream Keeper Initiative, which are helping to bring Black businesses, like mine, back to the Fillmore. I have received some grants from the Dream Keeper Initiative, and they have been very helpful as I gear up to open my new space.

My experience as a Black business owner in the Bay Area has been challenging. I initially wanted to open my business five plus years ago in the Fillmore (the neighborhood I grew up in), but there weren't any landlords that would take a chance on me. As I mentioned, that's why I'm grateful that I opened at Public Market, as it gave me a chance to prove myself and my business.

In order to make San Francisco a more sustainable place for small/diverse businesses, which are the heart of this city, we need to limit the barriers to entry for business owners by providing more access to capital and making the business permitting process more seamless and approachable.

TF: Last question…I hear that you were a Muni driver in San Francisco?! What was that like? I've never thought about driving a bus and being a chef as being similar…but they actually do seem to have a lot of similarities when it comes to being precise, punctual, and resolutely focused.

FM: Yes, I was a Muni driver for about two and a half years while I was in the early stages of starting my food truck. I drove the 38 Geary, 8X, and 14 Mission. It was an awful and dangerous experience, but it pushed me to accomplish my dreams of opening my own food business. However, I will admit that the experience of driving that sixty-foot bus in San Francisco made me better at driving my food trailer and dealing with people overall, something you definitely have to be able to do working in the service industry.

FERNAY'S SAUTÉED COLLARD GREENS

MINNIE BELL'S SOUL MOVEMENT, FERNAY MCPHERSON

From growing up in San Francisco's Fillmore District to driving for Muni to participating in the La Cocina culinary incubator program to crossing directly across the Bay Bridge to the Emeryville Public Market to launch her soul food business, Minnie Bell's Soul Movement, McPherson not only is one of the region's leading chefs these days but is someone who also is truly making an impact on the region she has always called "home." Her soul food dishes always have compelling little catches and/or personal twists to them.

These aren't your traditional collard greens, just my take on my favorite greens.

—**Chef McPherson**

YIELD: 3 to 4 servings

---

1 TABLESPOON BUTTER

2 TABLESPOONS OLIVE OIL

4 OZ. SMOKED SAUSAGE, THINLY SLICED

1 MEDIUM BELL PEPPER, CUT IN HALF, SEEDED, AND THINLY SLICED

1 SMALL ONION, CUT IN HALF AND THINLY SLICED

4 BUNCHES COLLARD GREENS, DESTEMMED AND THINLY SLICED

½ TEASPOON ONION POWDER

PINCH CAYENNE PEPPER, OR MORE TO TASTE

SALT AND FRESHLY GROUND BLACK PEPPER, TO TASTE

½ CUP CHICKEN STOCK, PLUS MORE AS NEEDED

1. In a large skillet or pot over medium-high heat, heat the butter and olive oil until the butter melts. Add the sausage, bell pepper, and onion and sauté until the onion is translucent.

2. Add the collards and cook them down for 2 to 3 minutes.

3. Add the onion powder, cayenne, and salt and pepper and stir for 1 minute to combine.

4. Add the stock and simmer, stirring occasionally, until most of the liquid has evaporated. Feel free to add more stock as needed, but be careful not to overcook your greens; they should still have a bite to them. Serve as a side dish and enjoy.

CORNBREAD MUFFINS WITH CURRY BUTTER

INTERNATIONAL SMOKE, AYESHA CURRY

There is no bigger restaurant ownership duo in San Francisco than Ayesha Curry and Michael Mina. Sure, they both love seeing Ayesha's husband, Stephen, win basketball games over at Chase Center, but they've also won over SF diners for years with this Downtown restaurant's excellent smoke- and grill-filled ensemble—don't just call it BBQ. For me, though, the main event is always Ayesha's cornbread recipe. It's fair to say that it's the greatest version of cornbread I've found anywhere in the country and will be a perfect companion at your next backyard BBQ.

YIELD: 24 muffins

2½ CUPS ALL-PURPOSE FLOUR	6 EGGS, AT ROOM TEMPERATURE
2 TEASPOONS BAKING SODA	2⅔ CUPS YELLOW CORNMEAL
1½ TEASPOONS BAKING POWDER	1⅔ CUPS SOUR CREAM
1⅝ CUPS BUTTER, AT ROOM TEMPERATURE	1 TABLESPOON THAI RED CURRY PASTE
2¼ CUPS SUGAR	1 (13½-OZ.) CAN COCONUT MILK
¾ TEASPOON KOSHER SALT	¼ CUP MINCED SEEDED JALAPEÑO CHILI

1. Preheat the oven to 325°F/163°C. Spray a muffin tin with pan-release spray.

2. In a bowl, sift together the flour, baking soda, and baking powder and mix until halfway combined.

3. Using a whisk or stand mixer fitted with a whip attachment, whip the room-temperature butter, sugar, and salt until light and fluffy, about 3 minutes.

4. Add the eggs, one at a time, mixing well after each addition and scraping down the bowl.

5. Add the cornmeal, mix until incorporated, and scrape down the bowl.

6. Add the sifted flour, baking powder, and baking soda and mix until halfway combined.

7. Add the sour cream, curry paste, coconut milk, and jalapeño and mix until homogeneous.

8. Fill the muffin cups three-quarters full with the batter.

9. If baking with convection, bake for 12 minutes, then rotate the pan and bake for another 8 minutes. If using a conventional oven, bake for 30 minutes total. The cornbread should be golden brown and baked all the way through. If not, give it another 3 to 4 minutes.

10. Let the muffins cool before taking out of the tin.

CURRY BUTTER

1 LB. BUTTER

1½ CUPS MILK

1¼ TABLESPOONS RED CURRY PASTE

½ CUP HONEY

1. In a small pot, combine the butter and milk and warm until the butter melts.

2. Whisk in the curry paste and honey to emulsify.

3. Cool the butter down to room temperature.

4. Use the butter to glaze the top of the cooled muffins.

LAZY BEAR, DAVID BARZELAY

The mezzanine level Den at Lazy Bear is the wittiest, most sharply decorated kind of funky hunting lodge meets upscale private club meets summer camp cabin you'll ever encounter. It's a lot of a lot. This is where you'll open and/or close dinner at the celebrated fine dining tasting menu–dinner party restaurant. Chef/owner David Barzelay is from the Southeast originally, and, since he's one of the great fine dining chefs of the Bay Area, you know this is not exactly going to be your typical ham and biscuits.

YIELD: about 10 servings/biscuits

LAZY BEAR DEN CITY HAM

3,000 ML COLD WATER	10 G CLOVES
340 G SALT	5 CALIFORNIA BAY LEAVES
450 G BROWN SUGAR	3,000 G ICE
50 G PINK CURING SALT	1 PICNIC HAM OR PORK SHOULDER, DEBONED
30 G BLACK PEPPERCORNS	
18 G STAR ANISE PODS	

1. Bring half of the water up to a boil with all the remaining ingredients, except the ice and ham. Once it reaches a boil, remove from the heat and let steep for 20 minutes.

2. Strain and add the remaining water, then add the ice. Stir to melt the ice. Once cold, add the ham to the brine and weight it down to keep it submerged. Brine for 8 to 14 days in the refrigerator, repositioning it every few days.

3. Once fully cured, remove the ham from the brine, pat dry, and leave in the refrigerator for a day or two to form a sticky pellicle (thin skin) before smoking.

4. Hot-smoke for a couple of hours, then chill.

5. Vacuum seal and cook sous vide for 5 hours at 180°F/82°C.

6. Chill and let rest for at least a couple of days before slicing thinly.

continued...

LAZY BEAR DEN HONEY AND FERMENTED CHILE BUTTER

450 G BUTTER (ABOUT 1 LB.), FULLY TEMPERED TO ROOM TEMPERATURE

50 G FERMENTED OR PICKLED SPICY PEPPERS

100 G HONEY

40 ML DRY SHERRY

20 ML CHAMPAGNE VINEGAR

4 G SMOKED PAPRIKA

4 G KOCHUKARU

4 G SALT

2 G FINELY GROUND MSG

1. Robocoupe everything together and use within a couple of hours, or else refrigerate for up to a couple of weeks. Temper and stir before using.

LAZY BEAR DEN BUTTERMILK BISCUITS

300 G (2 CUPS) ALL-PURPOSE FLOUR, PLUS MORE FOR ROLLING (KING ARTHUR OR ANOTHER RELATIVELY HIGH-PROTEIN AP FLOUR WORKS WELL)

12 G (2 TEASPOONS) SALT

50 G (¼ CUP) SUGAR

15 G (2½ TEASPOONS) BAKING POWDER

2.5 G (½ TEASPOON) BAKING SODA

80 G (ABOUT ¾ STICK) BUTTER, COLD, STRAIGHT OUT OF THE REFRIGERATOR

285 ML (1¼ CUPS) BUTTERMILK

MELTED BUTTER, FOR BRUSHING

1. Preheat the oven to 450°F/232°C (or 425°F/218°C with convection).

2. In a bowl, sift the dry ingredients together and whisk to combine uniformly.

3. Working quickly to keep the butter cold, grate the butter into the dry ingredients, using the large holes of a box grater, stopping occasionally to toss the butter bits in the flour mixture to make sure the individual bits stay separate. Cut the butter into the flour, using the tines of a whisk or fork, or a pastry blender, until there are no pieces of butter larger than a pea. You can do all of this in advance if you'd like, and refrigerate for up to a week or freeze for a month before proceeding.

4. Add the buttermilk and stir until the dough comes together into one shaggy but fully integrated mass, with no remaining dry flour. Don't be worried about any risk of overmixing. There is so much butter and buttermilk in this dough that it's pretty hard to overmix by hand.

5. Dump the dough out onto a floured work surface. With floured hands, flatten the dough to about 1½ inches thick by patting it down. Sprinkle the top liberally with flour, and then flip the whole thing over. That flip will keep the dough from sticking to the table when cutting the biscuits. Pat the dough down to 1 inch thick.

6. Cut out the biscuits using a round cutter, or just use a long knife to cut squares if you'd prefer. Dip the cutter into flour between each cut for a clean release. Gather the dough scraps together, re-form into a ball, pat out 1 inch thick, and cut more biscuits. Repeat until all the dough is used.

7. Transfer the biscuits gently to a baking sheet lined with parchment paper.

8. Just before baking, brush the tops of the biscuits liberally with melted butter. Add a second sheet pan underneath the first to keep the bottoms of the biscuits from browning too quickly. Bake until fully golden brown on top, about 13 to 16 minutes. When they're done, the outsides will feel set and a bit crispy, but the insides will still feel soft.

9. As soon as they come out of the oven, brush them again with melted butter (yes, even more butter). Transfer to a plate or bowl and wrap with a clean and dry kitchen towel to keep them fresh and warm.

10. Cut them open, slather with the chile butter, lay in a slice or two of ham, and enjoy.

Q&A, DAVID BARZELAY

OWNER/EXECUTIVE CHEF, LAZY BEAR AND TRUE LAUREL

TF: Many folks who watch the industry from afar (like yours truly) often cite Lazy Bear as the pop-up turned full-time restaurant that sort of started what is now a very common path for new restaurants. How did being a pop-up help you succeed when it was time to go full-time?

DB: As an underground restaurant (never actually a pop-up), we were uniquely successful in building a huge amount of pent-up demand, due to the limited number of guests we could serve, and an incredible base of customers who sang our praises. When opening in the current space, we knew we would at least get plenty of people in the door to try it. All we had to do was to make sure they left raving about it.

I also learned a ton during the five years of Lazy Bear Underground. No one is ever "ready" to open a restaurant until they've done it, but I was vastly closer to ready than I would have been at the start, or even than I would have been two years in, when I officially started looking for the right space to open. I knew much more who I was as a chef, a leader, and even as a person. That gave me the self-assurance to try the unique format for which Lazy Bear initially became known.

TF: Beyond, of course, being seasonal driven and using top-tier ingredients, how would you personally describe Lazy Bear's cuisine and cooking style?

DB: Our cuisine is all about tapping into nostalgia for shared American culinary experiences, expressing a reverence for the wild, and evoking a sense of place in the San Francisco Bay Area. The flavor memories we're going for are drawn from the American cuisine of the twentieth century, and we often lovingly reimagine the most lowbrow things we ate growing up! But we do it using the best local ingredients, both foraged and cultivated, and cook with high technique, effort, and attention to detail.

TF: One thing that guests note about Lazy Bear compared to other fine dining peers is how fun and friendly it is. There's the communal dinner party vibe and little touches like the camping theme, the suave upstairs den, the notebook and pencil "menu" . . . How did you think about all of these clever things?

DB: We thought very deliberately before opening about making the experience fun, rich with unique details and conversation starters. We felt like the worst thing we could do would be to make you sit next to strangers and then bore you.

I've always told our staff that we should conduct ourselves like we are hosts of a dinner party, not like we are servants at a dinner party. The best way to make sure that our guests are having fun is to make sure that we are having fun.

TF: Can you talk us through your strategy of taking a perfect seasonal ingredient and turning it into a Lazy Bear dish? Let's say a tomato in August or asparagus in late April?

DB: Our creative process usually involves identifying some awesome seasonal ingredient that we want to use—usually starting with produce, rather than protein—and then figure out some lowbrow thing our moms made that reminds us of the ingredient. Then we go from there.

TF: How do you incorporate your background growing up in the Southeast into the Lazy Bear equation?

DB: I ate very well growing up in Florida, with tons of Gulf seafood, not to mention fish my dad caught. My mother grew up on a farm in the Florida Panhandle and cooked almost everything from scratch, breakfast and dinner every day, even though she worked a demanding job. Most of what we ate was at least a bit Southern in cuisine. I grew up cooking all of the time with my mom, and I still incorporate lots of Southern inspiration in Lazy Bear's dishes and flavors.

TF: Finally, as a San Francisco resident, where do you like to eat? Do your kids have any favorite restaurants?

DB: Some of my SF favorites, in no particular order: Californios, San Ho Won, Benu, Koi Palace (Daly City), Birdsong, Las Palmas, Monsieur Benjamin, Che Fico, Absinthe, Z&Y, Swan Oyster Depot, Cotogna, House of Prime Rib, Yank Sing, Taqueria Cancun, Royal Feast (Millbrae), Dragon Beaux, Farmhouse Thai, WesBurger 'N' More, Han Il Kwan, Izakaya Rintaro, Anchovy Bar...

My kids love Italian food. Pizzeria Delfina, Gialina, Fiorella, and Original Joe's are all in our regular family rotation.

CARROTS ROASTED OVER HAY WITH KUMQUATS, SESAME, AND SALTED DATE ICE CREAM

VILLON, JASON FOX

Ever cooked with hay at home before? Now is your chance. Chef Jason Fox quietly has been one of San Francisco's most thoughtful and innovative chefs for years, first at his outstanding Mission restaurant Commonwealth, and now at the spectacular Villon in Mid-Market's Proper Hotel. His style of cooking is creative and rustic, balancing the best of both worlds, just like how this dish surprisingly and delightfully uses hay...and ice cream...to help carrots thrive. Yes, that's correct.

One of my favorite dishes is Carrots Roasted Over Hay with Kumquats, Sesame, and Salted Date Ice Cream. I like this dish because it combines very old techniques, such as roasting over hay, with some modern flairs, which is our salted dated ice cream. Texture and temperature [are] very important in our dishes, and this highlights some variations in temperature on the plate, as well as different textures. For a flavor profile, it bridges both savory and sweet flavors, with the earthiness of the carrots offset by the salted date ice cream and nettle puree. I think it really represents our ethos of merging classical and modern elements.

—**Chef Fox**

YIELD: 12 servings

CARROTS OVER HAY

6 QUARTS BABY CARROTS

EXTRA-VIRGIN OLIVE OIL, AS NEEDED

SALT, TO TASTE

ORGANIC HAY, AS NEEDED

2 CUPS WATER

continued...

1. Toss the baby carrots with olive oil and season to taste with salt.

2. Line the bottom of a 4-inch hotel pan with organic hay (about 2 inches deep, roughly spread). Lightly char or blowtorch in areas, 25 to 30 percent, then pour the water to put the flames out.

3. Cover with cheesecloth, and place a layer of carrots on top. Wrap the pan tightly with aluminum foil. Roast at 350°F/177°C for 25 to 30 minutes.

4. Remove the foil, turn the oven temperature to 425°F/218°C, and roast until the carrots are tender and slightly dried out, another 10 to 15 minutes.

NETTLE PUREE

3 QUARTS PACKED NETTLES	SALT, AS NEEDED
1 QUART PACKED SPINACH	ICE WATER, AS NEEDED
	XANTHAN GUM, AS NEEDED

1. Blanch the nettles and spinach in salted water.

2. Transfer to an ice bath and chill until cold.

3. Press the water out of the nettles and spinach.

4. Transfer to a Vitamix (note: the Vitamix should not be filled above one-third of its volume). Add the smallest amount of ice water to make it spin, and process to a perfect puree.

5. Add xanthan gum to thicken (1 teaspoon per Vitamix) and season with salt.

6. Pass through a chinois.

continued...

DATE ICE CREAM

1,000 G PITTED DATES

2,000 ML MILK

1,000 ML HEAVY CREAM

30 G SALT

400 G GLUCOSE

300 G TRIMOLINE

10 SHEETS GELATIN

1. In a medium pot, combine the dates, milk, cream, and salt and bring to a boil. Remove the pan from heat and steep until the dates are soft.

2. In a separate pot, combine the glucose and Trimoline. Warm through until combined and pourable.

3. Hydrate the gelatin in cold water.

4. Mix all the ingredients in an 8-quart container. Transfer in batches to a Vitamix, puree, and pass through a chinois. Refrigerate overnight and process the next day.

ASSEMBLY

FRESH FRUIT (KUMQUAT SLICES, CITRUS SEGMENTS, BERRIES, DEPENDING ON THE SEASON)

CHRYSANTHEMUM LEAVES

VADOUVAN OIL

SESAME SEEDS

1. Combine 2 tablespoons chopped parsley, 2 tablespoons chopped cilantro, 2 tablespoons fresh lemon juice, 6 tablespoons extra-virgin olive oil, and 1 minced garlic clove and then toss the carrots in the dressing. Spoon some nettle puree at the bottom of the plate, and then carefully place the carrots around.

2. Top with the fruit, chrysanthemum leaves, and drizzle of vadouvan oil around. Roll a scoop of date ice cream in sesame seeds and set it on top.

SQUID HEAD TARE

LE FANTASTIQUE, ROBBIE WILSON

At the edge of Hayes Valley, Le Fantastique's name says it all when it comes to chef/owner Robbie Wilson's ode to vinyl and champagne, with a tempting selection of cured fish and wonderfully composed warm savory dishes, plus caviar eclairs and tempting fondue-like melted butter compositions.

This Japanese-inspired, all-purpose basting sauce can do all the heavy lifting for any grilled meats, seafood, and vegetables, imparting a perfect balance of salt, sweetness, and umami. Ideally, you will baste with this sauce during the last few minutes of grilling and not in the beginning, as the sugar will burn quickly over high heat. Also, warm tare . . . whisked aggressively [with an equal amount of cold butter] . . . makes for a memorable sauce for dipping.

—Chef Wilson

SQUID H$_2$0

1,000 G SQUID HEADS AND/OR BODIES, CLEANED (INNARDS AND CARTILAGE REMOVED) AND CUT INTO 4-CM PIECES

1 GARLIC CLOVE, GERM REMOVED

150 ML KOMBU WATER (100 G KOMBU SOAKED IN 150 ML WATER OVERNIGHT) OR DASHI

2 STRIPS ORANGE PEEL

1 BAY LEAF

1. Combine all the ingredients in a sous vide bag, scald the bag in boiling water for 5 seconds, and shock until cool.

2. At 162°F/72°C, cook for 12 hours. Strain.

3. In a medium pot, simmer the squid water until reduced by 50 percent.

continued...

TARE

500 ML SQUID H$_2$O (SEE PAGE 187)	50 G BROWN SUGAR
500 ML TAMARI	50 G GRATED FRESH GINGER
200 ML SAKE	20 G SPRUCE TIPS
200 ML MIRIN	

1. In a medium pot over medium-high heat, bring all the ingredients to a boil.

2. Reduce the heat to a simmer and reduce the tare by 50 percent.

3. Strain. Tare may be refrigerated for up to 2 weeks.

SPECIAL SAUCE

ERIC EHLER

There's the secret sauce to many successful dishes—and then there's Eric Ehler's "Special Sauce." And we're in luck that he's sharing this magical sauce/condiment from his time cooking at a Lower Haight brewery-gastropub with us.

Black Sands was the first restaurant I was the chef at in San Francisco. It was a super-special place and honestly ahead of its time. The food menu was anchored by the Black Sands Burger. Just like many legendary burgers of San Francisco, if you bring this one up in conversation, folks will likely wax poetic. The burger definitely was a sum of its parts, but I think what people loved most about it was that it was fast, always juicy, and consistent, and it had a special sauce that was actually . . . SPECIAL!

The secret ingredient in this sauce is Maggi Seasoning or Bragg Liquid Aminos. You can also sub out a really cheap soy sauce. This is real umami. Put this on anything and people will think you have added crack to it.

—Chef Ehler

YIELD: generous 2 quarts

2 QUARTS MAYONNAISE (HOMEMADE AIOLI IS AMAZING TOO!)

½ CUP KETCHUP

1 TABLESPOON MAGGI SEASONING

1 TABLESPOON PICKLE BRINE

1 ONION, MINCED AND CARAMELIZED

1. Mix everything together and put on your favorite burger or sandwich. Add some horseradish if you are feeling crazy.

Q&A, ERIC EHLER

PRINCIPAL OWNER, OUTTA SIGHT PIZZA

TF: Most readers might already know this about your career, but I'll try to explain it here. It's fascinating how you're a chef who has worn many hats for many different kinds of places—sous chef, executive chef, consultant, owner, you name it. And the restaurants you've worked at represent such a wide variety of styles and cuisines—Mister Jiu's, Outta Sight, Fort Point, Lazy Susan, Serpentine, and more. Seriously, how are you able to specialize in so many things as a chef?

EE: (Laughs audibly.) I've been obsessed with food and cooking since I was like five years old. I love it. If I grasp onto something, I have to go a billion percent. When I was a kid, it was comics and action figures. When I was an adolescent, it was music and skateboarding, and when I was an adult, it was food and cooking.

It sometimes can be mistaken for "work" when chefs tirelessly work toward learning and educating themselves about cooking and techniques. I miss so much of the days when my friends and I would grab drinks after work and talk about new techniques learned or new ingredients we were just finding out about.

I've worked with so many great chefs and worked at so many different places. And [at] each place I've given it my all. Sometimes that means staying up all night reading cookbooks or researching the internet to come up with or learn dishes. Sometimes that means traveling thousands of miles to find the best version of something. Sometimes it's working seven days in a row to figure something out. To answer the question simply, if I'm going to make something, I do want it to be the best. I am competitive.

TF: Can you tell us a little more about your experience working with Brandon at Mister Jiu's?

EE: Brandon and I have been friends for over ten years. It definitely can be difficult working with a friend, but I saw his vision and wanted to help execute it. Brandon has always been so supportive of me. Right when I left Black Sands, he hit me up. He saw potential in me and gave me an opportunity I wasn't sure I was ready for. I went from running a neighborhood bar and restaurant to being a sous chef at the hottest restaurant in the city, probably the West Coast.

I wanted nothing more than to get a four-star [Michael] Bauer review, to get a Michelin star, and to be that kind of chef. I pushed as hard as I could for excellence, and, yes, that was very hard at times.

TF: It was at Mister Jiu's when you suffered a terrifying cardiac arrest on New Year's Eve of 2017. When you look back at that frightening episode, how does that drive you every day? For so many of us, your determination to return to the kitchen has been absolutely inspiring.

EE: Yes, it is something that I have to live with every day. Some days it is harder than others. Most days I just "live normally." The drive has always come from the idea that nothing is promised. I've lost so many people in my life that it has always been for them. Almost losing myself was a continued drive to keep pushing. I'm not religious or that spiritual, but I would like to think it just wasn't my time. That drives me to keep pushing for the "what-ifs." If I still can do it, then fuck it, let's go!

Thanks for being inspired. It is often toughest on those who are trying to inspire, but hearing over time that it did actually push others to do better, that means it was all worth the while.

TF: You're one of the biggest champions for San Francisco chefs and oft-ignored corners of the San Francisco dining world—that chefs need support, that the Tenderloin is more than what you read in the headlines, that the city still has lots of bright spots that should be highlighted, that there are many small and lesser-known restaurants worth visiting. It seems like you truly do love and appreciate San Francisco in a way that even many of us longtime residents don't.

EE: San Francisco has given me everything. My story isn't a rags-to-riches story, but I went through a lot as a kid. I love where I grew up, but it ultimately wasn't for me. I arrived [in] the city barely out of my teens. I had never been to California before. When I got here, I was welcomed with open arms to a gritty city full of weirdos that left their homes to find somewhere they belonged. I came here with a backpack, my knives, and my skateboard. And a dream!

TF: Speaking of those smaller and lesser-known restaurants, where are some of your favorite places to dine at? [I will note that I often note down the many under-the-radar places Ehler mentions he visited on Instagram. He could honestly write his own restaurant guide.]

EE: Hai Ky Mi Gia, Mộng Thu Cafe, Pho Tan Hoa, Lapats, Pho 2000, Capital, Punjab, Beep's, L'Ardoise, Begoni Bistro, New Fortune, Castillito Yucateco, Cocina Mayah, Dagwood & Scoops, El Tomate, La Espiga De Oro, Plain Jane, Sushi An, Kazan, Menya Kanemaru . . . I get takeout a lot . . .

TF: I also wanted to ask about your innovative work with Black Sands and Fort Point (both being breweries, though the latter subsequently took over the former's location). Why do you think we see much more culinary excitement at wine- or cocktail-centric bars than at beer bars/breweries?

EE: That is a great question! I think that because breweries can be so big, that they lend to being better food truck or pop-up spots. They also can be very unpredictable with business. I also think that breweries tend to be more family friendly. You have to be a little bit more casual. Beer is the every person's drink. Wine and cocktails are too fancy for some folk. Black Sands and FP both wanted something more untraditional than the common brew pub menu, so we were allowed to get funky with the menu! Great times. Thanks for remembering Black Sands.

TF: Finally, I have to ask, since you grew up in Iowa—when will a loose meat sandwich place open in SF?

EE: It'll never happen, but I'll have a pop-up just to confuse people!

HOMESTYLE FRA DIAVOLO SAUCE

ROSEMARY & PINE, DUSTIN FALCON

The Omakase Restaurant Group is one of the most intriguing of the handful of influential small restaurant groups in San Francisco. The group features the Japanese restaurants Omakase and Okane, plus the very popular local minichain, Dumpling Time. Then there's the splashy contemporary Niku Steakhouse and a vintage ole diner, Breakfast at Tiffany's. Finally, there's the superb contemporary Italian spot Rosemary & Pine, which opened in the Design District.

While it might be a group restaurant serving a cuisine that is seen in every corner of this city, Rosemary & Pine happens to be one of the most unique openings of the pandemic era. It's a refreshing, delightful place, both in terms of the upscale, breezy setting and Chef Dustin Falcon's menu (he's also executive chef at Niku Steakhouse). For this book, Falcon shared a sauce that the restaurant uses for its signature crispy burrata, but it can also be applied to pasta, pizza, or whatever your heart and palate desire.

YIELD: 12 cups

INFUSED FRESNO OIL

275 ML EXTRA-VIRGIN OLIVE OIL

50 G GARLIC

5 G FRESH THYME SPRIGS

15 G FRESNO CHILIES, SLICED

1. Combine all of the ingredients in a 4-quart saucepan and bring to a simmer. Turn off the heat and let the oil infuse while you prepare the sauce.

continued...

Homestyle Fra Diavolo Sauce
See page 193

TOMATO BASE

100 ML EXTRA-VIRGIN OLIVE OIL

500 G ONIONS, JULIENNED

40 G GARLIC, SLICED

1 (28 OZ.) CAN OF
BIANCO DI NAPOLI TOMATOES,
CRUSHED BY HAND

1. Warm a large rondeau over medium-high heat. Add the olive oil and warm until it shimmers. Add the onions and cook, stirring occasionally, for 3 to 4 minutes.

2. Add the garlic and cook for 2 minutes. Add the tomatoes and cook until the water has been cooked out of them, about 20 minutes.

FRA DIAVOLO SAUCE

TOMATO BASE (SEE ABOVE)

35 G PHXG

275 ML INFUSED FRESNO OIL
(SEE PAGE 193)

WATER, AS NEEDED

SALT, AS NEEDED

1. Place the Tomato Base in a blender, add the PHXG, and puree until combined. With the blender running, slowly drizzle in the infused oil until it has emulsified. Add water as needed if the sauce starts to break.

2. Weigh the sauce, add 0.8 percent of that weight in salt, and serve as desired.

Q&A, MARCIA GAGLIARDI

COLUMNIST AND CURATOR, *TABLEHOPPER*

TF: First off, *tablehopper* is seventeen years old now...seventeen years! That's a pretty incredible run. What's the key to the newsletter's success?

MG: Thanks! It's primarily two things: first, my deep passion for documenting our restaurant and bar industry. There's always an interesting story to tell, good people you want to support, a new place to discover, a taco you want everyone to know about. It keeps me going. And secondly: my dedicated audience who likes to read! I have subscribers who have been with me since the beginning, so we have a pretty special relationship.

TF: A *lot* has changed when it comes to covering the restaurant scene and the restaurant scene itself since you started. What are some of the most significant changes as a journalist and in terms of the restaurants that you're constantly visiting?

MG: Sadly, so many print media outlets are gone, along with their ability to pay writers more than online outlets can afford to, so that has been tough for journalists who write about food. Instead, we now have the flurry of influencer culture, since restaurants are able to reach thousands of people via social media—but I don't see their story being told, just cheese pulls.

TF: What are you most excited about/where do you absolutely love dining at these days? And, any favorite classics that hopefully never retire?

MG: I always love it when chefs can tell the culinary story of their roots: Chef Sri Gopinathan at Copra, Chef Heena Patel of Besharam, Chef Rob Lam of Lily, Chef Shawn Naputi at Prubechu. All of these places have a special energy and resonance.

Oh, I am such an SF classics lady. You have to eat it to save it! I adore Henry's Hunan, Yank Sing, Sam's Grill for seafood, and Kokkari is such a steady force!

TF: You've been one of the leading voices for the SF restaurant scene in the past two decades. What is it that makes our not-giant city (compared to LA or NY) such a culinary powerhouse?

MG: Of course, our ingredients and produce and commitment to seasonal and sustainable sourcing and small farmers all make our dishes sing year-round. I really noticed the difference when I was living in New York; the produce was often pretty lackluster, because it's at least a few days older than what our Bay Area chefs use! We have a pretty tight chef community, which I love to see, and so many multigenerational family restaurants. And our Cal-Italian scene here is unique. But honestly, I do think L.A. has the most exciting food scene right now.

TF: When you think about SF dining history—the pre-1970s/1980s farm-to-table movement—what do you think about? Was there even such a thing as Gold Rush cuisine?

MG: As a collector of vintage SF restaurant menus and ephemera, you would be blown away with the restaurants that sprang up after all that money was coming in here. (The dish hangtown fry tells the story of this newfound wealth.) Of course, French cuisine was highly esteemed, but it was the Barbary Coast! Places like Jack's and the Old Poodle Dog had bordellos upstairs! What a scene. Chinese cuisine has deep roots here—from the very beginning of the Gold Rush—and Italian immigrants knew how to fish and built up the Wharf. Boudin's sourdough starter is as old as the Gold Rush!

TF: If I'm correct, you grew up on the Peninsula, right? Any marquee food memories from growing up nearby and visiting the city?

MG: I did! San Mateo! I grew up going to Romolo's for cannoli and Woodside Deli, and eating with my grandparents at Kwoh Wah and Kee Joon's (they loved Chinese food). I remember coming into the city to dine at The Magic Pan and Hippo Burger, and then Sam Wo in my teens! Dining at Buca Giovanni made a big impression on me, and my grandpa liked Capp's Corner and the Gold Spike. Oh, and going to Il Fornaio and Prego with my parents and sister—it was the beginning of Cal-Ital in SF, and we loved those spots.

TF: I tend to fall into the loop of hyping the same generally already-hyped restaurants again and again. Yet, you seem to always know about restaurants that I've never heard of! So, what are some of the underrated restaurants and dining neighborhoods in the city?

MG: The Mission is always a hotbed of new spots, since there's so much turnover and there are tiny spaces where businesses can get their start, like the oh-so-delicious Al Carajo, and La Vaca Birria in the old Discolandia! I visit Chinatown all the time, whether it's America's oldest dim sum parlor at Hang Ah, or I'm picking up chicken wings at Capital, or feasting at Great Eastern. I actually lead private curated tours of Chinatown—I'm so passionate about sharing its many stories and charms.

MAIN COURSES

LAZY MAN'S CIOPPINO

SCOMA'S

O f all the gin joints in all the towns . . . ok, well if Humphrey Bogart's Sam Spade character from San Francisco–based *The Maltese Falcon* said the line, it would probably be more like, "Of all the iconic San Francisco dishes of all time, there is none more iconic than cioppino." It's part of the whole bouillabaisse-fisherman's stew family. And yet, cioppino is its own revered entity. It seems to be on tourists' itineraries right next to Alcatraz and the Golden Gate Bridge. Originally created by Italian fishermen at SF's Fisherman's Wharf in the early twentieth century (the exact time and place are heavily debated and basically not known), it's best enjoyed with the smell of salt water in the air and waves within view. That means go enjoy a bowl of cioppino at a Fisherman's Wharf institution like Scoma's (opened in 1965), and don't forget a bib.

YIELD: 4 to 6 servings

CIOPPINO SAUCE BASE

¼ CUP RICE BRAN OIL OR OLIVE OIL

1 MEDIUM ONION, DICED

2 TABLESPOONS CHOPPED GARLIC

½ CUP VEGETABLE STOCK OR WATER

3 TABLESPOONS RED WINE VINEGAR

2 (28-OZ.) CANS HIGH-QUALITY CHOPPED TOMATOES

2 TABLESPOONS TOMATO PASTE

½ TEASPOON DRIED OREGANO (PREFERABLY SICILIAN)

2 TEASPOONS KOSHER SALT

LEAVES FROM ½ BUNCH FRESH BASIL, THINLY SLICED

RED PEPPER FLAKES (OPTIONAL)

1. In a medium-size heavy-bottomed pot over low heat, warm the oil.

2. Add the onion and sauté until it just starts to soften, then add the garlic and sauté for 10 minutes.

3. Add the stock and vinegar and cook down until almost dry.

4. Add the tomatoes, tomato paste, and oregano and simmer for 30 to 40 minutes.

5. Add the salt and basil and cook for another 5 minutes.

6. Adjust the seasoning to your liking (red pepper flakes are a nice addition).

7. Cool rapidly. Refrigerate, tightly covered, for up to 2 days.

continued...

CIOPPINO (PER SERVING)

1 TABLESPOON OLIVE OIL

5 LITTLENECK CLAMS

5 MUSSELS

1½ CUPS CIOPPINO SAUCE BASE
(SEE PAGE 202), HEATED

2 PIECES LINGCOD OR OTHER
WHITE FISH (3 OZ. TOTAL)

3 LARGE GULF SHRIMP, PEELED

3 DRY-PACK DAYBOAT SCALLOPS
(NO CHEMICALS)

1¾ OZ. COOKED CRABMEAT

1 SPRIG FRESH FLAT-LEAF PARSLEY

1 PIECE TOASTED GARLIC BREAD

1. In a cold pan over medium heat, warm the olive oil.

2. Add the clams and mussels and move them around in the pan. Be careful not to let the pan flame up. Remove each clam and mussel as it opens to a plate. Add the base about 1 minute after you add the clams and mussels.

4. Add the fish, shrimp, and scallops and let simmer gently until almost cooked through.

5. Return the clams and mussels to the pan to heat through.

6. Plate in a large bowl with the lingcod in the middle, the shellfish around the perimeter, and the sauce base ladled in the center. The crabmeat should be sticking up on top.

7. Garnish with the parsley and serve with the garlic bread.

TURKEY TETRAZZINI

I t's one of the most recognizable early twentieth-century American dishes—a casserole that many of our parents and/or grandparents surely have made for us at some point. And it started right here in San Francisco at the historic, magnificent Palace Hotel, where it was named after...an opera singer staying at the hotel! Who knew that opera, a luxury hotel, and a spaghetti casserole were connected?

YIELD: 2 to 3 servings

5 TABLESPOONS UNSALTED BUTTER	3 CUPS COARSELY CHOPPED COOKED TURKEY, INCLUDING COOKED GIBLETS, IF DESIRED
10 OZ. MUSHROOMS, THINLY SLICED (ABOUT 4 CUPS)	1 CUP COOKED PEAS
¼ CUP ALL-PURPOSE FLOUR	
1¾ CUPS MILK	SALT AND FRESHLY GROUND BLACK PEPPER, TO TASTE
2 CUPS CHICKEN BROTH	⅔ CUP FRESHLY GRATED PARMESAN CHEESE
¼ CUP DRY WHITE WINE	
10 OZ. SPAGHETTI	⅓ CUP FRESH FINE BREAD CRUMBS

1. In a large, heavy saucepan over medium heat, melt 4 tablespoons of the butter, then add the mushrooms and cook, stirring, until most of the liquid they give off has evaporated. Stir in the flour and cook over low heat, stirring, for 3 minutes.

2. Add the milk, broth, and wine in a stream, stirring. Bring to a boil, stirring, and simmer for 5 minutes.

3. Cook the spaghetti in a large pot of salted water until al dente; drain well.

continued...

4. In a large bowl, combine the spaghetti, mushroom sauce, turkey, peas, and salt and pepper to taste. Stir in half of the Parmesan, and transfer the mixture to a buttered, shallow 3-quart casserole.

5. In a small bowl, combine the remaining Parmesan, the bread crumbs, and salt and pepper to taste. Sprinkle the mixture evenly over the tetrazzini, and dot the top with the remaining 1 tablespoon butter, cut into bits. (The casserole may be prepared to this point up to 1 month in advance and kept frozen, covered.)

6. Bake the tetrazzini in the center of a preheated 375°F/190°C oven until it is bubbling and the top is golden, 30 to 40 minutes.

MODERN CHICKEN TETRAZZINI

THE GARDEN COURT

Here's a livened-up, present-day version of the aforementioned classic from the Palace Hotel. Why not gather a few friends and have a tetrazzini-off (with some opera music as the soundtrack, of course) to determine which version you prefer?

YIELD: 2 to 3 servings

---

1 WHOLE BONELESS, SKINLESS CHICKEN BREAST

2 TEASPOONS DIJON MUSTARD

½ CUP CHOPPED FRESH PARSLEY

6 SPRIGS THYME

¼ CUP OLIVE OIL

2 ARTICHOKES

2 CUPS WHITE WINE

6 GARLIC CLOVES, PEELED

8 OZ. CASARECCE PASTA

SALT AND FRESHLY GROUND BLACK PEPPER, TO TASTE

8 OZ. KING OYSTER MUSHROOMS, CUT INTO ¼-INCH SLICES LENGTHWISE

½ CUP HEAVY CREAM

4 OZ. PEA SHOOTS, BLANCHED, OR MICROGREENS

GRATED PARMESAN CHEESE

1. Cut the chicken breast in half and pound flat.

2. In a small bowl, mix together the mustard, ¼ cup of the parsley, 2 sprigs of the thyme, chopped, and 2 tablespoons of the olive oil.

3. Coat the chicken with the mustard mixture, cover, and marinate in the refrigerator for 2 to 24 hours.

4. Clean the artichokes, removing the tough outer leaves and trimming the tips and stems. Cut into quarters and remove the heart fibers.

continued...

5. Put the artichokes in a medium saucepan and add the wine, garlic, and remaining 4 sprigs thyme. Bring to a boil, then reduce the heat and simmer for 20 minutes.

6. Drain, reserving the wine, and cool the artichokes.

7. Cook the pasta in salted water and drain.

8. Remove the chicken from the marinade and season with salt and pepper. In a sauté pan, heat 1 tablespoon of the olive oil and sauté the chicken until golden brown and cooked through, 8 to 10 minutes. Set aside to rest for 5 minutes. Shred into bite-size pieces.

9. In a large sauté pan, heat the remaining 1 tablespoon olive oil. Add the mushrooms and let caramelize.

10. Add the artichokes and toss for 1 minute.

11. Add the reserved wine and deglaze, scraping up any browned bits from the bottom of the pan. Add the cream and reduce for about 2 minutes. Add the chicken, pasta, and remaining ¼ cup parsley and toss to heat through. Season with salt and pepper.

12. Serve in warm bowls topped with the blanched pea shoots or microgreens and Parmesan.

SHRIMP AND GRITS

BOUG CALI, TIFFANY CARTER

Po'boys? Gumbo? Shrimp & grits? Black-eyed peas followed by banana pudding? The New Orleans via California specialties from Tiffany Carter at Boug Cali in the La Cocina Municipal Market (and the Chase Center) always call for some difficult lunchtime decision-making for indecisive diners. Here is a recipe for a tried-and-true favorite from the San Francisco–raised chef that is a perfect choice for brunch, lunch, or dinner any day of the week. This is delicious with pan-fried sliced fresh okra, shaved roasted corn, and scallions as add-ins.

YIELD: 4 servings

GRITS

2 CUPS WATER	2 TABLESPOONS UNSALTED BUTTER
2 CUPS GRITS	1½ TABLESPOONS SALT, PLUS MORE TO TASTE
1 CUP MILK	

1. In a saucepan, bring the water to a boil. Whisk in the grits until smooth. Add the milk, butter, and salt. Turn the heat to low, cover, and cook for 15 minutes, whisking frequently to avoid lumps.

continued...

BLACKENED SHRIMP

1½ LBS. LARGE SHRIMP, WITH TAILS ON

½ TEASPOON SMOKED PAPRIKA

½ TEASPOON GARLIC POWDER

½ TEASPOON CREOLE SEASONING (BOUG CALI USES TONY'S CREOLE SEASONING)

1. Toss the shrimp with the paprika, garlic powder, and creole seasoning.

2. Heat a cast-iron skillet over medium-high heat. Add the shrimp and char for 2 to 3 minutes on each side. Transfer them to a plate and set aside.

CREAM SAUCE

2 TABLESPOONS BUTTER

⅔ CUP FINELY CHOPPED HOLY TRINITY (EQUAL PARTS ONION, CELERY, BELL PEPPER)

1½ CUPS HEAVY CREAM

1 TABLESPOON SMOKED PAPRIKA

CREOLE SEASONING, TO TASTE

1. In a saucepan, melt the butter. Add the holy trinity and sauté until really soft. Add the cream, paprika, and creole seasoning and bring to a simmer. Let simmer, whisking, until it is reduced by half.

ASSEMBLY

1. Spoon grits into a bowl, drizzle with some cream sauce, then top with 2 to 3 blackened shrimp and more cream sauce.

Q&A, TIFFANY CARTER

CHEF/OWNER, BOUG CALI

TF: Growing up in the Bayview, did you always want to be a chef? What inspired you to pursue the culinary profession route and cook California soul food/New Orleans cuisine?

TC: I always knew I wanted to be an entrepreneur, not necessarily a chef, even though from a young age I was always whipping something up in the kitchen and cooking family recipes with my grandmother and aunts. I didn't realize I wanted to be a chef until my twenties. One summer it all just clicked for me. My cousins and I decided to sell plates of food using family recipes at our grandfather's church in the Bayview on 3rd Street. We were having fun but also making money, and that's when I realized I could actually make a business out of this. From there, I enrolled in Le Cordon Bleu. Today my California soul food is the legacy of the Great Migration. It's the food my grandparents brought to California from Louisiana and Alabama, but with my personal twist that reflects my Bayview roots, the California coast, and my French culinary training. It's authentically inauthentic California soul food.

TF: Any favorite food memories from your youth in SF?

TC: I have so many favorite food memories. Growing up in the Bayview, my favorite spots were Mozelle's for soul food and Constanso's for my Dutch crunch turkey sandwich. These family-owned restaurants made the neighborhood and my childhood special.

Another favorite memory was exploring the Mission and the Castro for off-campus lunch while I was attending Mission High School. I would eat at places like Orphan Annie's and Pancho Villa on 16th Street. Pancho Villa is still my favorite—the super steak and prawn burrito is my go-to.

TF: What was your experience like with La Cocina, and how were you connected to that program?

TC: After I graduated from culinary school, I saved up and opened a food truck in Bayview. La Cocina's executive director at the time, Caleb Zigas, came to try my food, and we talked about the challenges of running a food business. He encouraged me to apply to the incubator program for additional support. When I was accepted into the new La Cocina cohort, it was perfect timing, as I had just secured my spot as a vendor at the new Chase Center. La Cocina supported me in the negotiations with that deal. I then got accepted to be a vendor in La Cocina's Municipal Marketplace. I feel privileged to be a part of La Cocina, privileged for the first time in my life.

TF: When you think of the restaurant scene in SF and what makes it unique, what comes to mind?

TC: The mom-and-pop shops and the diversity of the food and the culture are what makes San Francisco's restaurant scene unique. San Francisco is a small city, and it's amazing the variety of food that is offered here. Of course, it saddens me that there aren't many Black restaurants left and that I'm one of very few Black-owned restaurants in the city.

TF: How has the city's dining scene changed since you grew up? How do we make this expensive, competitive city for operating a restaurant into a friendlier, more sustainable climate for chef entrepreneurs?

TC: A lot of diverse businesses have been pushed out because of pricing. The city needs to cap the rent wherever they can and should offer more equitable leases, similar to La Cocina's Municipal Marketplace model, because a majority of small-business owners can't afford these astronomical rents. Restaurants create the culture of this city. Let's keep the culture what it is and support the mom and pops and small-business owners.

TF: Can you tell us about SF Black Wallstreet, the organization that you helped cofound, and what is the mission for it?

TC: Gentrification and cost of living have pushed the Black community out of San Francisco, and with that their businesses and culture. SF Black Wallstreet's mission is to sustain Black culture and people in San Francisco. We focus on providing the Black community with opportunities for homeownership, economic development, and spatial justice. I believe that Black entrepreneurship is the highest form of activism, as it inspires the Black community to create their own financial freedom while also providing jobs and opportunities to others.

TF: Finally, Boug Cali is at both the La Cocina Municipal Marketplace and the Chase Center. Very different locations! What's it like operating at both places? A po'boy sounds like a perfect dinner pairing with watching a Warriors game!

TC: My dream was always to have a restaurant on Hyde Street and in the Dogpatch, so having my business at both of these spaces is literally a dream come true. While both locations are very different, each is a unique space to operate my business. Being at La Cocina's Municipal Marketplace, I'm able to build community and interact with customers on a daily basis. Being at the Chase Center stadium, I'm able to serve a larger volume and variety of people (and Warriors fans!). As a San Francisco native and lifelong Warriors fan, it's a pinch-me moment to think about Warriors fans eating my po'boys while watching the games. I totally agree that my po'boys are the perfect pairing for watching the Warriors game.

CHICKEN MOLE

LA GUERRERA'S KITCHEN, OFELIA BARAJAS

After spending many years as a tamale vendor in the Mission District, Ofelia Barajas and her daughter Reyna Maldonado joined the La Cocina incubator program to help them grow a business serving dishes from their home region of Guerrero in Mexico (situated between the Pacific Coast and Puebla/Mexico City in the general center of the country). The result is that Bay Area diners have been able to enjoy their wonderful cooking at various stops in Oakland. They are currently operating at the historic Swan's Market in Old Oakland.

YIELD: 8 servings

8 PIECES BONE-IN CHICKEN, A MIX OF THIGHS AND DRUMSTICKS

3¾ CUPS VEGETABLE OIL (ANY HIGH-SMOKE-POINT OIL)

12 CLOVES GARLIC, PEELED

8 ROMA TOMATOES, DICED

2 YELLOW ONIONS, DICED

2 CHILIES MULATO (WHOLE, DRIED, AND DESTEMMED)

4 CHILIES ANCHO (WHOLE, DRIED, AND DESTEMMED)

3 CHILIES PASILLA (WHOLE, DRIED, AND DESTEMMED)

8 CHILIES GUAJILLO (WHOLE, DRIED, AND DESTEMMED)

6 CHILES DE ÁRBOL (WHOLE, DRIED, AND DESTEMMED)

½ CUP SESAME SEEDS, PLUS MORE FOR TOPPING

½ CUP SHELLED PUMPKIN SEEDS

3 CORN TORTILLAS

1 BOLILLO OR DEMI BAGUETTE, TORN INTO PIECES

1½ DISCS (ABOUT 3¹⁄₁₀ OZ.) MEXICAN CHOCOLATE (OFELIA LIKES DANDELION OR IBARRA)

1 TABLESPOON SALT

HOT COOKED RICE, FOR SERVING

continued...

1. Bring a large pot of salted water to a boil, then add the chicken and reduce the heat to medium-low and cook until it is tender, about 30 minutes. Using tongs or a slotted spoon, remove the chicken to a large plate and reserve 4 cups of the chicken cooking liquid.

2. In a 10- or 12-inch skillet over medium-high, heat ¼ cup of the oil, then add 8 of the garlic cloves and cook until fragrant. Add the tomatoes and onions and sauté until the onions are translucent, about 8 minutes.

3. In a blender, process the tomato mixture until smooth. Remove from the blender and set it aside.

4. Using the same skillet, heat 3 cups of the oil over medium-high heat. Submerge all the chiles and remaining 4 cloves garlic for 2 seconds each (make sure not to burn them), using a slotted spoon to set them aside in a large bowl.

5. Using the same oil and skillet, place the sesame and pumpkin seeds in a medium metal sieve and submerge it in the oil for 2 minutes. Transfer the fried seeds to the same bowl with the chiles and garlic.

6. Fry the tortillas in the oil until golden brown, about 1 minute. Cool and break into pieces.

7. Add the chiles, sesame seeds, pumpkin seeds, tortillas pieces, and bolillo pieces to the reserved chicken cooking liquid and let sit for 10 minutes.

8. Transfer the mixture to the blender and blend until smooth (you may need to do this in batches).

9. In a medium pot over medium heat, heat the remaining ½ cup oil. Add the tomato mixture and heat to a simmer. Add the chile-and-seed puree and bring to a simmer. Add the chocolate and stir well to combine ingredients. Let simmer for 20 minutes.

10. Add the salt, stir, and then add the chicken, cover, and simmer to reheat it, 10 to 15 minutes.

11. Serve with rice and top with more sesame seeds.

GHAPAMA: RICE PILAF IN KABOCHA SQUASH

DALIDA

The marquee restaurant opening of 2023 was this excellent Presidio restaurant, where excellent modern eastern Mediterranean cooking is served in a renovated late nineteenth century military barrack alongside the Main Parade Lawn. It's a fascinating mix of contemporary and historic San Francisco. Dalida is also another wonderful pop-up to permanent story, where many city diners have been following wife-and-husband team Laura and Sayat Ozyilmaz since they started their Istanbul Modern dining concept in 2016. Fast-forward seven years and here they are with their own, truly special restaurant that has swiftly become one of the dining stalwarts (and hottest reservations) of present-day San Francisco. For this recipe, Sayat wants to mention that the dish has its roots in Armenia but the name of the dish is Turkish, which reflects the interconnectedness of cultures in that region before the invention of borders. It's a great representation of the regional cuisine that diners will find at Dalida.

YIELD: 2 to 4 servings

---

1 LARGE KABOCHA OR KOGINUT SQUASH (ABOUT 3 LBS.)

2 CUPS JASMINE RICE (MAY VARY DEPENDING ON THE VOLUME OF THE SQUASH)

½ CUP MIXED DRIED BERRIES (WE PREFER CURRANTS AS THEY DISPERSE AND POP BETTER, BUT RAISINS, MULBERRIES, AND BARBERRIES ALL WORK)

½ CUP MIXED NUTS (CASHEWS, HAZELNUTS, PINE NUTS, PISTACHIOS, AND WALNUTS ARE SOME TRADITIONAL ONES THAT GO INTO THIS PREPARATION)

2 OZ FINELY CHOPPED HERBS (FRESH TARRAGON, PURPLE BASIL, AND CILANTRO)

continued...

PINCH OF CINNAMON

PINCH OF ALLSPICE

PINCH OF GROUND CLOVES

1 TEASPOON BLACK PEPPER

¼ OZ. SALT

3 CUPS WATER, VEGETABLE STOCK, OR MUSHROOM STOCK (MAY VARY DEPENDING ON THE VOLUME OF THE SQUASH)

4 OZ. UNSALTED BUTTER

1. Preheat the oven to 400ºF/204.4ºC.

2. Before slicing into the squash, microwave it on medium for 3 minutes. The skin becomes easier to penetrate this way. The squash also becomes less brittle, so that it doesn't crack as easily when you cut into it.

3. Remove the top of the squash. You can trim and make the edges more visually pleasing with a peeler or a paring knife. Carve out the gills and seeds from the inside. Make sure you do not create any holes or cracks in the squash, as it will become the vessel to cook the rice.

4. Every squash is different. Measure the inside volume of the squash by pouring water into it. Pour the water out of the squash into a measuring pitcher. You should anticipate that the rice will double in size, so feel free to scale the amount of rice and water to fit the squash.

5. Parcook the squash in the microwave for 4 to 5 minutes before adding the rice, berries, and nuts. This helps to retain the shape and structure of the squash.

6. Add all of the herbs and dry seasonings to the squash and mix well. Bring the water or stock to a simmer and add to the squash. Finally, top with the butter.

7. Cover the squash with aluminum foil, making sure the top of the squash is as insulated as possible. Cook the squash in the oven for 40 minutes or until the rice and squash are both cooked. Remove from the oven and serve immediately.

Q&A, PETE SITTNICK

MANAGING PARTNER, EPIC STEAK AND WATERBAR

TF: Being a restaurateur is one of the hardest professions in the world, yet you've opened over twenty restaurants during your esteemed career. How in the world do you do it??

PS: The motivation for opening and operating restaurants comes from the joy and satisfaction of helping to make people happy. Ultimately, you want to develop a restaurant that is financially successful and sustainable, but that only happens when you can deliver a memorable dining experience for the guests and a gratifying work environment for the employees.

TF: Growing up in Michigan, were you always interested in restaurants and/or running a business?

PS: I really just fell into restaurants in Michigan as a part-time job in high school, then dormitory food service at the University of Michigan and an off-campus bar called Dooley's. Once I figured out that I did not want to be an accountant, I wound up getting a manager job with Houlihan's and they sent me out to California!

TF: The late Bill Kimpton was a great mentor for you. What did you learn from him and opening several notable places like Harry Denton's Starlight Room?

PS: Bill Kimpton was a great mentor, based on his humility and gratitude for the people that worked for him. He once told me, "Pete, I have no idea how to run a restaurant. That is why you are here. All I know is just how it should feel when I am a guest." He knew how to surround himself with good people because a restaurant truly is the summation of all the employees striving to do their best.

TF: You started working with Pat Kuleto back in the 1980s and went on to open some of San Francisco's most iconic restaurants. Can you tell us a bit about Pat and how your restaurants thrived at combining beautiful design with excellent food?

PS: Pat Kuleto is a creative force when it comes to designing restaurants. He looks at every detail that goes into creating a restaurant and how it will impact the guest perception and emotion. His designs evoke a sense of feeling extra special while still being very comfortable. The ambiance impacts the energy of the restaurant, so that it feels like a place you want to be. When you sit in a dining room surrounded by smiling, happy people, it just makes you feel better. Kuleto has a deep appreciation for good food, but he knew that talented chefs would be the key to cooking delicious food on a day-in, day-out basis, so that is who he partnered with. The whole experience would come together with great service and hospitality, so that his restaurants became extremely popular and built their reputation for every level of the dining experience.

TF: Waterbar and Epic Steak not only combine great design and great food, but the views are arguably the most picturesque in the city. It's so rare to find a "view restaurant" that also truly emphasizes the food and drink quality. How do these two restaurants pull it off?

PS: Waterbar and EPIC Steak have built their reputations in San Francisco by enhancing the iconic Bay Bridge view with the "in-the-moment" elements of great restaurants that our staff can provide——food, service, and hospitality. From the beginning, we wanted to be restaurants that became favorites of the locals. We tried to pay attention to the dynamics of all of the restaurant meal segments—lunch, dinner, after work, and private events. Once we gained the loyalty of the locals, we knew that out-of-town guests would visit Waterbar and EPIC not only for the view but for the quality of the experience.

We value and respect the opportunity to make each and every guest, regardless of where they are from, feel special when they visit Waterbar and EPIC. We continue to build the reputation of the restaurants by creating memories that live forever and inspire others to come back often. In many ways, we consider ourselves the "ambassadors of the waterfront." This means that we have a responsibility to make sure that locals and visitors to our restaurants leave with a smile on their face and joy in their heart.

TF: You're also a key voice for restaurants across the city through your work with the GGRA. How does that organization directly help San Francisco's restaurants?

PS: Restaurants are an important industry to the overall success of San Francisco as a city and as a destination. Hospitality is the largest employer in San Francisco and the biggest tax revenue generator. Restaurants are also one of the biggest supporters of nonprofit and charity causes—in fact, Waterbar and EPIC have raised close to a half million dollars for causes that help those less fortunate.

It is important that restaurants have a voice toward laws and regulations that make it easier to do business in San Francisco. That is where the Golden Gate Restaurant Association acts as a consolidated advocacy group. The public just sees a busy restaurant and thinks that it must be making money hand over fist. The reality is that profit margins are low, hours of operation are grueling, and staffing has become a real issue. The GGRA helps to promote the hard work and good intent that restaurant operators bring to the table.

TF: Besides your restaurants, where do you like to dine in SF?

PS: The great thing about San Francisco is that there are restaurants for every occasion or reason for going out. That means it could be a multicourse dinner or a burger at the bar. I enjoy eating in restaurants where I have relationships that have been built over time and often via past work together. Many of these restaurants are legends in the city, such as Boulevard, Delfina, Perbacco, Wayfare Tavern, Zuni Café, and Kokkari. I always need to have at least one dinner a year at House of Prime Rib—the whole vibe is truly San Francisco, and the place is always packed.

KUNG PAO "FIRECRACKER" CHICKEN

CHINA LIVE, GEORGE CHEN

George Chen is one of the true SF restaurant lifers—cooking at and/or running restaurants across several decades. His signature project is the ambitious, wonderful China Live. Right on Broadway at the edge of North Beach and Chinatown, it's multiple stories that combine a ground-floor restaurant, a shop, a great bar, and the haute Chinese tasting menu destination Eight Tables by George Chen. It all sounds overwhelming and complex. In reality, it's a fantastic place to visit for multiple reasons from noon to midnight.

YIELD: 4 servings

¼ CUP RICE BRAN OIL, PLUS JUST ENOUGH TO COAT PAN

8 OZ. CHICKEN THIGH MEAT, CUT INTO 1-INCH CUBES

CORNSTARCH, AS NEEDED

EGG WHITES, AS NEEDED

½ CUP EACH CHOPPED GREEN AND RED BELL PEPPERS

½ CUP DRIED CHILIES (GEORGE PREFERS FRESNO CHILIES AS THEY ARE SWEETER)

½ CUP SCALLION WHITES, CUT INTO 2-INCH LENGTHS

GARLIC, SLICED THIN, TO TASTE

¼ CUP SOY SAUCE MIXED WITH 1 TEASPOON EACH MINCED GARLIC AND MINCED FRESH GINGER, AND 1 TABLESPOON BLACK VINEGAR

1 TABLESPOON PEPPERCORN-INFUSED CHILI OIL

1 TABLESPOON RICE WINE

continued...

1. Over high heat, heat a wok or heavy saucepan with a coating of oil until hot, then add the ¼ cup oil and heat until the pan is just smoking. Dredge the chicken in the cornstarch and egg whites, add it to the pan, and turn down the heat. Let it cook slowly until the chicken is about 80 percent done (the chicken becomes white on the outside). Drain off the oil and reserve.

2. Add some water to the same pan and heat to a boil. Add the bell peppers and turn off the heat. Drain.

3. Clean and dry the pan. Add the dried chilies, scallions, and garlic to the skillet and cook until they just start to char. Add 1 tablespoon of the reserved oil and heat to just smoking over high heat. Add back the chicken and bell peppers, and add the soy sauce mixture. Toss the ingredients together.

4. When almost done, add the peppercorn oil, then the rice wine to finish. Remove from the pan and serve immediately.

PEKING DUCK

Z&Y

Chef Han of Z&Y has cooked for celebrities, political dignitaries, and Chinese presidents. So, it's quite an honor to be able to share his recipe for one of the most beloved and famous dishes of regional Chinese cooking. Chef Han was born in Beijing, and Beijing-style Peking duck is indeed the most famous dish from the capital city, and it's no surprise that it is one of Chef Han's signature dishes. Here's your chance to try making Peking duck from someone who has spent a career perfecting the dish.

We have translated Chef Han's techniques into a recipe suitable for home kitchens and cooks. With enough skill, and lots of patience, you too can master the art of Peking Duck. Marvel at its intricacy and its beauty: tender, juicy duck meat encased in its own crystalline skin.

—Z&Y

YIELD: 4 to 6 servings

---

1 WHOLE DUCK, ABOUT 4 LBS., THAWED IF FROZEN

25 ML CHINESE RED VINEGAR

500 ML WATER

35 G MALTOSE

PEKING DUCK PANCAKES, FOR SERVING

HOISIN SAUCE, FOR SERVING

SCALLIONS, WHITE AND LIGHT-GREEN PARTS ONLY, SLICED LENGTHWISE, FOR SERVING

CUCUMBER, CUT INTO MATCHSTICKS, FOR SERVING

continued...

---

1. Remove the wings and innards from the duck.

2. Bring a large pot of water to a boil. If your pot is big enough to submerge the duck fully, then submerge it in the water for 15 to 20 seconds. If not, set the duck on a wire rack in the sink. When the water comes to a boil, gently and slowly (take 15 to 20 seconds to do it) pour half of it over the top surface of the duck. Make sure to cover the surface evenly. Flip the duck over and repeat with the remaining water.

3. Let the duck cool slightly, then place on a wire rack set on an aluminum foil–lined rimmed baking sheet.

4. In a medium bowl, combine the vinegar, water, and maltose. Brush this solution over the entirety of the duck, making sure it is thoroughly covered.

5. Transfer the duck, with the wire rack, to a fresh foil-lined rimmed baking sheet. Place the duck in the freezer for 24 hours.

6. Remove the duck from the freezer and let defrost for 7 hours at room temperature.

7. Preheat oven to 400°F/204°C. Roast the duck for 50 minutes to 1 hour, until a deep golden brown.

8. Transfer the duck to a cutting board. Carve and serve immediately with pancakes, hoisin sauce, scallions, and cucumber.

SPICY FISH WITH FLAMING CHILI OIL

Z&Y

The Sichuan dishes at Chinatown's Z&Y often dial up the málà sensation (a quick one-two punch of heat and numbing) that its cuisine's ample use of peppercorns and chilies is known for. Chef Han's recipe for this signature spicy fish is powerful, delightful, packs quite the kick, and giant rivers of flavor. It's without question one of the most memorable and popular large-format dishes in San Francisco.

YIELD: 3 to 4 servings

2 TEASPOONS CHINESE COOKING WINE

60 G POTATO STARCH

10 G WHITE PEPPER

5 G SALT

1,000 G BASS FILLETS

300 G NAPA CABBAGE

200 ML CANOLA OIL

50 G CHINESE BEAN PASTE

30 G DRIED CHILIES, SLICED

20 G GREEN PEPPERCORNS

300 ML WATER

25 G GINGER, CHOPPED

5 G STAR ANISE

5 G CHINESE CINNAMON STICKS

5 G GALANGAL

25 G SCALLIONS, CHOPPED

30 G MINCED GARLIC

1. In a baking dish, combine the Chinese cooking wine, potato starch, white pepper, and 2 g of the salt. Add the fish and turn to coat on both sides with the marinade.

2. Cut the cabbage into slices (roughly 3 fingers wide), rinse with hot water, and place in a bowl.

3. In a pot over high heat, heat half of the canola oil until sizzling hot. Add the bean paste and half of the sliced dried chilies and green peppercorns. Stir-fry until aromatic.

4. Add the water, ginger, star anise, cinnamon, galangal, and remaining 3 g salt. Cook for 10 minutes.

5. Fish out the spices and add in the fish. Cook for 2 to 3 minutes. Transfer the fish to the bowl with the cabbage. Add the scallions and garlic.

6. In another pan over high heat, heat the remaining canola oil until smoking and add in the remaining green peppercorns and sliced dried chilies. Add to the bowl with the fish and cabbage.

PHYLLO-CRUSTED SOLE

ESTIATORIO ORNOS

First it was Aqua, then Michael Mina, and now this renowned California Street restaurant address is a wonderful Santorini-meets-urbane-Greek-Middle-Eastern restaurant from Michael Mina with fellow chefs Girair "Jerry" Gourmroian and Nikolaos Georgousis.

Nowadays at 252 California Street, make sure to start with the grilled octopus, finish with the tableside grilled baklava sundae, and enjoy wonderful fish preparations like this phyllo-crusted sole in between those courses.

YIELD: 2 servings

CAVIAR CREMA

1 TABLESPOON SMALL-DICED SHALLOT

1 SPRIG FRESH THYME

1 TABLESPOON OLIVE OIL

½ CUP CRISP WHITE WINE

1 CUP HEAVY CREAM

2 OZ. COLD BUTTER, DICED

SALT AND FRESHLY GROUND BLACK PEPPER, TO TASTE

JUICE OF ½ LEMON

½ OZ. CAVIAR

1. In a sauce pot, heat the shallot, thyme, and oil. Once it starts to sweat, add the wine and bring to a boil. Reduce until almost dry.

2. Add the cream and reduce by half.

3. Strain, then whisk in the cold butter slowly over low heat until fully emulsified. Season with salt and pepper.

4. Once ready to serve, add the lemon juice and caviar, stir, and serve. *continued...*

SKORDALIA

1 CUP ALMONDS, LIGHTLY TOASTED

1 TEASPOON SALT

¼ TEASPOON GROUND WHITE PEPPER

1 TEASPOON BALSAMIC VINEGAR

1 GARLIC CLOVE, PEELED

1 CUP SOAKED WHITE BREAD

½ CUP WATER

1 CUP OLIVE OIL

½ CUP CANOLA OIL

JUICE OF ½ LEMON

1. Place the almonds, salt, pepper, vinegar, and garlic in a food processor. Process for 5 minutes.

2. Squeeze the excess water from the bread, then add to the processor in small increments with half of the water. Continue to process.

3. Drizzle in the oils slowly with the processor running until fully emulsified.

4. Add the lemon juice. If the mixture is too thick, add some of the water that was squeezed from the bread. Adjust the seasoning if needed.

PETRALE SOLE

2 CUPS CLARIFIED BUTTER

1 EGG WHITE

2 (6 OZ.) PETRALE SOLE

1 TEASPOON SALT

5 DRIED PHYLLO SHEETS (LET DRY OVERNIGHT), CRUSHED INTO CORNFLAKE-SIZED PIECES

5 BRUSSELS SPROUTS

1. In a sauté pan over medium heat, warm the clarified butter; be careful to not let it get too hot.

2. Gently whisk the egg white to break it apart.

3. Season the fish with the salt and add to the egg white, turning to coat it fully.

4. Remove the fish from the egg white and dredge in the crushed dried phyllo. Make sure the sole is fully coated; you can help by gently pressing the phyllo into it.

5. Place the sole in the clarified butter and cook until golden brown, about 2 minutes per side.

6. Once golden brown, transfer to a wire rack in a 350°F/177°C oven for 2 to 3 minutes to finish cooking.

7. Pull apart the Brussels sprout leaves and quickly sauté them in the olive oil.

ASSEMBLY

1. Make a bed of skordalia and place the fish on top.

2. Place the Brussels sprout leaves facing up on top of the fish, creating little "cups" to catch the caviar crema.

3. Once ready to enjoy, spoon over the caviar crema, filling all Brussels sprout "cups," and serve.

Feta-Brined Roast Chicken
See page 236

FETA-BRINED ROAST CHICKEN

SOUVLA

Charles Bililies's wildly popular Greek Californian "fast-fine" concept (take-out is very popular, but it ultimately is not fast-casual in that it's easy to have a proper three-course meal with wine if you desire, and the ingredients and techniques are on par with an upscale downtown restaurant) is the definition of a successful concept that revolves around a concise, smartly composed menu of wraps and salads (plus the very popular Greek frozen yogurt). There are a few exceptions to this tidy menu—some mezé and the tremendous feta-brined rotisserie chicken. It's sort of the hidden gem of Souvla since it isn't a salad, wrap, or frozen yogurt, yet everyone already knows about it, and for good reason. It's easily among the most vaunted roast chicken renditions in this roast chicken–crazy town.

YIELD: 4 servings

---

4 OZ. FETA CHEESE, CRUMBLED

3½ TEASPOONS KOSHER SALT

1 (3½- TO 4-LB.) WHOLE CHICKEN

1 TO 2 TABLESPOONS CRACKED BLACK PEPPERCORNS, TO TASTE

2 TABLESPOONS DRIED GREEK OREGANO

2 LARGE LEMONS

¼ CUP OLIVE OIL, PLUS MORE AS NEEDED

1 LARGE BUNCH ARUGULA OR OTHER STURDY SALAD GREEN, FOR SERVING

---

1. The day before serving, combine 2 oz. of the feta, 2 teaspoons of the salt, and 4 cups water in a blender and blend until smooth. Put the chicken in an extra-large resealable plastic bag or a container large enough to submerge it, and cover with the feta brine. Refrigerate for at least 8 hours or overnight. *continued...*

2. Before cooking, remove the chicken from the brine and transfer to a paper towel–lined tray. (Discard the brine.) Pat the chicken dry with paper towels and allow to come to room temperature for 1 hour.

3. In a small bowl, combine the remaining 1½ teaspoons salt and the pepper, oregano, and grated zest of the lemons (about 1 tablespoon). Liberally cover the chicken with the herb mix and gently massage the entire bird with it. Halve the lemons and place 3 halves in the cavity (save the remaining half for serving). Using kitchen twine, tie the legs together.

4. Preheat the oven to 450°F/232°C. Place a large, ovenproof skillet over high heat. Add the oil and heat until it just smokes. Place the chicken, breast side up, in the pan. Transfer the entire pan to the oven. Cook, basting once or twice, until the juices run clear when the chicken is pierced with a knife at the thigh, 50 to 60 minutes.

5. Remove the pan from the oven and stir the remaining crumbled feta into the pan juices. Let the chicken rest for 10 minutes in the pan before slicing and serving on a bed of greens, with the feta-laced pan juices on top, drizzled with a little lemon juice from the reserved lemon half.

Q&A, CHARLES BILILIES

FOUNDER AND CEO, SOUVLA

TF: It's safe to say that Souvla is a phenomenon here in SF. What are the key ingredients that make this concept thrive at its handful of locations around the city?

CB: Thank you for saying that; it means a lot. We feel very fortunate that Souvla has become a part of the cultural fabric of the city of San Francisco in ways we had never anticipated. First, there's no one secret or one key element—it's many things being done each and every day as consistently as possible that compound over many years. It's a group of very talented, very committed individuals coming together to serve thousands of people a day and provide them with delicious, nourishing meals and memorable dining experiences. None of this happened overnight, and none of this was done by any one person. Souvla has been both a personal and collaborative journey over a decade long, and the result of a lot of thought, effort, and risk by many individuals. There is a heart and a soul to the Souvla brand that is difficult to replicate without all of those elements, and consumers are savvy in distinguishing restaurant brands that are genuine versus ones created in a boardroom or by other artificial means.

TF: Can you tell us a little bit about what inspired you to open Souvla? And, how is the Dogpatch location a little different from the others?

CB: The Souvla story is told in two parallel stories—the product, and the format, which ultimately come together as a representation of my relationship with my Greek heritage. On the product side, I had an epiphany almost fifteen years ago with a leftover sandwich I made, which prompted the question as to why no one had modernized the gyro or souvlaki sandwich in America. On the format side, I wanted to leverage my background in ultra fine dining with a business model that was both scalable *and* profitable, and could be executed in a very challenging and expensive city like San Francisco. That's how the fast-fine format came about.

With our Dogpatch location—that restaurant sort of fell into our laps, and it had this amazing vintage bar that was too nice to remove. We had been cooking a lot of more traditional Greek dishes for weddings and other special events, and we saw this as an opportunity to expand our all-Greek wine list and pair it with more traditional mezés, or small plates.

TF: Souvla has been pretty innovative with its partners, like Delta Airlines and Black Sheep Foods. What drives those relationships?

CB: Most of those are inbound opportunities that present themselves, and from there it's mostly driven by my or a member of our team's passion and/or interest. I'm a huge Delta fan and frequent flyer, so the opportunity to work with the biggest and best airline in the world was an incredible experience. With Black Sheep Foods, we debuted their product nationally and remain advisers (and neighbors) with the team. We remain very protective of the Souvla brand, and so are careful as to whom we partner with, but overall they have been great opportunities to expand our brand awareness and work together with other talented, driven teams.

TF: Prior to Souvla, you worked with two of the true Bay Area culinary legends— Thomas Keller and Michael Mina. What were those career experiences like, and how did they help shape Souvla's menu and format?

CB: I did, and quite closely with each of them, as a matter of fact. I created the Culinary Assistant role at the Thomas Keller Restaurant Group and later brought that to the Mina Group. They were both incredible opportunities that gave me extraordinary insight into the inner workings of very high-performing organizations, both from an operational and a business standpoint. From attention to detail, to consistency, to operating restaurants as a business, there is a lot from my time with both Thomas and Michael that [is] baked into Souvla. That said, there is also a lot that is quite a bit different, from the simple, streamlined menu, to our company culture, which is ultimately expressed in our motto: "Make it nice & be nice."

TF: Finally, in the big Northern California picture, what really stands out to you that makes our region such a marquee, unique place for chefs and diners alike?

CB: Honestly, we're very spoiled here in Northern California when it comes to the quality of ingredients, the creativity among chefs and restaurateurs, and the overall savviness of the Bay Area diner. For example, just the year-round quality of the produce alone is almost enough, but you get to combine that with reasonably moderate weather and an abundance of natural beauty always in close proximity. We're excited to bring Souvla to more and more areas in the Bay Area in the years to come.

FISHERMAN'S STEW WITH PAPRIKA AND EGG NOODLES

BAR TARTINE, NICK BALLA

Nick Balla's career has been one of the most fascinating ones for me to follow. He's cooked thrilling Japanese izakaya food, yet also opened the eyes of this city to his Central European heritage with the cuisine of that region and specifically Hungary (with strong elements of Japan and California throughout the menu), plus the mind-boggling, wonderful world of fermentation and pickling when he and his then partner, Cortney Burns, ran the kitchen and immense larder at the much-missed Bar Tartine in the Mission (yes, it was affiliated with Tartine Bakery). Nowadays, Balla can be found cooking outstanding lunches at Coast Gallery and Café in Big Sur.

The Hungarian town of Baja is famous for its fish stew, and its citizens are locked in an unending argument with the nearby town of Szeged (and every other town in the country) as to whose fish stew is best. In Baja, the bright-red broth is usually poured over spiral egg noodles and the fish is served on the side. We've included a recipe for a simple noodle dough, but dried spaghetti broken into random-sized pieces makes a good substitute.

—Chef Balla

YIELD: 4 to 6 servings

½ CUP (60 G) '00' FLOUR	2 TABLESPOONS KOSHER SALT
½ CUP (60 G) G ALL-PURPOSE FLOUR	2 TABLESPOONS LARD
8 EGG YOLKS, BEATEN	2 GREEN BELL PEPPERS, SEEDED AND DICED
2 (1 LB./455 G) CARP OR CATFISH, CLEANED AND CUT CROSSWISE INTO STEAKS 1 INCH/2.5 CM THICK	4 SWEET WHITE ONIONS, DICED

---

12 GARLIC CLOVES, THINLY SLICED	SEA SALT, TO TASTE
½ CUP (55 G) HOT PAPRIKA, CHILI POWDER, OR A MIXTURE OF HOT AND SWEET PAPRIKAS	CHOPPED FRESH CHIVES, FOR GARNISH
2 CUPS (480 ML) DRY RED WINE	FRESH CURLY-LEAF PARSLEY LEAVES, FOR GARNISH
6 CUPS (1.4 L) FISH STOCK	SOUR CREAM, FOR GARNISH

1. Set a large bowl on a wet towel. Sift the flours into the bowl. Make a well in the center and pour the egg yolks into it. Starting from the yolks and working out to the edge of the bowl, swirl the mixture with your hands or a spoon, slowly and gradually pulling the flour into the yolks until a cohesive dough forms; add a bit of water if the dough is dry.

2. Remove the dough from the bowl and place it on a dry, clean work surface. Knead the dough until it is silky and taut, about 5 minutes. Flatten into a disk and wrap with plastic wrap. Rest at room temperature for at least 1 hour and up to 6 hours, to relax the glutens.

3. Unwrap the dough and gently flatten it as much as possible with the heel of your hand. If rolling by hand, lightly flour the work surface and roll the dough to ⅛ inch/3 mm thick. If using a pasta machine, set it to its widest setting. Lightly flour the dough and run it through the rollers, folding the dough in half and then rolling again. Continue folding and rolling until the dough is silky smooth, 6 to 8 passes. Continue rolling, setting the machine one setting lower each time to produce a dough that is ⅛ inch/3 mm thick.

4. Have a small bowl of water at hand. By hand or using a cutting attachment, cut the noodles into strips about ⅛ inch/3 mm thick. Now cut the long ribbons into 2-inch/5-cm pieces. Cover the extra dough with a damp cloth while you work. Take two pieces in your hand and pinch them together at the top, using a bit of water to adhere them. Twist until the other ends meet, and secure them with a bit of water and a good pinch. Set aside and continue twisting until you have formed all of the noodles. Use immediately, or leave to dry, uncovered.

5. Season the fish steaks on both sides with 2 teaspoons of the kosher salt and refrigerate for 1 hour.

continued...

6. In a heavy-bottomed Dutch oven over medium-low heat, melt the lard, then add the bell peppers, onions, and garlic. Cook, stirring occasionally, until the onions are soft but not browned, about 20 minutes. Add the paprika and stir constantly until fragrant, about 1 minute. Add the wine and simmer until much of the alcohol aroma has dissipated, about 10 minutes.

7. Add the stock and simmer for another 40 minutes. At this point, the onions should be tender and the broth flavorful. Add the remaining 4 teaspoons kosher salt, then taste and adjust the seasoning if needed. If not using right away, let cool, transfer to an airtight container, and refrigerate for up to 1 week. Pour the broth into a Dutch oven and bring to a simmer over medium heat when ready to finish.

8. Bring a large pot of salted water to a boil over high heat. Add the noodles and cook until just tender, about 4 minutes for fresh, 8 minutes for dried, then drain.

9. When the paprika broth is simmering gently with no bubbles visible, lower the fish steaks into it and cook just until the fish flakes easily, about 5 minutes.

10. Using a slotted spoon, carefully transfer the fish steaks to a serving platter. Ladle the broth into a large serving bowl and add the cooked noodles.

11. Garnish the broth and noodles with the chives, parsley, and sour cream. Serve the fish alongside the noodles and broth.

Q&A, MELISSA PERELLO

CHEF/OWNER, FRANCES AND OCTAVIA

TF: Can you tell us a little bit about what inspired you initially to pursue a career as a chef and what led you to San Francisco? It sounds like your grandmother Frances (the namesake of Frances the restaurant) was a key influence?

MP: Even as a child I was always drawn to cooking. It was my first curiosity. After summers cooped up at my grandparents' home in Texas, watching the gamut of cooking programs on PBS, I'd land back home with a list of recipes I wanted to learn how to cook. It was my parents' largesse allowing me to run wild in the kitchen at home in my younger years that really gave me the confidence to consider cooking as a career.

My grandmother Frances was a big part of that, and I've kept her with me in every kitchen along the way. When you open your first restaurant, you never know for sure if there will be a second, so if there were only one, it should be named for her.

TF: Before opening Frances and Octavia, you worked at some of the most important restaurants in SF of the 1990s and early 2000s—Aqua, Charles Nob Hill, and Fifth Floor. For readers who didn't follow the local restaurant scene at that time, can you tell us a bit about those pivotal restaurants?

MP: Ron Siegel at Charles Nob Hill was the one who really gave me the tools to develop collaborative relationships with farmers on the vision of a dish. That was a hugely important lesson for me—one that impacted the way I approach cooking every day.

TF: Frances and Octavia are two of the most commonly named "quintessential" restaurants of San Francisco by locals and tourists alike—they're fun, in that middle ground between casual and upscale, very welcoming, very seasonal and local ingredient focused. What is the magic at both places that has made them such beloved restaurants? Besides the physical dining room sizes (Frances is smaller than Octavia), what would you say are some of the major differences between the two restaurants?

MP: We were very fortunate to open Frances with a small team of fine dining expats that were deeply invested-in delivering the nuances of fine dining but wanted to create something more relaxed and accessible. I can't say it's always easy to balance precision with comfort or value with luxury, but we're constantly trying to celebrate the harmony between those points.

TF: What major changes have you seen in the SF restaurant scene since you first arrived in town? Has your cooking style/philosophy changed in those years?

MP: When I opened Octavia, the focus was really on translating the signature essence of Frances to another, larger space in a different area of the city. Both spaces have taken on their own identities pretty naturally. Frances is certainly a little smaller and has more foot traffic. It's filled with the energy of the Castro. There's designated walk-in space at the counter (versus Octavia, which is reservation only), so the feeling, to me, is a shade less formal than Octavia—which is a larger space with a stately flavor reflective of its Pacific Heights neighborhood.

On that note, the additional space at Octavia has provided opportunities that were never possible at Frances, given the limited space. We were able to expand our bread program with a full-scale sourdough operation, and we offer our house levain for sale out the side door at this location only. Octavia also has a bigger setup for things like whole animal butchery and pasta production, so the logistics of the space have allowed us to develop a robust pasta menu at this location. Though I didn't envision it this way, they really are kind of the perfect complement of uptown and downtown as a duo.

TF: When you have free time to dine out, where do you like to go in the city?

MP: Well, free time is sparse these days, running around with a one-year-old in tow, but when we have time we love to visit The Progress and The Anchovy Bar, Delfina, Rich Table, and Flour + Water.

EGG HOPPERS AND SEENI SAMBOL (ONION SAMBOL)

1601 BAR AND KITCHEN BRIAN FERNANDO

Most San Francisco diners knew very little, if anything, about Sri Lankan cuisine before Chef Brian Fernando went off on his own (after working in Spain and California fine dining kitchens) and opened this small, cheery SoMa restaurant that serves fascinating classic and contemporary takes on the Sri Lankan cuisine that California-born Fernando learned about from his father, who was from the country. The restaurant hasn't fully reopened since the COVID-19 pandemic, but they are still serving special public and private dinners, which often feature these always-wonderful hoppers. Here's Fernando's recipe for what is definitely considered one of the island country's most famous dishes.

YIELD: 25 servings (this can easily be halved)

---

500 G RICE FLOUR	16 G DRY ACTIVE YEAST
105 G GRANULATED SUGAR	50 ML WARM WATER
800 ML COCONUT MILK	5 G SUGAR
200 TO 300 ML WATER	200 G COOKED BASMATI RICE

1. Combine the rice flour, 100 g of the sugar, 400 ml of the coconut milk, and the water in a large bowl.

2. In a separate container, combine the yeast, warm water, and remaining 5 g sugar and let proof for about 10 minutes, until it triples in volume.

3. Blend the rice and remaining 400 ml coconut milk in a commercial blender at high speed to form a thick paste.

continued...

4. Combine the yeast mixture and contents from the blender with the rice flour mixture. Using a whisk, stir until no lumps of flour remain. Place in an oven with the pilot light on for about 3 hours. The mixture should double in size. Cook in hopper pans until cooked through and golden brown. The batter is rather simple but, unfortunately, is useless without hopper pans, small, wok-like shaped pans that are about 7 inches in diameter. We get ours directly from Sri Lanka. They sell nonstick versions in the United States that can be ordered online.

SEENI SAMBOL (ONION SAMBOL)

100 ML NEUTRAL OIL

A FEW SPRIGS CURRY LEAVES

500 G RED ONIONS,
SLICED VERY THIN

10 G SALT

20 G SUGAR

2 G CAYENNE PEPPER

10 G ALEPPO PEPPER

10 G MALDIVE FISH

3 G TAMARIND PASTE

1. In a large sauté pan over medium-high heat, heat the oil until it just begins to smoke. Immediately add the curry leaves, then the onions. Cook until the onions begin to slightly caramelize.

2. Add the salt, sugar, cayenne, Aleppo pepper, and Maldive fish and mix well. Lower the heat and continue to cook for another 15 minutes, until the onions are completely tender.

3. Remove from the heat and stir in the tamarind paste. Allow to cool, refrigerate overnight, and then serve at room temperature.

Q&A, RAY TANG

CHEF/OWNER, PRESIDIO SOCIAL CLUB

TF: It's hard to believe that Presidio Social Club opened back in 2006. Where does time fly?? How has this journey been for the restaurant? Can you tell us a bit about the opening stages and early years?

RT: Trevor, PSC was and still is such a hard-fought and hard-won restaurant. Opening in 2006 meant that the Great Recession of 2008–2010 was just about to take hold. Sandwich that with the pandemic of 2020, PSC had a renaissance period of about ten years. In those ten years, our brand became stronger, clearer, and more trustworthy. We never flaunted ourselves as a chef-driven restaurant. Instead, we made pleasing people our goal. As we are not a private club, we just had fun pretending to be a club and came up with so many themed events over the years. So, to answer your question, we just pivoted every time there was a challenge. And then when we realized our customers would return for those events, we just kept evolving while keeping our core brand strong.

TF: What's it like running a restaurant in the far northeast corner of the city...in what's essentially a national park?

RT: You know, we are not quite Balboa, not quite Spruce, and not quite Tipsy Pig. I think most people who think of the northeast think of these thematic restaurants. That's why over the years we have worked harder to be a little quirky and yet not too clubby and not too much of a party place. Being in the park centers us. Trees, open sky, and the thought of discovering a retreat in the city, that's what we work hard on to convey. So far, we are still here. The upside is that all of us here work in a park. And that in itself is super unique.

I often tell our delivery drivers to stop and smell the trees. No one is honking and you are not double-parked.

TF: How would you describe PSC's menu and cuisine style? It's one of the very few San Francisco restaurants that seem to effortlessly balance comfort and innovation together.

RT: Over the years and through the many talented and dedicated chefs that PSC has had, all knew how to please our customers. The basics are American throwback. But each of the chefs was thoroughly trained in the European style. So the techniques have always been solid here.

I say that our food has always been brasserie food disguised as American comfort food.

TF: Brunch has always been a hallmark of the restaurant. What's it like at PSC every weekend day around noon?

RT: Funny thing is that Saturday noon is very different than Sunday noon. If the weather is nice on Saturday, people trickle in either after a morning outing or before they start their weekend. On Sundays, it's completely battle royale. Think of all the Hollywood epic scenes of invaders storming the castle. Waves and waves of hungry brunchers, Lululemon dads, stroller patrols, bridal and baby showers, sun seekers and spritz sprawlers...get the picture?

TF: Ha, definitely! Ok, shifting from that scene...this is a book about San Francisco food past *and* present. Can you tell us a bit about working at the legendary Postrio back in the 1990s?

RT: Postrio, a brilliant name alluding to the trio of chefs on Post Street, with the famous Wolfgang Puck. I worked there on two tours of duty. First, with the opening chefs, David and Anne, then again with the Rosenthal brothers, Mitchell and Steven. I still look up to these brilliant mavericks as my mentors.

Postrio was about style, amazing ingredients, impeccable service, and bold cross-cultural flavors. We as line cooks always collaborated on dishes using the finest local ingredients NO ONE could get their hands on besides us. Berries from Sebastopol. Sonoma lamb. The best seafood available locally and from around the world. There was no talk of farm to table because there was nothing that wasn't.

The theater crowd would hit us at five p.m., then the socialites, then anyone who was anyone, and by ten p.m., we [would] have served over four hundred plus high-end, fun-to-execute, delicious, and innovative plates of food and wood-fired pizzas.

To this day, most of my best friends are friends that I made while working there in the 1990s.

TF: Finally, I know that you could also be a culinary tour guide of San Francisco. What restaurants/bakeries/markets do you return to on a regular basis?

RT: I am super boring BECAUSE I love the classics so much. House of Prime Rib. Swan Oyster Depot. Joe's of Westlake. Marin Farmer's Market. And my new favorite old Cantonese restaurant that I cannot tell you about.

**Fried Red Trout with Beech Mushrooms
and Pickled Ginger Butter**
See page 256

FRIED RED TROUT WITH BEECH MUSHROOMS AND PICKLED GINGER BUTTER

THE PROGRESS, STUART BRIOZA

The Progress is hardly just the next-door neighbor and sibling of State Bird Provisions. It's its own unique, fantastic place, residing in a stunning former theater. The food is dramatic but not in a theatrical way—in a genuine, honest, compellingly delicious way. This excellent fish preparation is a great example of that.

This is a fun dish to construct as a cook, and deconstruct and devour as a diner. At The Progress, meals are built around several large platters that serve as a family-style menu.

—Chef Brioza

YIELD: 4 to 6 servings

TROUT

1 (2-LB.) WHOLE TROUT

SALT AND FRESHLY GROUND BLACK PEPPER, TO TASTE

1 CUP BLACK RICE POWDER

RICE BRAN OIL, FOR FRYING

1. Remove the trout's head by cutting through the bone at an angle toward the head about ½ inch behind the neck and collar. Remove the tail by cutting through the bone at the same angle as the head, leaving 3 to 4 inches of flesh on the tailbone.

2. Fillet the center of the fish, remove any pinbones, and cut into 2-inch pieces. Season liberally with salt and pepper. Dredge the center-cut pieces only in the black rice powder.

3. In a deep, heavy-bottomed saucepan or a Dutch oven, heat the oil to 350°F/177°C. Deep-fry the trout head and tail for 3 to 4 minutes. Transfer to a wire rack. Fry the dredged fish pieces for 2 to 3 minutes. Transfer to the rack.

SAUCE

1½ OZ. FISH SAUCE (RED BOAT)

1½ OZ. FRESH LIME JUICE

1½ OZ. WATER

1 TEASPOON GRATED GINGER

½ TEASPOON GRATED GARLIC

2 TABLESPOONS PICKLED JAPANESE GINGER

2 TEASPOONS GINGER PICKLING LIQUID

2 TABLESPOONS BUTTER

½ CUP BEECH MUSHROOMS, SEPARATED, BUT NOT CHOPPED

1. Combine all the ingredients in a cold sauté pan. Bring to a boil and quickly remove from the heat.

ASSEMBLY

TINY LETTUCE LEAVES, FOR GARNISH

SHAVED TOKYO TURNIP, FOR GARNISH

MANDARIN ORANGE WEDGES

GROUND LONG PEPPER

1. Pour the sauce into a large serving platter. Arrange the fish on top, piecing it back together with a pile of the rice powder–dredged body in the center, flanked by the head and tail.

2. Garnish with the lettuce leaves and shaved turnip, and scatter mandarin wedges around. Finish with a sprinkling of long pepper.

PETRALE SOLE WITH CELTUCE

ANOMALY, MIKE LANHAM

Arguably the newest of the very notable and ambitious tasting menu spots in San Francisco is the result of incredible commitment and skill—and just a sheer love of restaurants and bringing smiles to customers' faces. Everyone roots for Chef Mike Lanham, as he battled back from a frightening spinal injury, worked at fine dining restaurants, then saw his Anomaly concept bounce from pop-up to pop-up location around town as he kept seeking a permanent space—and then he still had to persevere through the COVID-19 pandemic, serving his dishes in ways that could be enjoyed at home (and not screwed up by terrible home chefs like me). Now, here he is, with a splendid Lower Pacific Heights–Presidio Heights area home for Anomaly at long last. He didn't give up on his dream, and it certainly paid off. Bravo, Mike! I'm so thrilled that we could include Anomaly and his excellent sole (or salmon, if you prefer) recipe in the book.

YIELD: 1 serving

---

1 BUNCH SCALLIONS

NEUTRAL OIL, AS NEEDED

750 ML SPARKLING WINE BRUT

250 ML HEAVY CREAM

100 ML WATER

SALT, TO TASTE

1 PETRALE SOLE OR SALMON FILLET (ABOUT 3 OZ.)

1 MEDIUM CELTUCE OR KOHLRABI

A FEW TABLESPOONS BUTTER

FINGER LIME, FOR GARNISH

continued...

1. Roughly chop both the green and white parts of the scallions. Put them in a blender and cover just barely with oil. Blend for about 30 seconds. Transfer the mixture to a pot over high heat and bring to a boil. Cook for 90 seconds. Allow to cool to room temperature and place in the refrigerator. Once cool, strain the solids out by running the scallion oil through a chinois or a fine mesh strainer lined with cheesecloth.

2. Reduce the sparkling wine by three-quarters, then add 60 to 65 ml of the reduced wine to the cream and water. Season with salt to taste.

3. Sear the fish fillet lightly and place into a 118°F/48°C sous vide for 15 minutes. To finish, pull the fillet out, pat it dry, and place in a convection oven at 400°F/204°C for 45 seconds to 1 minute to finish.

4. Use a melon baller to shape five pieces of celtuce or kohlrabi. Make a beurre monté by bringing 2 tablespoons water to a simmer in a saucepan over medium heat, then reducing the heat to medium-low and whisking in a few tablespoons of butter, one at a time, stirring continuously to emulsify. Salt to taste and poach the celtuce or kohlrabi in this mixture until tender.

5. To assemble, place the fish fillet on the plate and season to taste with salt. Arrange the celtuce artfully and add three small piles of finger lime next to the celtuce. Finally, put the cream sauce into a pourer and incorporate a few spoonsfuls of the scallion oil, depending on your personal taste. The goal is to have green swirls of oil in the otherwise white sauce. Pour the desired amount of sauce onto the plate.

Q&A, BORIS NEMCHENOK

PARTNER/DIRECTOR OF OPERATIONS, FIORELLA, BAR NONNINA, VIOLET'S, AND UVA ENOTECA

TF: Let's start with your early, early dining days in SF. Any food memories from growing up in the city?

BN: As a kid I grew up going to a ton of Russian banquet halls (think large tables packed with caviar and blintzes, salads, beef tongue, adult beverages . . .). However, as I was going through high school, I discovered the amazing taquerias the Mission and, back then, Upper Haight Street had. When I turned nineteen, I got a busser job at EOS in Cole Valley, working for Arnold Wong, and the rest is history. I was hooked on amazing food.

TF: How are things different these days compared to back in your youth, when it comes to the restaurant scene and dining out in SF?

BN: It's pretty different these days, however, I had very different expectations of what dining was in my early twenties to now. I think in general the restaurant scene in SF had somewhat of an old-school feel with a sprinkle of farm to table coming up. Now it seems to me that the new generation of chefs and restaurateurs [is] pushing the boundaries a bit more but also working with the limits of doing business in San Francisco.

TF: What brought you back after working in NYC restaurants? Is that where you caught the restaurant industry bug?

BN: I came back to SF as I wanted to be back home, close to my family. My father passed away while I was in NYC, and it felt right to come back. I also was really interested in bringing back the feel of NYC to SF. The Italian food, especially the Italian wine bar scene, was so strong in NYC, and I felt that was missing in SF at the time. I was so inspired by Jason Denton's INO in Lower Manhattan at the time. I really wanted to show that to SF.

TF: Can you tell us a little bit about the start of Fiorella? I know the first location in the Richmond is particularly special for you, since that was the neighborhood you grew up in and it's never had the most robust restaurant scene, especially later at night.

BN: I had Uva Enoteca open for a while at this point and had just parted ways with my partners at Citizen's Band in SoMa. I was itching to get back into doing more Italian food, and my investor at Uva Enoteca introduced me to Brandon Gillis to help out with Uva for a bit. We both had worked in NYC and loved Italian food, so we started talking about doing a project in SF. We were kind of kidding around one day, as Brandon lived in the Richmond District, and he said, if you find something a few blocks from my house, I'll open up an Italian concept with you, and then, boom, it happened. It was really special to open something in my old neighborhood, and I was so glad to see the neighborhood response.

TF: I remember when Fiorella started, and we (I don't think just me) were all very excited for the clam pizza. Now, Fiorella has grown into a little phenomenon with an outstanding variety of pizzas, a beloved salad, incredible wallpaper, and much more. How did this exciting growth happen that made Fiorella one of SF's favorite restaurant concepts?

BN: This really came organically for us. We opened our first Fiorella location on a shoestring budget and had no idea what the response would be in the Outer Richmond. It's pretty sleepy out there, and the dining scene was pretty mellow. We realized the neighborhood

Italian was something missing there and in other parts of SF, so we kept going with this concept and now have three locations with more to come in and outside of SF.

TF: Of course, Fiorella wasn't even your first restaurant in SF. That was Uva Enoteca! Can you tell us a bit about that wine bar/restaurant and Violet's?

BN: Uva Enoteca was my first! It was really inspired [by] my time working at Otto in NYC and hanging out after work at INO and InoEnoteca. Uva just had its fifteen-year anniversary, and I could not be more proud of the team there.

We felt, being in the Outer Richmond, that it was missing a good place to have a cocktail and some delicious American food, so we decided to open Violet's.

TF: Finally, you've worked for over two decades in restaurants in arguably the two most competitive markets in the country. What lessons have you learned that seem to be the keys to success in a culinary capital like SF?

BN: Being able to adapt with the times and needs of the guests is key. Dining, economy, and habits change consistently and it's important to adjust. I learned a lot of this during the 2008 financial crisis when Uva first opened.

OVER THE CALABRIAN RAINBOW PIZZA

TONY'S PIZZA NAPOLETANA, TONY GEMIGNANI

The biggest name in pizza in San Francisco is a true pizza champion—as in, champion of the World Pizza Cup (yes, it's a thing). Tony Gemignani is the rare pizzaiolo who specializes in multiple styles. At his flagship North Beach restaurant, there are nine styles (!). Don't ask me for a favorite.

On a nonpizza note, Gemignani might be quite a celebrity chef, but he is also just a truly friendly, super-kind guy. A few years ago, I visited the George Mark Children's House in the East Bay with Tony and two San Francisco Giants players. Not only does he bring joy to hundreds of San Francisco diners each day, but it was so special to see the heartfelt cheer that Tony and the Giants brought to these pediatric patients who have devastatingly difficult medical conditions or illnesses.

YIELD: 1 to 2 servings

---

8 MEDIUM-SIZE TRIMMED PIECES RAINBOW CHARD

LIGHT OLIVE OIL, AS NEEDED

SALT AND FRESHLY GROUND BLACK PEPPER, TO TASTE

3 OZ. BULK CHORIZO

3 TO 4 OZ. TOMATO SAUCE

¼ TEASPOON MINCED CALABRIAN CHILI IN OIL

PINCH RED PEPPER FLAKES

2 TEASPOONS HEAVY CREAM

1 (12-OZ.) BALL PIZZA DOUGH (SEE PAGE 266)

6 (1-OZ.) SLICES WHOLE MILK MOZZARELLA

2 OZ. SLICED PANCETTA OR SMOKED BACON

7 GIGANTE WHITE BEANS, SLICED IN HALF

EXTRA-VIRGIN OLIVE OIL, AS NEEDED

LEMON WEDGE, FOR SERVING

1. Set up the oven with one pizza steel or stone on the upper oven rack and one on the lower oven rack.

2. Preheat the oven to 500°F/260°C to 520°F/271°C for at least 1 hour.

3. Blanch the chard and lightly sauté in olive oil. Season with salt and pepper and set aside. Keep warm.

continued...

4. In a medium-size sauté pan over medium heat, sauté the chorizo in oil. Once it has lightly cooked, add the tomato sauce, Calabrian chili, red pepper, and cream. Stir continuously for 2 minutes over low heat. Season with salt and pepper and set aside.

5. Shape and stretch your pizza dough into a 12- to 14-inch circle. Add the cheese, leaving a ¼-inch border, and add the pancetta or bacon. Carefully add the warm tomato cream sauce, leaving a ¼-inch border.

6. Place the pizza on the upper stone or steel. Cook for 5 minutes.

7. Using the peel, take the pizza out of the oven, turn it 180 degrees and place it on the bottom surface until golden brown, another 5 to 6 minutes.

8. When the pizza is finished baking, take it out of the oven and cut into desired slices. Add the rainbow chard, white beans, and lemon wedge. Don't forget to squeeze your lemon. Serve and enjoy.

TONY GEMIGNANI'S PIZZA DOUGH

5 G ACTIVE YEAST

60 ML WARM WATER (80°F/27°C TO 85°F/29°C)

435 G HIGH-GLUTEN HIGH-PROTEIN FLOUR (13.5% OR HIGHER)

5 G LOW DIASTATIC MALT (PREFERABLY AB MAURI)

215 ML COLD WATER (38°F/3°C TO 40°F/4°C)

10 G FINE SEA SALT

5 G EXTRA-VIRGIN OLIVE OIL

1. Using a wire whisk, vigorously mix the yeast into the warm water for 30 seconds and set aside.

2. Using a stand mixer fitted with the dough hook, add the flour and malt to the bowl, then mix at low speed for 1 minute.

3. While mixing on low speed, carefully add the yeast mixture to the bowl. Use some of the cold water to rinse any excess yeast from the warm water bowl if necessary and slowly pour 80 percent of the cold water into the bowl while mixing on low speed.

4. Continue mixing for 30 seconds. Slowly add the remaining cold water down the inner side of the bowl to gather up any excess flour that wasn't incorporated.

5. After 30 seconds of mixing, stop the mixer if the dough starts to gather up onto the dough hook. Pull it off the top of the hook and back into the bowl. Mix at a faster speed for 1 minute.

6. Add the salt and continue mixing on the faster speed for 1 minute. While mixing, carefully pour the olive oil close to the center of the dough hook onto the dough.

7. Continue to mix for approximately 1 minute on high speed.

8. Stop the mixer, take the dough out, and, using your hands, turn the dough onto a clean, hard work surface, preferably marble, granite, or stainless steel.

9. After hand forming for 30 seconds, cover the dough with a warm, damp cloth and let sit for 30 minutes.

10. Stretch and fold the dough three times and let sit, covered with a damp towel, for another 30 minutes.

11. Divide the dough into two equal parts (about 367.5 g each) and ball your dough. Place the dough on a clean cookie sheet or half sheet pan and loosely wrap with plastic wrap, keeping it airtight. Refrigerate for 24 to 36 hours.

12. Take the dough out of the refrigerator 1 hour before use. Keep the dough covered until use. This should give you a dough ball that weighs between 12 and 13 oz.

TRADITIONAL DELUXE TAVERN CRACKER-THIN PIZZA

CAPO'S, TONY GEMIGNANI

Tony Gemignani kindly thought that readers would want to try making a different kind of pizza. Besides, the weekend is two days, not one. So, here's a second pizza project to try!

Tavern-style pizza has gained popularity in the last few years. This recipe is a combo you will see everywhere in Chicago. Traditionally, green bell peppers, white onions, and sliced mushrooms are used. I prefer a sautéed button mushroom, roasted red peppers, and sliced red onions for mine. I also prefer to add the ingredients above the cheese and not under it. It's all up to you. This recipe is similar to how I make it at my restaurants Capo's and Pizza Rock. It all depends on if you are a traditionalist or want to kick it up a notch.

—**Chef Gemignani**

YIELD: 1 to 2 Servings

---

1 (12-OZ.) BALL PIZZA DOUGH (SEE PAGE 266)

FLOUR OR CORNMEAL, FOR DUSTING (TONY PREFERS CORNMEAL)

5 TO 6 OZ. TOMATO SAUCE

7 TO 8 OZ. SHREDDED PART SKIM OR WHOLE MILK MOZZARELLA

3 OZ. ROASTED RED PEPPERS OR CHOPPED GREEN BELL PEPPERS

1½ TO 2 OZ. SLICED RED ONION OR CHOPPED WHITE ONION

5½ OZ. SAUTÉED BUTTON MUSHROOMS OR SLICED MUSHROOMS

6 TO 7 OZ. BULK ITALIAN SAUSAGE (DIME-SIZE PIECES)

PINCH 50/50 MIXTURE GRATED ROMANO AND PARMESAN CHEESES

PINCH DRIED OREGANO

---

1. Set up the oven with one pizza steel or stone on the upper oven rack and one on the lower oven rack.

2. Preheat the oven to 500°F/260°C to 520°F/271°C for at least 1 hour.

3. Dust the dough with flour or cornmeal. Using a rolling pin, roll the dough into a 16- to 17-inch circle. Dock the dough.

4. Using a pizza wheel, trim the pizza into a 14-inch circle. Push down the edges and place on a pizza peel. Slide the pizza onto the upper stone or steel, and parbake for 2 minutes.

5. Take the pizza out of the oven and add the sauce and cheese. Make sure the sauce and cheese are as close to the edge as possible.

6. Add the peppers, onion, and mushrooms, then the sausage. Finish with the grated 50/50 cheese and oregano. Place the pizza on the upper stone or steel. Cook for 5 minutes.

7. Using the peel, take the pizza out of the oven, turn it 180 degrees, and place it on the bottom surface until golden brown, 5 to 6 minutes.

8. When the pizza is finished cooking, take it out of the oven and cut into 16 squares. Enjoy.

Q&A, ADRIANO PAGANINI

OWNER/OPERATOR, BACK OF THE HOUSE, INC. (A MANO, BERETTA, LOLINDA, STARBELLY, SUPER DUPER BURGERS, THE TAILOR'S SON, WILDSEED, AND MORE)

TF: First off, were you always interested in restaurants and food growing up? How did you catch the restaurant bug?

AP: I was lucky enough to have a mother who was a fantastic home cook and grew up with her making two or three meals from scratch daily. Her food wasn't fussy, which really showed me that food that is honest, tastes good, and is made well is what I prefer to eat. This philosophy is still what gets me excited today. From Milan, I moved to France and worked under Paul Bocuse, who taught me that consistency is the most important skill of a chef. With repetition, you get perfection, and that is why you see so many of our restaurants thriving after ten plus years. We work really hard to deliver our guests a consistent experience time and time again—it's all about precision in our technique and quality ingredients that make our food stand out above the crowd.

TF: You're one of the most prolific restaurateurs in modern SF history. How do you navigate the seemingly endless challenges of running restaurants in this competitive, unique market?

AP: Things are always changing. That is a fact of life. You can either roll with it or you can get pulled down by it. I've always liked the fact that no two days in this industry are the same, and that motivates me and our team to constantly be innovating, improving, and modifying our systems. There is never a dull moment, for better or worse!

TF: Can you briefly describe your thought process in starting a new restaurant? Most of us have no honest idea how all these wonderful restaurants get started. Does the concept or location come first usually?

AP: It happens both ways, actually. Sometimes a great location comes up, and then we think of what would work in that space and best serve the neighborhood from a conceptual standpoint. Other times, there are concepts or styles of cooking that I am really interested in, so I think of a location where that particular concept would be a good fit, but this way usually takes more time and patience for the right spot to open up in the right location.

TF: Your restaurants vary greatly in terms of cuisine and format. What would you say might be a unifying theme among them?

AP: For me, it has always been important to create restaurants that serve the neighborhood that they are in and are affordable enough for our guests to visit regularly. Again, I don't like fussy food and stuffy service, so I am always trying to create spaces that I would want to hang out in (because I spend a lot of time in my restaurants!): casual, transportive, comfortable, and elegant in their simplicity. That's kind of our formula for success.

TF: Your restaurants always seem to be a little bit ahead of the trends in SF. Beretta and Lolinda arrived just before the Mission became arguably the city's hippest dining neighborhood. Beretta was a game changer for the artisan pizza movement in SF. It's hard to imagine Hayes Street now without a Mano, since it's such a beloved place there. Wildseed arguably made the city understand the term "plant-based" and that it truly tastes great. I could go on and on. How do you stay one step ahead of everyone?

AP: Restaurants are my obsession. I have been very lucky that I have had my finger on the pulse of trends throughout my career, and that the kind of restaurant I like to operate is the kind that a lot of people like dining in. Travel always inspires me, and I generally take several international trips a year, just to see what the dining scenes are like around the world. This helps to keep our restaurants feeling hip and on trend without feeling cheesy or kitschy.

For Beretta, combining artisan pizza with craft cocktails happened a bit by luck—and the idea that people would come to a restaurant for the drinks was unusual at the time. Lolinda was born because I liked the idea of a steak house, but I was tired of the boring "business dinner" steak houses, and I wanted a place that was a lot more fun and inclusive. I was also really turned off by the waste that you usually have in a steak house (portions are too big, and half of the food goes to waste), so we came up with the idea of a sharable steak house where we do not focus on increasing the check average, but we want guests to order the right amount of food for them. The result is a lower average check, but people come back again and again. Super Duper came about because I wanted a quintessential American burger made with high-quality ingredients and really good meat, and we wanted to be a place that supported the community. I was inspired to create Wildseed because I wanted to cut down on my meat consumption, but I also really wanted a vegan place that felt fun and exciting, with food anyone could enjoy, regardless of their dietary preferences or restrictions.

TF: From your decades here in SF, what do you think are some of the defining characteristics that make our city's dining scene so strong?

AP: We have the benefits of proximity to great product, great weather, and a lot of diversity. San Franciscans are always willing to try something new, and it keeps our chefs and bartenders nimble and creative. There are no rules here, which makes it really fun to dine out. You can have one of the best meals of your life at a Michelin-starred restaurant, or at a taco truck. There is something for everyone here.

SPAGHETTI WITH BOTTARGA

LA CICCIA, MASSIMILIANO CONTI

I'm already salivating just thinking about this signature dish of the beloved Noe Valley restaurant that, as far as I know, put Sardinian cuisine on the map for San Francisco diners—so much so that it's even common for home chefs to think to themselves, hmm, maybe this dish could use a little bottarga. It's all because of this truly special—even sacred—dish from Chef Massimiliano Conti. He and his wife, Lorella Degan, sold La Ciccia in 2022 to a longtime regular of the restaurant, but the chef kindly shared this SF hall of fame recipe with me, so all of you at home can be transported to Sardinia and/or Noe Valley.

The bottarga pasta is traditional from the center and southern part of Sardinia coastal villages; this is my version. In many parts of Sardinia it is made with only pasta, olive oil, and bottarga.

In Sardinia, the best bottarga comes from the gray mullet fish roe from the Cabras lagoon in the Sinis Peninsula, but you can find bottarga in many other villages in Sardinia and in other parts of Italy, as well other coastal Mediterranean places like Greece, Tunisia, Turkey, Egypt, Algeria.

It's believed that bottarga, or butarik in Arabic (to describe salted and dried fish roe), has Phoenician origins and was introduced in Sardinia and Sicily during their commercial trading trips to the islands where they founded multiple colonies on the coastal sites.

—Chef Conti

continued...

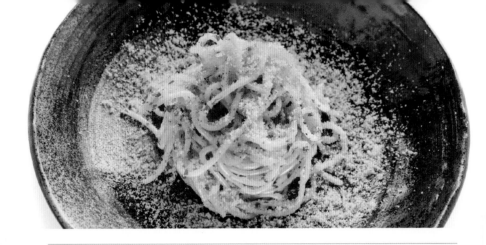

YIELD: 4 servings

1½ TABLESPOONS SALT,
PLUS MORE TO TASTE

1¼ LBS. FRESH SPAGHETTI
OR 1 LB. DRY SPAGHETTI

5 TABLESPOONS EXTRA-VIRGIN
OLIVE OIL

2 GARLIC CLOVES, CRUSHED

½ TEASPOON RED PEPPER FLAKES

5 OZ. GRATED MULLET BOTTARGA

1 BUNCH FRESH PARSLEY, CHOPPED

1. Bring a large pot of cold water to a boil. Add the salt, then add the spaghetti and cook until al dente, 4 to 6 minutes for dry pasta, 2 to 3 minutes for fresh pasta.

2. Meanwhile, in a 12- to 14-inch sauté pan over low heat, heat the olive oil, garlic, and red pepper flakes until just fragrant, about 2 minutes.

3. Remove from the heat and remove the garlic. Add 6 to 8 tablespoons of pasta cooking water and half of the bottarga. Mix gently in order to create a sauce with a creamy consistency; adjust the salt to your liking.

4. Drain the pasta and add to the oil mixture. Add the parsley and toss to mix well over medium heat.

5. Pour the pasta into warm serving bowls, sprinkle the rest of the bottarga on top of each bowl, and serve immediately.

PASTA WITH RAGU NOSTRANO

DELFINA, CRAIG STOLL AND JOHN ARCUDI

Yes, in fact, it is possible to go to Delfina and *not* order the legendary spaghetti pomodoro. I'm not necessarily recommending that, but more just want to really highlight how Delfina is so great at so many dishes and different kinds of pasta. For a quarter century, chef/co-owner Craig Stoll has proven to be one of San Francisco's true maestros of the pasta art. When he speaks about pasta or provides a recipe, you should listen. Here's a unique meat ragù pasta preparation from Stoll and John Arcudi, Delfina's chef de cuisine, who has worked at the restaurant and Pizzeria Delfina for the past decade.

YIELD: 4 servings (ragù recipe yields 4 quarts)

---

1 "10" CAN WHOLE PEELED PLUM TOMATOES

1 CUP EXTRA-VIRGIN OLIVE OIL

2 LBS. GROUND BEEF

2 LBS. GROUND PORK

KOSHER SALT AND FRESHLY GROUND BLACK PEPPER, TO TASTE

¼ LB. CHICKEN LIVERS, CLEANED

3 OZ. PANCETTA, FINELY CHOPPED OR GROUND

1 CUP FINELY DICED ONION

½ CUP FINELY DICED CELERY

½ CUP FINELY DICED CARROT

2 TABLESPOONS 50/50 MIX FINELY CHOPPED FRESH ROSEMARY AND SAGE

1½ OZ. GARLIC, "SMASHED AND SMEARED"

⅔ OF A 750-ML BOTTLE WHITE WINE

1 GALLON MEAT STOCK

1 QUART WHOLE MILK

1 LB. FRESH TAGLIATELLE

2 TABLESPOONS BUTTER

¼ CUP GRATED PARMIGIANO REGGIANO CHEESE

continued...

1. Clean the tomatoes by breaking open each one over the top of the open can and pulling out the seeds. Drop each tomato into a container as you go. When done, break up the tomatoes a little bit with your hand and strain the juice back over the cleaned tomatoes. Discard the seeds.

2. Heat some of the oil in a heavy-bottomed pot. The ideal pot for this is shallow and wide. Add the beef and pork, in batches if necessary, season with salt and pepper, and cook over high heat. Stir the meat, breaking it up and browning it lightly. Once the meat is browned, turn it out into a colander set over a pan or a bowl to collect the drained fat.

3. Add some more of the oil to the same pot and set it back over the heat. Season the chicken livers with salt and pepper and sauté them gently. The livers should be lightly browned and still a little pink inside. Remove them to a plate to cool. Chop finely when cool and set aside.

4. Add the pancetta to the same pot and cook over low heat in order to render out all of the fat.

5. Add the veggies and raise the heat to medium, stirring and scraping the bottom of the pot with a wooden spoon in order to loosen and incorporate the built-up fond. Cook for about 10 minutes, until mostly soft and 50 percent cooked.

6. Add the herbs and garlic and a little more oil, if needed, and cook over low heat until the sofritto is aromatic and the veggies are cooked through, about 10 minutes.

7. Add the tomatoes with their juice and continue to cook over medium heat until most of the liquid has evaporated. Add the browned meat back to the pot, then add the wine. Cook over medium heat to reduce the wine until almost dry.

8. Flood the pot with enough stock to almost cover the meat. Cook over medium to medium-low heat until almost dry. Flood the meat again and repeat until all of the stock has been incorporated and the sauce is juicy and soupy but not flooded. The meat and sauce should be homogeneous at this point.

9. Add the milk and chopped chicken livers, and reduce to the consistency in the previous step. Check the seasoning, adjust if necessary, and transfer to a container if not using immediately. Cool rapidly before storing in the fridge.

10. To make the pasta, add the tagliatelle to a pot of boiling salted water.

11. Meanwhile, heat 3 cups of the ragù and the butter in a large pan, until the butter melts and melds with the ragù.

12. Just before the pasta is al dente, remove from the water and put in the pan with the sauce.

13. Heat the pasta in the sauce until the sauce starts to naturally stick to the noodles. Add the Parmigiano Reggiano and toss in the pan until the cheese has melted. At this point, no sauce should be pooling around the noodles.

14. Serve by splitting into four portions.

Q&A, CRAIG STOLL

CHEF/CO-OWNER, DELFINA AND PIZZERIA DELFINA

*This phone interview with the legendary chef has been edited for clarity and brevity.

TF: It's 2023 and Delfina is 25 years old this year. What comes to mind when thinking about that quarter century, and can you tell us a little about those early years?

CS: Well, first of all, they're dog years—so it's more than 25. At the time we opened in 1998 and started working on it in 1997, the first dot com boom was amping up. Everybody was opening really fancy places with lots of bells and whistles with incredible interiors. Our idea was to open a place our friends could afford to eat at. We wanted to open our own business and be our own bosses.

We lived in the Mission and still looked all over town for a spot, but when we found a spot in the Mission, we were very confident it was a great location, even though friends kind of thought we were nuts, and I get it. We went to Bi-Rite [Market] shortly after they opened, just getting groceries, and Sam said, "Hey, are you still looking for a spot?" and he showed us this Brazilian café two doors down (on 18th Street). There was a little piece of torn paper in the window that said "restaurant for sale." We met the guy the next morning, gave him all the money we had, which was $30,000, and we had ourselves a space.

The idea was really to have a neighborhood restaurant where we could do what we wanted to do and strip away the formality (not that we could afford it anyway). We let the servers wear what they wanted. Annie was at Scala's at the time, so we kind of stole some of the servers from Scala's. When you take them out of their bow ties and their black-and-whites, they're just incredible people full of great personality, and that's what Annie encouraged. She wanted warm service and people connecting with people.

I just wanted the food to speak for itself. People wanted to make "tall food" back then. You go to a trattoria in a town in Italy or a bistro in France, it's not about these brilliant dishes. It's about thoughtful cooking and connecting good ingredients.

TF: It must be remarkable to look back from the Mission District in 1998 and now, in 2023, there are tourists who come to San Francisco just to literally eat their way through this particular neighborhood, with how many wonderful restaurants, taquerias, bakeries, shops, and such are there. How would you say that the Mission has shaped Delfina itself?

CS: I think we were just in the right place at the right time more than anything. When I was living and working in the Mission before we opened, we were eating incredible food all over the place, like Timo's [where The Beehive is now], this incredible tapas mash-up place. So, all of the businesses up and down the [Delfina space] block had iron gates that you close up at night. The first thing we did was cut these gates off, almost like a sign saying "we're done with this." Foreign Cinema opened a year later, and Bi-Rite right before us. Tartine opened a couple years later. It's amazing and great to see how it's evolved.

TF: Many people use the kind of nebulous term of "Californian-Italian" or "Cal-Ital" to describe your style of cooking at Delfina. How would you describe the cooking style, since you have so much experience in San Francisco and time cooking in Italy? And what led you to become a chef and drew you to Italy to learn in-depth about Italian cuisine there?

CS: I started cooking, washing dishes, bussing tables in Florida. I'm from New York originally, then my family moved to Florida when I was twelve. In high school, I got a job so I could have a car so I could have girlfriends. I also needed something to steer me and focus me, because I wound up in an adolescent drug rehab when I was younger. Cooking helped me on a number of levels. I fell in love with it. The camaraderie and the instant gratification. My family [members] were huge foodies before anyone heard the term. That kind of carried through; I got a job in the kitchen and really loved it. I was either going to go to school for journalism or to culinary school. I picked culinary school and went to the CIA, then got a bachelor's [degree] in hospitality at FIU in Miami because I wanted to make sure I had a college degree and wanted to learn some of the business aspects. But I kind of majored in hacky sack, I like to say.

I moved out to SF in '88 to work for Bradley Ogden at Campton Place. I got thrown in this kitchen and thought I knew a lot and got humbled pretty quickly. From the week I moved here, Bradley took me to the Marin Farmers' Market, and I met some amazing people. I got to make goat cheese with Laura Chenel in Santa Rosa when she was still based out of her home. Just some incredible experiences. And coming out here as a 22-/23-year-old in 1988, I was like, "Craft beer! Reggae on the river! The Fillmore!" I was just never going back.

Then I got a job at Postrio, which was a Wolfgang Puck restaurant, now long gone. At both of those restaurants, there were just amazing people who went on to open restaurants. My sous chef at Campton Place, Chris Major, opened Splendido and I went there to work as a sous chef. Then I got an opportunity to go to Italy. The Italian Trade Commission put together this program where they set up a culinary school at a conference center in Torino, and they took thirty American students (which I wasn't at the time . . . long story short, I got my way into this program). It was three months, and every day there would be a chef from some region of Italy or some specialty who would do a demonstration and a lecture and a little bit of hands-on [experience]. On the weekends, we went to visit prosciutto or Parmigiano production or wineries. They took us on truffle hunts. They had a bus and would take us all over. They just really wanted to kind of, no pun intended, force-feed us Italian culture and food.

Then we all got jobs. I got a job at a place called Da Delfina, just outside of Florence. Obviously, hence the name Delfina. It's located in like central casting for "Italian hilltop village," surrounded by vineyards and olive groves, and there's only one guy working in the restaurant who spoke English. It was an incredible experience. Working in Tuscany, I was just blown away by how similar the products, climate, and land were to Northern California. It was just like opening Delfina—right place at the right time.

[After returning] I bounced around [various jobs in San Francisco, including about three years at Palio d'Asti] and found myself in Mill Valley as the chef of a restaurant called The Frog and The Peach, a short-lived restaurant with a terrible name. So, while I was working at this little restaurant as the chef, [over] at the Depot Café, right there on the square [in Mill Valley], there was this woman who made my coffee in the morning, Annie. We started dating, and on our second date, we decided to open a restaurant together. Annie had worked all over town as well. We both worked at the Kimpton Group at the same time. We knew all the same people, but we had never met. She had always wanted to open her own restaurant and had a similar trajectory. She's from Philly and worked in restaurants since she was in high school. She was always hoping to find a chef to [open a restaurant] with and I was always trying to find a front-of-the-house partner.

TF: I want to ask about two of the Delfina classics—the panna cotta and the spaghetti. What's the secret sauce that makes them so simple yet robust and consistent every single time?

CS: The panna cotta was developed by one of our early pastry chefs. What sets it apart are the buttermilk and the lemon in it, so they give it a tang. Your normal panna cotta doesn't have that in it, so it's really one-dimensional and almost bland. Our panna cotta has a zing to it, so people really dig it. And, it's a great way to make use of whatever seasonal fruit is around—to highlight that and kind of combine them. It's just a mainstay.

The spaghetti was inspired by a visit to a friend's house in Milan and by the spaghetti at Bistro Aix [a now-closed restaurant in SF's Marina District that was owned by one of Craig's good friends]. I just thought, you're a neighborhood joint, you need a bowl of spaghetti with tomato sauce. You should be able to come in on a Wednesday night, sit at the counter when your family is out of town, and have a bowl of spaghetti and a glass of wine. It is a particular expression of tomato sauce—kind of light and bright. It's just a style, not a simmer-on-the-back-of-the-stove-all-day, nonna-style tomato sauce, which is delicious and I love as well.

But this is cooked quickly at a high heat, so it retains a lot of acidity and sugar. We use California tomatoes for this (kind of like California grapes, there's this sugar and acidity that come to a peak), as opposed to using the San Marzanos, which have a lot more of a vegetal, earthy flavor. So, it's like a higher-pitched flavor from the tomatoes we use. It's a quick cook, and there's the technique of finishing the pasta in the sauce in the pan with some of that pasta cooking water. That helps a lot and pulls it together.

TF: Switching gears to your other restaurant, how did you develop the pizza and learn about Neapolitan-style pizza?

CS: In 1998, there was not an authentic Neapolitan pizzeria on every block of the city. There were some pizza places we kind of liked but nothing like we grew up with, in other words, New York and Philly. So, we really wanted to open a pizzeria. I thought, hey, let's go to Naples and learn from the source and really get into it. I quickly learned it was very, very different from the pizza that we grew up with but also incredible. We really spent a lot of time there [in Naples] working on this. The thrift store [next to Delfina] got evicted, so we wound up opening the pizzeria right next door [after a search all over town for a space]. The space was so small that we didn't have room for a wood-fired oven, so we went with these deck ovens. Long story short, the style of pizza we wound up developing is kind of a New-York-meets-Naples mash-up.

TF: Final question—besides the whole local-seasonal emphasis in San Francisco, is there another key ingredient when you step back and think about what makes our dining scene so world-class and a tourist destination, yet we're a fraction of the size of your home city, New York??

CS: Obviously, access to incredible ingredients. I think there's an open-mindedness of everyone here. The Bay Area is a place of innovation, from the Beats to the psychedelic era. Silicon Valley...people feel supported when they follow their dream. People are really open-minded and always have been here. Hopefully it will stay that way.

UNCLE MIKEY'S CHICKEN ALLA CACCIATORA

CAFE ZOETROPE

Along with being one of the greatest film directors and producers of all time and a well-respected winery owner and hotel entrepreneur, the legendary Francis Ford Coppola also owns a restaurant in...San Francisco! Coppola bought the historic Sentinel Building in North Beach in 1972 and eventually added this cafe-restaurant in 1999, where this recipe handed down from his uncle has always been on the menu. As with all homemade stews, the next day the taste is even better!

YIELD: 6 servings

SALT AND FRESHLY GROUND BLACK PEPPER, TO TASTE

5 LBS. CHICKEN THIGHS, CUT INTO 12 PIECES

2 TABLESPOONS ALL-PURPOSE FLOUR

2 TABLESPOONS EXTRA-VIRGIN OLIVE OIL

2 TABLESPOONS PAPRIKA

8 OZ. CARROTS, CUT ½ X ¼ INCH

8 OZ. STALKS CELERY, CUT ½ X ¼ INCH

8 OZ. CREMINI MUSHROOMS, SLICED

5 BAY LEAVES

1½ BOTTLES RED WINE

6 CUPS WATER

1 TABLESPOON BUTTER (OPTIONAL)

1. Salt and pepper the chicken thighs, then coat them with the flour.

2. In a Dutch oven, heat the oil. Add the chicken and brown until golden on both sides.

continued...

3. Add the paprika and turn to coat all sides of the chicken with the paprika. Add the carrots, celery, mushrooms, and bay leaves, and salt and pepper to taste.

4. Add the wine and water, bring to a boil, and let simmer until the chicken is cooked through, about 30 minutes.

5. Remove the chicken from the pan and reduce the sauce for about 45 more minutes.

6. Return the chicken to the pan to reheat and finish with the butter, if desired. The sauce can be served on the side.

Q&A, GIANLUCA LEGROTTAGLIE

PROPRIETOR, MONTESACRO PINSERIA; PARTNER,
GENERAL MANAGER, AND WINE DIRECTOR, 54 MINT

TF: First of all, for our readers who haven't been to Montesacro—what's a pinsa??

GL: Distinctly Roman and similar to pizza, pinsa is created using three different types of flour—soy, rice, and wheat (all GMO-free)—a proprietary combination imported directly from Rome. Once the dough is made, it rises for 72 hours before being stretched by hand with additional rice flour to give it extra crispiness. Due to its composition and long leavening process, pinsa is lower in fat, lower in calories, and easier to digest than most traditional pizza. With its crispier crust and unique flavor, a pinsa is meant to be savored. Montesacro is the United States' very first pinseria.

TF: Can you tell us a little about what inspired you to work in restaurants and eventually open 54 Mint and Montesacro?

GL: I found out about pinsa during a trip back to my native neighborhood in Rome 8 years ago. The crunchiness and overall texture of this product blew me away. By the time I returned to SF, I decided to import the pinsa flour from Rome to the US and start a pinseria. When we signed the lease for the first Montesacro, I imagined a casual, rustic place for people to gather together, enjoying a pinsa with seasonal toppings that is gentle with the stomach, but a delicious experience for your palate.

TF: Your director of operations, Jacopo Rosito, is one of the most acclaimed cocktail minds in SF. How do your bar and wine programs work together with the food side?

GL: We worked to put together a thoughtfully curated wine list, featuring unique international wines, all of which are organic and made biodynamically. Guests will be challenged to explore lesser-known wines from around the world, including unique sparkling selections (no prosecco here!) like Glera, ProFondo, and Specogna, along with rosé, white, and red wine, vermouths, and dessert wines. We recently partnered with a wine producer in Sardinia to create our own in-house wine (a blend of Barbera and Cannonau). Seasonally inspired cocktails supplement the bar program, which is spearheaded by Jacopo, with spirits and ingredients that represent Italy found in every single libation, specifically highlighting small producers and distillers. In an effort to minimize waste in the restaurant, the mixology team also utilizes dehydrated and fermented ingredients as garnishes on their cocktails and mocktails. We pride ourselves on Jacopo's Negroni, which is one of our staples, and always will be.

TF: You have a unique perspective on the city's dining scene because you've also opened restaurants in other markets. What really stands out to you about San Francisco's dining scene and makes it so unique?

GL: The endless inspirations from traditional Roman cuisine are the heart and soul of our kitchen. We like to source local ingredients from the Bay Area purveyors and pair them with some Italian staples. We proudly make simple, authentic food.

TF: Montesacro has actually grown during the pandemic, and 54 Mint continues to be an Italian dining favorite in the city. What are your restaurants' keys to continued success in such a competitive, expensive market?

GL: The very true intent when creating our menu and overall experience was to take our patrons on a trip to Rome, without any plane tickets. People who dine with us are encouraged by our staff to share their food.

TF: Since the pastas at 54 Mint are all just so consistently wonderful, can you tell us the key to a perfect carbonara, cacio e pepe, and bucatini all'Amatriciana?

GL: One ingredient that not everyone knows about, acqua di cottura, that in Italian stands for "starchy water," a liquid gold for every Roman. It gives the quintessential kick to pasta. Pecorino is also a key, as it needs a bit of experience to get the right cheese that balances saltiness and texture.

TOFU BROCHETTES

GREENS, KATIE REICHER

It isn't a stretch to say that Greens is the most important vegetarian restaurant in Bay Area history. I don't really like saying that because carnivores and vegetarians alike have both enjoyed dining at this splendid Fort Mason classic for several decades because it's truly delicious—and it's also great that it has put vegetables on a satisfying pedestal rarely seen anywhere else. It never gets old and it never gets remotely boring. Originally founded in 1979 by Chef Deborah Madison and the San Francisco Zen Center, Greens deserves to be in the pantheon of San Francisco's historic restaurants. By virtue of being so local-produce driven, the menu of courses changes pretty frequently. But you can always count on a pizza, spring rolls, and tofu brochettes that have probably changed tens of thousands of minds by now that previously mumbled, "Oh, tofu is boring." No, it isn't. It can be a wonderful main event, as these brochettes always are.

YIELD: 8 skewers

CHIMICHURRI MARINADE

2 LARGE BUNCHES FRESH PARSLEY

1 BUNCH FRESH CHIVES

¼ CUP RED WINE VINEGAR

½ CUP REFINED OLIVE OIL
OR OTHER NEUTRAL OIL
(LIKE AVOCADO)

¼ TEASPOON RED PEPPER FLAKES

1 TABLESPOON MINCED GARLIC

¼ TEASPOON FRESHLY GROUND
BLACK PEPPER

1 TEASPOON SALT

1. Finely chop the parsley and chives.

2. Combine in a bowl with the remaining ingredients and mix until well combined. The sauce will not emulsify like a vinaigrette, but will have a loose, somewhat "broken" consistency. This is desirable.

continued...

TOFU BROCHETTES

16 CREMINI MUSHROOMS

1 BELL PEPPER,
CUT INTO 1-INCH TILES

1 LARGE ZUCCHINI,
CUT INTO ½-INCH ROUNDS

8 SMALL ONIONS (CIPOLLINI,
PEARL, OR RED)

1 BLOCK FIRM OR EXTRA-FIRM
TOFU, CUT INTO 1-INCH CUBES
(HODO FOODS BRAND PREFERRED)

16 (10-INCH) WOODEN SKEWERS,
SOAKED IN WATER

1. Cut all the vegetables to size and align each one in a container for easier grabbing.

2. Cap the end of a skewer with a mushroom, followed by a tofu cube, bell pepper, zucchini, and onion. Repeat the process backward to finish the skewer, finishing with a mushroom.

3. Place the skewers in the marinade and allow to marinate for at least 30 minutes or up to 1 day.

4. Grill over medium-high heat (400°F/204°C to 425°F/218°C), turning occasionally so that the vegetables cook through and the tofu browns evenly on all sides.

PISTACHIO-CRUSTED 38 NORTH DUCK BREAST

SPRUCE, MARK SULLIVAN

San Francisco isn't necessarily a city that considers itself glamorous or that loves to dress up. However, every night at Presidio Heights' always-bustling Spruce really does feel like *the* sophisticated, suave place to be, even on a cold February night. It carefully toes the line between fun and formal—three martinis or $3,000 Bordeaux first-growth wines. What ties it all together is the excellent and refined yet unfussy cooking of acclaimed Chef Mark Sullivan.

YIELD: 4 servings

DUCK SAUCE

(YIELD: 2 CUPS)

½ CUP THINLY SLICED CARROTS

½ CUP THINLY SLICED SHALLOTS

2 TABLESPOONS OLIVE OIL

½ CUP DRY SHERRY

¼ CUP ORANGE JUICE

1 QUART DUCK STOCK
(SEE PAGE 297)

½ CUP VEAL STOCK
(STORE-BOUGHT)

1 TABLESPOON BLACK
PEPPERCORNS

1 BAY LEAF

½ BUNCH FRESH THYME

1. In a large pot over medium heat, caramelize the carrots and shallots in the olive oil for 5 minutes.

2. Add the sherry and simmer for 2 minutes.

3. Add the orange juice and simmer for 2 minutes.

continued...

---

4. Add the stocks, peppercorns, bay leaf, and thyme, bring to a simmer, reduce the heat to low, and simmer for 90 minutes, skimming throughout the entire process. Do not boil!

5. Strain.

TURNIP PUREE
(YIELD: 3 CUPS)

4 OZ. UNSALTED BUTTER

1 LARGE YELLOW ONION, SLICED THIN

2¼ LBS. TURNIPS, SLICED THIN

½ TABLESPOON SALT, PLUS MORE TO TASTE

1 CUP HEAVY CREAM

1. In a large pot over low heat, melt the butter, then add the onion and cook slowly until tender. Do not caramelize!

2. Add the turnips and salt, cover, and cook for 30 minutes.

3. Add the cream and cook for another 15 minutes. The turnips should resemble a chunky puree.

4. Pass through a chinois until smooth. Add salt to taste.

BLANCHED BABY TURNIPS
(YIELD: 1 QUART)

2½ QUARTS ICE WATER

¾ CUP SALT

1 LB. BABY WHITE TURNIPS, TOPS TRIMMED

1. Prepare an ice bath by whisking together the ice water and ¼ cup of the salt. Set aside.

continued...

2. In a large pot over high heat, bring 2½ quarts water and the remaining ½ cup salt to a boil.

3. Blanch the turnips for 4 to 5 minutes or until tender.

4. Immediately cool in the ice bath for 10 minutes.

5. Drain and dry the turnips on paper towels.

CORIANDER AND PISTACHIO CRUST

½ CUP PISTACHIO NUTS, SHELLS REMOVED

½ CUP CORIANDER SEEDS

¼ TEASPOON CITRIC ACID

¼ TEASPOON SALT

2 TABLESPOONS DARK BROWN SUGAR

2 TEASPOONS ALMOND OIL

1 TEASPOON EXTRA-VIRGIN OLIVE OIL

1. Preheat the oven to 325°F/163°C.

2. On a baking sheet lined with parchment paper, lay out the pistachios. Toast until light golden brown, 10 to 15 minutes, stirring every 5 minutes. Set aside to cool.

3. In a sauté pan over medium-low heat, toast the coriander seeds for about 2 minutes. Set aside to cool.

4. Pulse the toasted pistachios in a food processor until coarsely ground. Set aside. Do the same for the toasted coriander seeds. Set aside.

5. In a sauté pan over low heat, combine the ground pistachios and coriander seeds and stir in the citric acid, salt, dark brown sugar, and oils. Cook for 2 minutes, until warmed and combined.

continued...

DUCK BREASTS

4 SKIN-ON DUCK BREASTS

2 TABLESPOONS SALT

2 TABLESPOONS OLIVE OIL

2 TABLESPOONS HONEY

CORIANDER AND PISTACHIO CRUST
(SEE PAGE 295)

1. Preheat the oven to 350°F/177°C.

2. Score the skin of each duck breast and season on both sides with the salt.

3. In a sauté pan over medium-low heat, coat the bottom of an ovenproof pan with the olive oil, place the duck breasts skin side down, and cook for 10 minutes.

4. Pour off the rendered fat, transfer the pan to the oven, and roast for 3 to 5 minutes.

5. Return the pan to the stove top over medium-high heat (still skin side down) and cook for 1 to 2 minutes.

6. Remove from the heat and the pan, and rest the duck skin side up on a wire rack for 8 to 10 minutes.

7. Brush the skin on each breast with the honey and coat with the coriander and pistachio mixture.

ASSEMBLY

1. Spoon the turnip puree off-center onto the left side of the plate. Place the duck breast off-center on the right side of the plate.

2. Slice the blanched turnips in half and place three pieces on the plate around the soubise.

3. Spoon the duck jus in the center of the plate between the puree and duck.

DUCK STOCK

A store-bought alternative would be to purchase a nicely made chicken stock (the ones in jars or buckets in the refrigerated section, not the ones in the cartons on the dry storage shelves). Duck stock is essentially the same as chicken stock but made with duck bones.

(YIELD: 1 QUART)

2 DUCK CARCASSES

2 LBS. CHICKEN FEET

1 CUP CHOPPED LEEKS

1 CUP CHOPPED YELLOW ONIONS

½ CUP CHOPPED CELERY

I CUP CHOPPED CARROT

¼ CUP GARLIC CLOVES, CRUSHED

½ BUNCH FRESH THYME

1 TABLESPOON BLACK PEPPERCORNS

2 BAY LEAVES

1. Preheat the oven to 365°F/185°C.

2. On two baking sheets lined with parchment paper, roast the duck bones and chicken feet separately until golden brown.

3. Place the roasted duck bones and chicken feet in a large pot and cover with 2 inches of cold water. Over medium heat, bring to a simmer, then reduce to low heat. Allow to cook for 1 hour, skimming frequently, and keeping the heat low enough to where the stock does not boil.

4. After 1 hour, add the remaining ingredients and simmer for another 2 hours.

5. Strain the duck stock and reserve.

BODEGA SF, MATT HO

As the name suggests, the anchor of this outstanding preparation is a whole branzino. "This dish is a reimagined Northern Vietnamese classic," says owner Matt Ho. "This dish is usually served with sole or catfish fillets on a sizzling plate. Instead, we keep the branzino whole and debone it to make it easier to eat while still using all the traditional flavors used in the marinade."

It's one of many reimagined Vietnamese classics at this year-old restaurant between Union Square and the Tenderloin. And it's a wonderful restaurant story, as Ho's family ran a Northern Vietnamese restaurant, Bodega Bistro, not far away in the Tenderloin from 2003 to 2017. Now the family is back, and they're serving some of SF's most riveting food.

YIELD: 4 servings

1 WHOLE BRANZINO

20 G YOGURT

5 G MINCED FRESH DILL

7.5 ML FISH SAUCE

7.5 G SHRIMP PASTE

1 TEASPOON TURMERIC

20 G MINCED GALANGAL

DILL, SAUTÉED, FOR GARNISH

ONIONS, DICED, FOR GARNISH

CRISPY SHALLOTS, FOR GARNISH

VERMICELLI, FOR SERVING

PERILLA LEAVES, FOR SERVING

RAU RAM, FOR SERVING

MINT, FOR SERVING

LITTLE GEM LETTUCES, FOR SERVING

1. Butterfly and debone the branzino.

2. In a bowl, combine the yogurt, dill, fish sauce, shrimp paste, turmeric, and galangal. Whisk until smooth.

3. Add the branzino and turn to coat completely. Marinate in the refrigerator overnight.

4. Preheat the broiler.

5. In a large, ovenproof pan over high heat, sear the branzino on both sides.

6. Transfer the pan to the oven and broil until it gets a nice char on the skin, about 7 minutes.

7. Remove from the oven and top with sauteed dill, onions, and crispy shallots.

8. Serve with vermicelli, perilla leaves, rau ram, mint, and little gem lettuce.

CAUSWELLS, ADAM ROSENBLUM

Chef Adam Rosenblum's modern-meets-retro menu at this Marina favorite is always fun and tempting, yet I'd venture to guess that almost half of the tables (maybe more) don't veer too far away from SF's most beloved and award-/list-winning burger. So, fire up the grill, and try to make it at home! Then head back to Causwells and see how your version compares (and don't forget to try other dishes like the banana bread "grilled cheese" while you're visiting the restaurant).

YIELD: 1 burger; about 2 cups sauce

CAUSWELLS BURGER SAUCE

1 CUP AIOLI OR MAYONNAISE

½ CUP KETCHUP

1 TABLESPOON DIJON MUSTARD

1 TEASPOON WORCESTERSHIRE
SAUCE

CHOPPED LACTO-FERMENTED
DILL PICKLE, TO TASTE

PINCH CAYENNE PEPPER

2 TEASPOONS FINELY CHOPPED
FRESH PARSLEY

1. Combine all the ingredients in a blender and mix on low until combined.

EACH BURGER

8 OZ. PREMIUM GROUND BEEF, FORMED INTO A BURGER

2 SLICES KRAFT AMERICAN CHEESE

1 SESAME SEED BURGER BUN

1 ($\frac{1}{16}$-INCH-THICK) SLICE YELLOW ONION

SLICED LACTO-FERMENTED DILL PICKLE

SLICED GREEN-LEAF LETTUCE

1. Grill the burger or sear it in a cast-iron pan over high heat to your desired degree of doneness, adding the cheese in the final 2 minutes to melt slightly.

2. Toast the bun and add a healthy dose of Causwells Burger Sauce.

3. Build your burger with the onion, pickle, and lettuce and enjoy.

JOE'S SPECIAL

ORIGINAL JOE'S

The original Original Joe's opened in the Tenderloin, but now the legendary Duggan family's restaurant resides in the heart of North Beach. This namesake dish is a kind of brunch mash-up, but nobody will judge you for ordering it at 8 p.m. The Duggan family also owns Westlake Joe's (an amazing retro space) just south of SF in Daly City and recently bought Zanze's Cheesecake, a longtime small-scale purveyor that defines "cheesecake in San Francisco" (the original owner/cheesecake virtuoso, Sam Zanze, retired in 2023 at 90 years old). So, amazing cheesecake, stiff yet delightful Manhattans, great burgers, Joe's Special—there are lots of things that make Original Joe's truly a special part of the city.

YIELD: 4 servings

---

2 TABLESPOONS OLIVE OIL

1 MEDIUM YELLOW ONION, CHOPPED

8 OZ. GROUND BEEF

1 (10-OZ.) PACKAGE FROZEN SPINACH, THAWED AND SQUEEZED DRY IN PAPER TOWELS

8 EGGS, LIGHTLY BEATEN

KOSHER SALT AND FRESHLY GROUND BLACK PEPPER, TO TASTE

¼ CUP FINELY GRATED PARMESAN CHEESE, FOR TOPPING

TOASTED SOURDOUGH BAGUETTE, FOR SERVING

1. Heat the olive oil in a skillet over medium-high heat. Add the onion and cook for about 5 minutes.

2. Add the ground beef and cook until browned and all the moisture evaporates, about 10 minutes.

3. Add the spinach and cook for about 2 minutes.

4. Add the eggs and cook until they are cooked and the mixture is slightly dry, about 4 minutes.

5. Season with salt and pepper and top with a sprinkling of Parmesan. Serve with a toasted sourdough baguette.

Q&A, NICK KELLY AND CALLI MARTINEZ

CO-OWNER/CHEF (NICK) AND CO-OWNER/WINE DIRECTOR (CALLI),
ALTOVINO

TF: Once upon a time, I lived right by where Altovino is now on Nob Hill (when it was Mason Pacific). It's one of the quintessential SF neighborhoods, right? What's it like running a restaurant there, literally on the cable car line?

NK: Yes, I think it is, with the older-style buildings, views of the bay, cable car lines, and the steep hills—really can't get more San Francisco than that. We love having our restaurant in this part of the city; it feels like a much smaller city over here—we see so many of our neighbors on a daily basis going about their day that stop by to chat, say hi, or wave as they pass by. We are really lucky to have so many people who live over here that just love good food and wine and are so happy and open to trying new things. Our regulars really are the ones who help us push through the pandemic, by being so patient, nice, and just happy to have us here, and as a result we have made such good friends with so many of them. Which is just very different compared to a lot of other restaurants I've worked at. We really do feel that we are a part of this neighborhood, not just operating here.

TF: Stepping back in time a little bit, what inspired you to pursue a culinary career?

NK: My family 100 percent inspired me to pursue this career. Growing up, my dad was/is still a chef and my mom a pastry chef, so food was always an important part of our life. Their production kitchen for the catering company was right next to my elementary school, so I spent lots of time after school in that kitchen, doing homework, peeling apples, pinboning salmon, making marzipan roses, playing in the walk-in, and it was always just fascinating being in the kitchen with everything going on. I still remember when I was in third grade and had just gotten out of school, and my dad was asking me about my school day while he sliced a case of button mushrooms, so fast, thin, and the whole time looking at me as I talked to him. That's when I decided that I wanted to be a chef and learn to cut and cook with the ease that my dad showed.

TF: What drew you in particular to become such a gifted chef and knowledgeable mind about regional cuisines of Italy? I know you worked at the great Barbacco in Downtown SF for several years.

NK: The majority of my family on both sides is Italian, so growing up we typically leaned toward cooking and eating Italian. My favorite memories are making gnocchi and fresh pasta at home. We always had a big garden growing up, and grew lots of tomatoes for canning and sauce making. So, I've always been really into Italian-style food, but Barbacco is where I really started diving into actual regional cuisines of Italy. While I was there, we started doing a monthly regional menu in addition to our regular menu, where each month I would create a menu focused on one region and the classic dishes from the area. In preparation for each menu, I would do a lot of research not only on the dishes themselves, but the culture, landscape, wine, produce, livestock, and traditions of the area. I just fell in love with the vast diversity of the food and cultures, the deeper I went. So, after I left Barbacco, I traveled to Italy with my now wife, and over the course of three months I worked and traveled from Alto Adige through Piemonte, down the west coast into Emilia-Romagna, Tuscany, and all the way to Sicily, and then [we] worked our way back up the east coast before ending in Verona. That trip let me experience all the differences that I had been reading about, and [it] had a profound impact on how I approach Italian cuisine then and now.

TF: Before Barbacco, you worked at the iconic Martini House in the Napa Valley. What cooking influences did you learn there?

NK: Martini House had a huge impact on my life as a chef; I was 19 when I started there, as green as they come. Up until that time my cooking experience was from a catering background, so [it was] my first real fine dining restaurant job, and it was eye-opening—so fast, so much attention to details. People were the best [there], and still my best friends to this day are from that restaurant. I think the organization, structure, being aware of everything going on around you, and how to work together as a well-oiled machine were my greatest takeaways. I could write a book about everything I learned there because I really grew up as cook there, from 19 as an extern to leaving there at 25 as a sous chef after six different other positions. Chef Todd [Humphries] and Chef [Christopher] Litts have had a lasting impact on my life in the most positive ways—[I] love them very much.

TF: Can you tell us a bit about the menu, your pasta making, the whole animal butchery program, and the cuisine philosophy at Altovino?

NK: Our philosophy is to cook like Italians in San Francisco, not as Californians, with French technique using Italian ingredients while applying "De maiale non si butta via niente" (you never throw anything away from a pig) toward all ingredients. We make vinegars from fruit trim [and] shrubs from overripe fruit, [and] we ferment/use vegetable trim in creative ways to avoid as much waste as possible. I guess we try to balance out the menu by having traditional, classic pasta dishes like all'amatriciana and modern pasta dishes that—while keeping the Italian cooking fundamentals—aren't traditional in any area in Italy just unique to us, like our Sacchetti filled with slow-roasted lamb shoulder, served with peperonata, zucchini fonduta, and herb salad. One thing we don't do anymore, though, is extruded pasta here in-house. I just really don't care for the texture of fresh extruded pasta, so if we want to do a dish that should have an extruded shape, we buy high-quality, Italian brass die, dry extruded pasta. Typically, we have one dry pasta and five or six fresh pasta shapes on the menu at any given time.

Our whole animal butchery program here is very important to me, because it really is the best way to make sure nothing from an animal goes to waste. We also work directly with farmers and ranchers that we've developed relations with over the years, and [it] cuts down the carbon footprint of the animals we use, while being better financially for both of us. Butchery also happens to be [the] favorite part of my prep day. It takes planning, but it also gives you the freedom to customize the cuts you get. I very rarely cut an animal the same way every time, just depends on what you want to get out of it. We always have rendered fats to cook with—bake with, preserve with. It really is the only way to do things, in my opinion.

TF: And, of course, your wife, Calli, is the co-owner and wine director at Altovino! How do you two work together to make the restaurant such a seamless, special place for matching great wines and food together?

NK: I love working with my wife—we have such a similar outlook about how we view food, wine, service, [and] restaurant culture, especially our own. We want to be happy at work, and we want the people around us to be happy, and in turn show happiness toward our guests in the restaurant. Everything else comes along with that. We focus on the people first, then the product. Of course, the quality product is very important as well.

TF: Calli, what initially drew you toward a career in hospitality and wine?

CM: There are two reasons that stand out for me. I grew up in a really active, outdoorsy family, and I've never really clicked with that lifestyle. So, my favorite memories from growing up are when we would all sit down to meals at restaurants on vacation or for special occasions. That mindset has never really changed! No matter where we are, I am always excited for meals. I love to try new restaurants, take in the ambience, read the menu, try the wine, and allow myself to get caught up in that. I also remember if my mom and dad went out on a date, they would come say good night to us when we were already in bed, and I always wanted to know the details of what they ate for dinner. I thought their descriptions of things like osso buco sounded so interesting and delicious. That's where the food aspect came into it.

Secondly, during high school and college I developed pretty bad social anxiety. I had a really hard time meeting new people, and I felt uncomfortable trying to hold a conversation. Going to work as a server helped me gain a lot of confidence and also helped me become more open-minded, because you are constantly meeting new people on both sides of the table. Working as a server was one of the first times I can remember feeling a sense of purpose. People talk down about restaurant jobs that don't come with a lot of clout attached, but I got so much out of it and I'm absolutely a better person for it.

My biggest goal growing up was to own my own business—there was no other option that I ever considered. I originally thought it would be a spa (I moved from the Seattle area to San Francisco in order to get my aesthetics license), but my experiences with food and working in restaurants were so impactful that it was a natural path to follow.

TF: I want to quickly ask about what used to be one of my favorite restaurants in the city...Aster! If I'm correct, you worked there back when it was open, 5 or 10 or so years ago? Can you tell us a bit about that influential Michelin-starred restaurant and Chef Brett Cooper's cooking style there?

CM: I did! Aster was a whole new experience for me. I had only worked in casual places (although they added fine dining touches). Being a Michelin-starred environment, Aster had a level of attention to detail and consistency that I hadn't really experienced before, but I really liked the style. At the time that I worked there, we had a great team—it just felt like a choreographed dance on the floor.

TF: Now, back to the present. What are some of your pairings of wines and signature dishes at Altovino?

CM: We change our wine list a lot, so it's fun to be able to try a lot of different wines up against our food. Recently I was pairing the Pappardelle Bolognese with a Montefalco Rosso from Bocale in Umbria, and I was really happy with that. The Bolognese, of course, is such an intense dish, with lots of flavors layered in, since Nick cooks the sofrito so long and then uses dry-aged beef and prosciutto, which also lend a savory quality. The Bocale matches its intensity, with really deep, dark fruit [and an] earthiness that I liked next to the rich flavors and, of course, some nice tannins from the Sagrantino, since it definitely has a strong fat content.

SMOKED DUCK

THE MORRIS, GAVIN SCHMIDT

When San Franciscans refer to "the duck," they're likely talking about the signature smoked duck from Chef Gavin Schmidt at this outstanding restaurant located where the Mission starts to blur into Potrero Hill. Long before The Morris, this address was the Slow Club, one of the definitive 1990s restaurants of SF, where Jim Moffat (who you can find now at the excellent Bar Acuda and AMA in Hanalei, Kauai) was one of the leading chefs of the big modern-California-cuisine movement when it started pivoting to being served in more high-octane, casual environs in more industrial corners of the city. It's wonderful to see this space evolve into another signature restaurant with The Morris. Besides the duck, The Morris has a number of staples—buckwheat doughnuts, charred broccoli, the amazing wine list from owner Paul Einbund, the Chartreuse Slushy, to name just a few—that are hardly just the supporting cast for this showstopping centerpiece dish.

YIELD: 4 to 6 servings

BRINE

2 L WATER	2 SPRIGS FRESH THYME
220 G SALT	3 GARLIC CLOVES, PEELED
340 G SUGAR	

1. In a large pot over high heat, bring the water to a boil. Whisk in the salt and sugar until they are dissolved. Add the thyme and garlic and allow to cool.

continued...

DUCK

1 (6-LB.) PEKIN DUCK

1. Cut off the neck and wings, chop them into 1½-inch pieces, and reserve for the jus.

2. Submerge the duck in the brine for 24 hours.

3. Remove from the brine and hang the duck to dry in a refrigerator with good air circulation around it for 7 to 10 days to dry out the skin.

4. Smoke the duck for 2 hours over hickory at 165°F/74°C.

5. Transfer to a preheated 425°F/218°C oven (convection) or 450°F/232°C oven (without convection) and roast to an internal temperature of 140°F/60°C (test at the thickest part of the breast or in the center of the thigh), 35 to 45 minutes.

6. Let rest for 15 minutes before carving into serving pieces.

JUS

100 G BUTTER

300 G DUCK WINGS AND NECK, CHOPPED

100 G MEDIUM-DICE CARROT

150 G MEDIUM-DICE ONION

20 G GARLIC CLOVES, PEELED

50 G MEDIUM-DICE FENNEL BULB

140 ML WHITE WINE

2 L POULTRY STOCK

1 CARDAMOM POD

½ CINNAMON STICK

2 CLOVES

5 G LONG PEPPER

2.5 G SZECHUAN PEPPERCORNS

4 G BLACK PEPPERCORNS

1 STAR ANISE POD

½ WHOLE NUTMEG

100 G MARSHALL'S FARM HONEY

12 G GROUND ESPRESSO

50 ML RED WINE VINEGAR

SALT, TO TASTE

1. In a shallow sauce pot, melt the butter until foamy and starting to brown. Add the duck wings and neck and cook in the browned butter until the skin on the wings is deep brown. Add the carrot, onion, garlic, and fennel and cook until they are well caramelized.

2. Deglaze with the wine and bring to a boil.

3. Add the stock and all the spices and simmer over low heat for 2 hours.

4. Stir in the honey and espresso and let steep for 3 minutes.

5. Pass through a fine-mesh sieve. Stir in the vinegar and season with salt to taste.

6. Serve on the side with the carved duck.

SISIG FRIED RICE

ABACÁ, FRANCIS ANG

From pastry chef to a typhoon to a tremendous pop-up to an early pandemic opening, wow, it's incredible how Abacá came about (more on that journey via the interview on page 315). This modern Filipino restaurant in Fisherman's Wharf from Francis and Dian Ang is, in my humble opinion, probably the most impressive SF restaurant to open during the turbulent first 2 years of the COVID-19 pandemic. There's nothing else even remotely like it in San Francisco. This dish from Chef Ang was an early influence in his career to pursue cooking Filipino food.

YIELD: 6 servings

---

1 LARGE PIG'S HEAD OR 1 LB. BONELESS PORK BUTT AND 1½ LBS. UNCURED PORK BELLY

1 TEASPOON KOSHER SALT, PLUS MORE TO TASTE

2 TABLESPOONS UNSALTED BUTTER

1 LARGE ONION, MINCED (ABOUT 2 CUPS)

2 TEASPOONS PLUS 3 TABLESPOONS MINCED GARLIC

4 OZ. CHICKEN LIVERS, CLEANED, RINSED, AND ROUGHLY CHOPPED

1 SERRANO CHILI, THINLY SLICED

3 TABLESPOONS SOY SAUCE

1 CUP WHITE VINEGAR

1 TABLESPOON SUGAR

¼ CUP MAGGI OR KNORR SEASONING

¼ TEASPOON FRESHLY GROUND BLACK PEPPER, PLUS MORE TO TASTE

3 QUARTS LEFTOVER WHITE RICE

PICKLED RED ONION, FOR SERVING

CRUMBLED CHICHARRÓN, FOR SERVING

FRIED SUNNY-SIDE EGG, FOR EACH SERVING

continued...

1. Place the pork of choice in a large pot. Add enough water to cover the meat, about 12 cups, and the salt. Bring to a boil over high heat, reduce the heat, and simmer until just tender, about 1½ hours.

2. As the pork cooks, add more hot water as needed to keep it covered.

3. Preheat the broiler with a rack placed in the middle of the oven. Line a rimmed baking sheet with aluminum foil.

4. Remove the pork from the liquid and place on the prepared baking sheet. If using the pig's head, use a knife to carve out as much meat as possible. Let the broth cool and save for another use.

5. Broil the pork until slightly charred, 10 to 15 minutes; watch closely to prevent burning. When the meat is cool enough to handle, chop into small bite-size pieces.

6. In a 12-inch skillet over medium-high heat, melt the butter. When bubbling, add the onion and 2 teaspoons of the garlic; cook until the onion is soft, 3 to 4 minutes. Add the chicken livers; cook, stirring occasionally, about 2 minutes. Add the chili, chopped pork, soy sauce, vinegar, sugar, and Maggi seasoning; simmer for about 10 minutes. Add the pepper.

7. Let cool overnight or cool to room temperature.

8. Mix in the rice and season with salt and pepper.

9. Heat a wok or nonstick pan. Add the remaining 3 tablespoons garlic and cook until lightly browned. Add the rice mixture and sauté until heated through.

10. Serve garnished with pickled red onion and crumbled chicharrón and topped with an egg fried sunny-side up.

Q&A, FRANCIS ANG

EXECUTIVE CHEF/OWNER, ABACÁ

TF: Many San Francisco diners have read in recent years about (and thoroughly enjoyed dining at) Pinoy Heritage and Abacá. But let's step back and first talk about your culinary journey that set the stage for these two concepts in San Francisco. After growing up both in SF and the Philippines, what led you to pursue a career in cooking?

FA: In the Philippines, I grew up watching cooking shows. Jacques Pépin, Julia Child, Martin Yan, *Iron Chef*, and Food Network with Alton Brown. Culinary arts was a popular curriculum at the time, and when I moved to the United States, I enrolled in City College of San Francisco. My first class was pastry. Immediately, I fell in love. I don't have any talents in singing/dancing or in sports. I couldn't draw or paint. But I saw a potential in being able to express myself through cooking, creating, and plating. I was even dubbed as Fancy Francis by my chef instructor.

TF: How did your experiences at Restaurant Gary Danko and Fifth Floor help shape your next steps?

FA: Each restaurant had an immense impact. At Gary Danko, I was able to learn the basics of production at a high-volume and high-caliber restaurant directly from Chef Gary Danko himself.

At the Fifth Floor I was able to utilize my basic knowledge from Danko and create flavors that are classic yet unconventional. I gained confidence in experimenting and leading. Through David Bazirgan, my journey as a young chef flourished. He helped promote my name in the culinary scene in San Francisco.

TF: Per my experience covering restaurants in SF, you're one of the very few chefs in the city who has had tremendous success as a pastry chef *and* on the savory side. How do the roles complement each other as a chef and also differ? Why do you think there doesn't seem to be much crossover between the two?

FA: To succeed in pastry, it requires dedicated time in learning techniques properly. It requires accuracy, practice, patience, and perseverance. Being a trained pastry chef first, it has given me a different vision when creating dishes. I was able to understand the flavor balance of sweet, sour, salty, and bitter. I understand aesthetics, textures, and temperature variations, all of which play a role in the final product of the dish.

TF: The story of how you and Dian started the Pinoy Heritage concept in 2013 is remarkable and inspiring. The devastation of a typhoon in the Philippines turned into a chance for you to make an enormous difference there in the aftermath of the storm, yet it also convinced you to pursue further research in bringing the country's cooking to the San Francisco audience. Can you talk us through these four-plus years leading to the pop-up starting?

FA: When we did the fundraiser for the typhoon, we created an all-Filipino menu. People loved it, and it felt so good when people told us how good it was. That was our "eureka moment." We started to have a few more pop-ups, but we quickly realized that as soon as we researched about Filipino food, the more we realized how little we know about the cuisine. Even though we grew up in the Philippines, it's a country with 7,000-plus islands. We dedicated several months out of the year to travel to different regions and different towns to understand and learn the cuisine. We asked local champions of their regions to teach us their heirloom recipes. After all, if we were to represent Filipino food, we had to learn what it truly is.

TF: Abacá is arguably the marquee San Francisco restaurant to have opened since the pandemic started. You opened a restaurant in a somewhat quiet (often tourist-centric) neighborhood in the midst of a pandemic *and* having a young child. It's amazing how you can do all of this! Looking back on what must have been a surreal few months, what have you learned in the first year-plus of Abacá?

FA: Oh, it was a lot of sacrifice. It still is. We just have to have faith that it'll all work out—that it's all worth it and people will continue to support us and our mom-and-pop restaurant.

I have learned to be patient. That we have to find solutions to problems and continue to evolve and progress. I have learned to look at things half-full and not half-empty. That we are blessed to be doing things we love and are passionate about.

TF: What are some of the dishes that seem to be the signatures or favorites of Abacá diners? And how about for the panaderia/brunch?

FA: Definitely the sisig fried rice, skewers, buns, and okoy. For brunch and panaderia, it has to be the Wagyu tapsilog, bibingka, and ensaymadas.

APPLEWOOD-SMOKED BACON-WRAPPED PORK TENDERLOIN WITH FUJI APPLES AND DANDELION "PERSILLADE"

ONE MARKET RESTAURANT, MARK DOMMEN

From its origins with one of SF's all-time greats as its chef (Bradley Ogden) to when the torch was later passed to another incredibly talented kitchen leader, Mark Dommen, One Market Restaurant continues to be one of the stalwarts of downtown San Francisco dining. Dommen has a knack for making comfort cuisine fresh and exciting (latkes with avocado and caviar, anyone?), and that particularly endearing style is exemplified by this recipe. Immediately your eyes go to bacon-wrapped pork tenderloin, right? Well, you're in San Francisco, folks. Dommen was inspired to create this recipe 18 years ago because he found a bunch of dandelion greens at a farmers market and wanted to use them in a dish. If that isn't a California local-seasonal-cuisine story, then I don't know what is.

YIELD: 4 servings

½ GALLON APPLE CIDER

2 PORK TENDERLOINS, ABOUT 16 OZ. EACH

8 OZ. APPLEWOOD-SMOKED, THINLY SLICED BACON

SEA SALT AND FRESHLY GROUND BLACK PEPPER, TO TASTE

4 GARLIC CLOVES, PEELED

5 TABLESPOONS GRAPESEED OIL, PLUS MORE TO SEAR THE PORK

¼ CUP HEAVY CREAM

2 FUJI APPLES

½ BUNCH DANDELION GREENS

½ BUNCH MUSTARD GREENS

3 TABLESPOONS BUTTER

1 LARGE SHALLOT, FINELY CHOPPED

CIDER VINEGAR, TO TASTE

1. In a large pot over high heat, reduce the cider down to about 1 cup. Set aside.

2. Trim the pork tenderloins to remove any fat and all the silverskin. About one-third of the way up each tenderloin, starting at the tail, make a cut about three-quarters of the way through, then fold the tail part under. This should give you a nice even filet.

3. Spread a large piece of plastic wrap out on a cutting board and lay half of the bacon in a shingle pattern, each slice slightly overlapping the previous one.

4. Season the pork tenderloin with salt and pepper to taste and place at one end of the shingle of bacon. Use the plastic wrap to help fold the bacon over the filet, wrapping it tightly to cover the entire tenderloin. Leave the plastic wrap on the filet until you are ready to cook the pork. Do the same with the second pork tenderloin.

5. Blanch the garlic cloves three times, in clean water each time.

continued...

6. Heat a small sauté pan with 1 tablespoon of the oil and sauté the garlic until lightly brown. Add the cream and reduce by half. Put the garlic and cream in a blender and blend to a fine puree. Set aside.

7. Peel the apples and cut into 12 nice round disks. Remove the cores with a round cutter.

8. Add the remaining 4 tablespoons oil to a hot sauté pan, then add the apple rings. Sauté until nicely caramelized. Remove to a plate lined with a paper towel.

9. Put a large pot of water on to boil and add enough salt to make it as salty as the sea.

10. Meanwhile, wash the dandelion greens to remove any dirt or sand.

11. When the water is boiling, blanch the dandelion greens, then transfer to an ice bath to stop the cooking. Drain the dandelions and squeeze out as much water as possible. Chop into small pieces. Do the same thing with the mustard greens— wash, blanch, shock, squeeze, and chop.

12. Preheat the oven to 400°F/204°C.

13. Season the bacon-wrapped pork tenderloins with salt and pepper and sear in a hot sauté pan with some grapeseed oil. When nicely browned all the way around, transfer the pork to a roasting pan with a wire rack and roast for 16 to 18 minutes, until medium (about 140°F/60°C). Remove from the oven and keep warm, but allow to rest for 10 minutes.

14. While the meat is resting, put the apples in the oven to warm them.

15. In another sauté pan, melt 1 tablespoon of the butter and sweat the shallot. Add the chopped dandelion and mustard greens and continue to sauté. Add the garlic cream and combine. Season to taste with salt and pepper.

16. Heat the cider reduction, whisk in the remaining 2 tablespoons butter, and season to taste with salt and pepper. If it needs it, add a couple of drops of vinegar to balance the sweetness of the sauce.

17. To plate, put 3 apple rings on each plate. Top each apple ring with some of the dandelion–mustard green mixture. Slice each pork tenderloin into 6 pieces and put 1 slice of the pork on top of each apple. Spoon the cider reduction around the plate. Serve.

Q&A, MICHAEL DELLAR

MANAGING PARTNER, ONE MARKET RESTAURANT

TF: As we sit here in the spring of 2023, One Market Restaurant just celebrated its thirtieth anniversary. Thirty years! That's remarkable in the restaurant industry. What are the secrets to the restaurant's success?

MD: No secrets. Just focus and lots of good blocking and tackling, a commitment to seasonal farm-fresh fare, and, above all, hospitality. We respect and value every guest.

TF: You have quite the dynamic duo of Mark Dommen running the kitchen and Tonya Pitts running the wine program. Can you tell us a little about both of them? How would you describe One Market's cuisine and drinks program?

MD: It's really a trio, not a duo. General manager/partner Lorenzo Bouchard is the only one other than myself who was there on opening day, February 16, 1993. With Lorenzo, Mark, and Tonya, there are over 50 years of service. We think each is the best at what they do... service, culinary, wine.

TF: Thirty years ago you started One Market with the legendary Bradley Ogden. No story about San Francisco food is complete without talking about Bradley. Can you tell us a little bit about him and those early One Market days?

MD: Bradley created the menu at One Market as a city-oriented rendition of what we had accomplished at The Lark Creek Inn in 1989. That was our country restaurant, whereas One Market would be our city restaurant. Both celebrated the seasons and curated ingredients with American tradition in mind, something that Brad had become the master of. It was his influence that pushed farmers and ranchers to create products like interesting fruits and vegetables, free-range chickens, and smoked meats that weren't available locally.

TF: What led you to a career as a restaurateur?

MD: It was a dark and stormy night . . .

My background is in consumer-packaged-goods marketing, starting with The Clorox Company in 1970 right out of business school at USC. I loved wine and food, had started my own wine and food society, and loved to cook—learning at my mother, Harriett's, knee. When Clorox bought a restaurant company in the East Bay called Emil Villa's Hickory Pit, I moved in as director of marketing and helped triple the business in size. Then in 1984, I joined Spectrum Foods with founders Larry Mindel and Jerry Magnin, who had created the best multiconcept restaurant business on the West Coast with restaurants like Chianti, Ciao, Prego, MacArthur Park, and Harry's Bar and American Grill. Soon we had created new ones like Chianti Cucina, Guaymas, Spiedini, Spuntino, etc. We sold our business and soon thereafter it was time to go out on my own with a great chef-partner like Bradley.

The Lark Creek Inn [a legendary Marin County restaurant] was our first concept together in 1989, then One Market in 1993. Many more followed. Subsequently, Brad went to Las Vegas to open another restaurant venture of ours, the eponymous Bradley Ogden at Caesars Palace in 2002. He stayed in Las Vegas, I stayed in San Francisco, and we both grew the business.

At one time, we grew our team to 15 restaurants with $50 million in operational sales—Lark Creek expanded to San Mateo, Walnut Creek, and SFO; Lark Creek Steak and Cupola landed at the Westfield San Francisco Centre, Yankee Pier opened in Larkspur, Lafayette, Santana Row, and SFO; Parcel 104 came to be at the Santa Clara Marriott; Arterra opened at the Del Mar Marriott; and many more. We had James Beard nominations and awards and Michelin stars at multiple restaurants. All of the restaurants that Bradley and I worked on together were closed around 2015, other than One Market.

Through it all, One Market, with its stellar team, was always our flagship. It all started with Jim Wood of the *San Francisco Examiner* naming it "best new restaurant" of 1993. The restaurant went on to win a coveted Michelin star during the award's first 5 years in San Francisco. Today, One Market exists with an incredibly experienced team of restaurant professionals led by Mark Dommen, Lorenzo Bouchard, and Tonya Pitts. Truly the A team.

TF: As an anchor of downtown San Francisco dining, how are things different these days, some 3 years after the pandemic started? The Embarcadero still looks as busy as ever (to me, at least), even if offices aren't full.

MD: I wish that were true. While the Ferry Building attracts many thousands of visitors for the Saturday farmers market, the business district is not as busy as before the pandemic. It really can't happen, as there aren't as many people working in the big office buildings. There aren't as many people commuting on public transportation, for which the area around One Market is a hub with Muni, BART, and multiple ferries converging. Eventually, it will get back to busier times. The area also may end up being more mixed-use, with additional residential spaces in the zone. The hope is that that will create the kind of excitement that developed in downtown Manhattan after 9/11.

TF: You've surely seen a lot and met a lot of interesting/powerful people over the decades while owning a prominent restaurant overlooking the Ferry Building. Any fun stories or particularly memorable ones?

MD: We like to say the important things happen at the foot of Market Street. We've entertained presidents and vice presidents, senators, congressional leaders, prime ministers, royalty, and other world leaders, Super Bowl heroes, World Series winners, NBA champions, and Academy Award winners…you name it. We have hosted parties for the leaders of virtually every major corporation and hundreds of nonprofits. One Market was chosen to be the NFL house for Super Bowl 50 and the annual Pride kick-off breakfast for thousands. The restaurant has hosted weddings and birthdays, graduations, and all sorts of celebrations of every kind for every type of person. One of the things that has endeared us to our audiences is that we've always extended the highest level of hospitality, but have not been inclined to talk about it. For us, it's all in a day's work, plying our trade and extending our welcome to one and all.

DÖNER KEBAB WITH HAUS PITA, TURKISH HOT SAUCE, AND TZATZIKI YOGURT–DILL SAUCE

RADHAUS

Now 30 years young, Suppenküche in Hayes Valley continues to be packed nightly for liter steins complemented by spaetzle, bratwurst, and more comforting, satisfying German fare in festive surroundings. Across town in Fort Mason Center is its sibling, Radhaus, with a totally different vibe (a spacious, sunlight-filled beer hall) and view (literally looking at the Golden Gate Bridge). Modern Germany is a diverse place and Turkish cuisine has a huge presence there, as anyone who has visited Hamburg, Munich, or Berlin and enjoyed döner kebab in recent years can attest. It's great that we can enjoy this Turkey-via-Germany-via-California classic dish right on the bayfront.

YIELD: 4 servings

DÖNER KEBAB

TURKISH HOT SAUCE
(SEE PAGE 326)

TZATZIKI (SEE PAGE 326)

MARINATED GRILLED CHICKEN
(SEE PAGE 327)

PICKLED SHALLOTS (SEE PAGE 327)

PITA (SEE PAGE 328)

DICED TOMATOES, TO TASTE

LITTLE GEM LETTUCE, TO TASTE

FRESH HERBS, TO TASTE

continued...

TURKISH HOT SAUCE

113 ML EXTRA-VIRGIN OLIVE OIL

12 G WHOLE GARLIC CLOVES

60 G JULIENNED SHALLOTS

30 G GROUND ALEPPO PEPPER

30 G GROUND URFA PEPPER

113 ML TOMATO WATER OR REGULAR WATER

20 ML APPLE CIDER VINEGAR

1. On low heat, add the olive oil and gently pan-roast the garlic until fragrant and golden brown. Just as the garlic becomes fragrant, add the shallots and sauté until translucent.

2. Remove the pan from the heat and while stirring constantly add the Aleppo and Urfa peppers to toast in the oil, taking caution not to burn the pepper powder. Exercise caution, as the peppers will become very fragrant very quickly and could cause some irritation; it is recommended to do this step with the overhead fan on high.

3. Fully cool the mixture to room temperature.

4. Add the flavored olive oil with all the spices, garlic, and shallots to a blender and begin to blend on high. In this fashion, now you will reverse-emulsify by adding the water and apple cider vinegar to the oil. The vinegar and water may be combined for this purpose.

TZATZIKI

250 G STRAINED GREEK YOGURT OR LABNEH

50 G FRESH DILL, ROUGH CHOPPED

40 ML CUCUMBER JUICE

20 ML EXTRA-VIRGIN OLIVE OIL

15 ML FRESH LEMON JUICE

SALT, TO TASTE

1. In a mixing bowl, combine all of the ingredients, mix well, and set aside.

MARINATED GRILLED CHICKEN

88 G PAPRIKA	11 G ONION POWDER
38 G ALLSPICE	11 G GROUND GINGER
34 G TURMERIC	11 G ALEPPO PEPPER
29 G CUMIN	OLIVE OIL, AS NEEDED
11 G GROUND CINNAMON	BONELESS CHICKEN THIGHS OR BREASTS, AS NEEDED
11 G GARLIC POWDER	

1. In a bowl, combine all of the ingredients, except the olive oil and chicken, and mix well.

2. Using enough olive oil to coat the chicken, add the spice blend to the chicken and distribute evenly. Marinate in the refrigerator for at least 4 hours, but preferably overnight.

3. Proceed to grill or roast the chicken until cooked through to an internal temperature of 165°F/69°C is reached.

PICKLED SHALLOTS

100 G SHALLOTS	35 G SUGAR
100 ML RED WINE VINEGAR	35 ML WATER

1. Julienne the shallots crosswise so individual rings are visible.

2. Combine vinegar, sugar, and water in a small pot and bring to a rolling boil.

3. Pour the boiled pickling liquid over the shallots and place a weighted object over the shallots to keep them submerged in the pickling liquid. After about 1 hour they should be cooled and pickled.

continued...

PITA

310 G ALL-PURPOSE FLOUR	7 G ACTIVE DRY YEAST
5 G KOSHER SALT	240 ML WARM WATER
5 G SUGAR	15 ML EXTRA-VIRGIN OLIVE OIL

1. In a large mixing bowl, combine the flour, salt, and sugar.

2. In a separate small bowl, dissolve the yeast in the warm water. Let it sit for about 5 minutes until it becomes frothy.

3. Make a well in the center of the flour mixture and pour in the yeast mixture and olive oil. Mix everything together until a dough forms.

4. Transfer the dough to a floured surface and knead it for about 5 to 7 minutes until it becomes smooth and elastic.

5. Place the dough in a greased bowl, cover with a clean kitchen towel, and let it rise in a warm place for about 1 to 2 hours until it doubles in size.

6. Once the dough has risen, remove it from the bowl and flatten it down, releasing the air bubbles. Divide the dough into small (golf ball)-size balls.

7. Roll each ball into a circle about 15 to 18 centimeters in diameter and about 6 millimeters thick.

8. Lightly flour each pita bread to prevent sticking.

9. Heat up a nonstick skillet or cast-iron skillet to medium-low heat and add enough olive oil to coat the pan, and proceed to shallow-fry each pita until golden brown.

To Serve

1. Build yourself a Doner Kebab using pita as your base. Add lettuce, chicken, diced tomatoes, Pickled Shallots, Tzatziki, and Turkish Hot Sauce and finish with some freshly chopped dill.

HANGTOWN FRY

TADICH GRILL

Growing up in California, you learn all about the mid-19th century Gold Rush in the foothills of the Sierra Nevada Mountains somewhere around 4th or 5th grade. However, for some reason, nobody ever taught us about the iconic dish that was created in (or around) Placerville at that time or that the town had an ominous nickname of "Hangtown").

At the end of the day, the Hangtown Fry is a collection of a few of our favorite ingredients (oysters and bacon!) held together in egg form. It is hardly an abstract or complex dish. But, it is a very important and historical dish. The City of Placerville even has a whole page about it on its website that describes the murky history of whether it was originally a celebratory dish or more of a dish that represents the darker side of the ol' Wild West. Regardless, this version comes from San Francisco's oldest restaurant, which was founded in 1849, right around when the dish would have been created, and it is absolutely delicious. I personally call it an oyster-and-bacon omelet, but it really exists in its own dimension, a beautiful reminder of a long-gone world.

YIELD: 1 serving

---

2 SLICES BACON

½ CUP SEASONED FINE BREAD CRUMBS, TOASTED; OR FLOUR SEASONED WITH SALT AND PEPPER

6 OYSTERS, SHUCKED

1 TABLESPOON UNSALTED BUTTER

3 EGGS, LIGHTLY BEATEN

3 TO 4 DASHES TABASCO

KOSHER SALT AND FRESHLY GROUND BLACK PEPPER, TO TASTE

continued...

1. Place a nonstick sauté pan over medium heat. Add the bacon and fry for 6 to 8 minutes, until crisp. Transfer to paper towels to drain.

2. Place the bread crumbs in a small bowl. Dredge the oysters in the bread crumbs, shaking off any excess.

3. Pour the bacon fat out of the sauté pan. Add the butter to the pan and melt it over medium heat. Add the oysters and sauté for about 1½ minutes on each side, or until they just plump up. Crumble the bacon and toss it with the oysters.

4. Pour the eggs into the pan. Season with the Tabasco, salt, and pepper, and cook for about 3 minutes, until the eggs are almost set, lifting the edges of the cooked eggs to let the uncooked eggs run underneath.

5. Carefully flip the frittata over and cook for about 2 minutes longer, or until the other side is set. Transfer to a plate and serve immediately.

BRAISED BEEF BOURGUIGNON

ABSINTHE BRASSERIE & BAR, IAN BEGG

San Francisco certainly loves its French cuisine, but it honestly doesn't have many bistros or brasseries (French-inspired bakeries/pastry shops are a different story). When you stroll off Hayes Street into Absinthe, you could absolutely be in Lyon or Paris—trust me, I lived in the 7th arrondissement of Paris for five months once upon a time, and Absinthe is almost more legit Parisian than any bistro/brasserie I actually dined at there. Absinthe is so good at so many things—pretheater dining, cocktails, lazy afternoons of snacks and conversations—but, to me, it's really about excellent French classics. What is a more timeless bistro standard than boeuf bourguignon? Allez-y à Hayes Valley.

YIELD: about 20 servings

BRAISED BEEF

¼ CUP COOKING OIL	2 QUARTS CELERY, CHOPPED
1 (25-LB.) CHUCK FLAT TAIL (BONELESS SHORT RIBS)	1 CUP GARLIC CLOVES, PEELED
	1.5 L RED WINE
SALT AND FRESHLY GROUND BLACK PEPPER, TO TASTE	2 CUPS RUBY PORT WINE
4 QUARTS YELLOW ONIONS, CHOPPED	3 GALLONS BROWN CHICKEN STOCK
	2 BUNCHES FRESH THYME
2 QUARTS CARROTS, CHOPPED	2 BAY LEAVES

1. Preheat the oven to 350ºF/177ºC. In a large rondeau, heat the oil almost to the smoke point. Season the beef with salt and pepper. Sear each piece on all sides until it has developed a deep brown color.

continued...

2. Once properly caramelized, place the beef in 2 (6-inch) hotel pans. Drain off some of the fat and add the onions, carrots, celery, and garlic. Caramelize the vegetables over low heat, stirring often.

3. Deglaze the rondeau with the wines and reduce by half.

4. Add the stock and bring to a simmer. Skim the stock well once and pour it into the hotel pans with the ribs. Add the thyme and bay leaves, tied into a bouquet garni with twine.

5. Cover the pans with aluminum foil and place in the oven for 2¾ to 3 hours, rotating the pans at the halfway point.

6. Once cooked, remove the foil and chill the hotel pans down in an ice bath.

7. To portion the ribs, pull the meat out of the gelatinous stock. Warm the stock until liquid and strain through a fine chinois.

CARROT PUREE

4 QUARTS CARROTS, PEELED AND CUT

¼ CUP SALT, PLUS MORE TO TASTE

1 LB. COLD BUTTER, CUBED

1. In a medium pot, place the carrots and cover with cold water by 3 inches. Bring the water to a simmer and add the salt.

2. When the carrots are tender, strain and puree in a Robot-Coupe with the cold butter. Adjust the seasoning with salt as needed.

3. Once smooth, pass the puree through a tamis sieve. Keep warm.

ASSEMBLY

6 OZ. BRAISED BEEF (SEE PAGE 331)

2 QUARTS BEEF BRAISING LIQUID

1 TO 2 TABLESPOONS BUTTER

CARROT PUREE

RICE BRAN OIL OR OTHER OIL WITH A HIGH SMOKE POINT, FOR FRYING

2 OZ. VEAL SWEETBREADS, CLEANED OF MEMBRANE AND CUT INTO 1-INCH PIECES

SEMOLINA FLOUR, AS NEEDED

SALT, TO TASTE

CELERY, SHAVED INTO THIN HALF-MOONS AND CHILLED IN ICE WATER, FOR GARNISH

FRESH FINES HERBES, CHOPPED, FOR GARNISH

1 TABLESPOON OLIVE OIL, FOR GARNISH

1. In a large saucepan, warm the beef in the braising liquid until hot and tender all the way through.

2. In a sauté pan, ladle 5 to 6 oz. of the braising liquid and reduce to a glaze or until it coats the back of a metal spoon. Add the beef to the glaze and the butter, stirring it in off the heat. Continue to glaze the meat until the sauce is sticking to the protein (you can flash the pan in a hot oven or salamander to achieve this).

3. In a shallow serving bowl, spoon about ¼ cup of the warm carrot puree. Place the glazed beef on top and spoon the glaze around the carrot puree.

4. Warm the rice bran oil to 350ºF/177ºC. Toss the sweetbreads in semolina flour and fry them in the rice bran oil for about 30 seconds. Season the crispy sweetbreads with salt as soon as they come out of the fryer.

5. In a small bowl, mix the shaved celery with the fines herbes, olive oil, and salt. Garnish the dish with the sweetbreads, celery, and fines herbes.

Braised Beef Bourguignon
See page 331

PACIFIC LONGNOSE SKATE, GREEN GARLIC PUREE, AND SMOKED FISH NAGE

APHOTIC, PETER HEMSLEY

Visionary chef Peter Hemsley is a gifted culinary artist and actual artist who opened a solo restaurant in SoMa (appropriately) called Palette that deftly wove together his own art and excellent cooking in a way that we had rarely, maybe never, seen before in this city. In early 2023, Hemsley closed that concept and swiftly reopened as Aphotic, bringing that innovative eye and gifted gastronomic skill set to fish and seafood.

YIELD: 4 to 6 servings

---

10 LBS. FRESH STOCKFISH, GUTTED AND GILLED, WITH HEADS INTACT (THEY USE LOCAL ROCK COD)

3 QUARTS MIREPOIX (CARROT, ONION, CELERY, FENNEL), ROASTED

10 LBS. SMOKED STOCKFISH

5 HEADS SMOKED GARLIC

½ CUP TOMATO PASTE

1 BOTTLE WHITE WINE

SPICE KIT (SACHET OF BLACK PEPPERCORNS, CORIANDER SEEDS, AND FENNEL SEEDS)

OLIVE OIL, AS NEEDED

SHERRY VINEGAR, TO TASTE

½ CUP BEEF JUS (OPTIONAL)

8 OZ. GREEN GARLIC OR SPRING GARLIC, FINELY CHOPPED

6 TABLESPOONS BUTTER

1 CUP HEAVY CREAM, PLUS MORE AS NEEDED

3 OR 4 LEEKS (WHITE PART ONLY), JULIENNED

1 BUNCH SPRING ONIONS

6 (5-OZ.) PORTIONS SKATE WING, TRIMMED OF SKIN AND CARTILAGE

ALL-PURPOSE FLOUR, FOR DUSTING

GREEN HERB OIL, FOR GARNISH

ONION BLOSSOMS (OPTIONAL), FOR GARNISH

continued...

1. Prepare the smoked fish "nage." Nage is a technique from the French culinary codex and means to "swim," referring to the way this kind of sauce is employed, typically as a bed for something to "float" or "swim" in; it is oftentimes the consistency of a beurre blanc. Here, the roasted fish stock will "float" the roasted skate wing, and the nage will have more of a meat jus consistency when it's finished. Roast the fresh stockfish in a large pan, being careful to break up the fish evenly to get nice caramelization and coverage in the pan's shallow bottom.

2. Add the roasted mirepoix, smoked stockfish (they do theirs in a wood-fired hearth, but a smoker will do), smoked garlic, and tomato paste, deglaze with the wine, then fill the pan up to the brim with water. Add the spice sachet and simmer for about 2 hours to develop the flavors.

3. Strain the sauce through a fine sieve, and reduce until the color takes on a dark amber/brown hue and has the consistency of a very thin puree. The sauce will be further reduced upon finishing the dish with a small splash of cream, mounted with a couple of knobs of butter, and seasoned with sherry vinegar and a spoon of beef jus for consistency and a more rounded mouthfeel, if needed.

4. In a medium nonstick pan, sweat the green garlic with some oil and butter, being careful not to overheat the pan, and caramelize the garlic. Garlic, like onion, has a healthy amount of sugar in it, and colors easily. Once sweated, add the cream and reduce by half, about 15 minutes. Puree, reserving half of the cream to regulate the consistency; it should be the texture of creamy polenta when warm. Keep warm.

5. Julienne the leeks and sweat in a pan with 8 oz. of the butter over very low heat. Cover the leeks with a cartouche (parchment paper lid) and stir often to avoid coloration. Keep warm.

6. Clean the spring onions, season with salt and olive oil, and grill until the bulbs are cooked, without charring the green stems.

7. Fold a skate wing portion like a book, or a pocket fold, so that it is the size of a deck of cards. Dust the fish with flour, season with salt, and pan sear in a hot pan with grapeseed or olive oil. Allow the fish to develop a nice color on one side, basting it with hot oil on its back side. Flip the fish, add a knob of the butter and a couple of garlic cloves, and baste the fish for 2 minutes constantly, regulating the temperature of the flame, until the fish is fully cooked.

8. To plate each serving, place a small amount of wilted leeks at the center of a warm plate. To its side, add a small spoon of green garlic puree. Place the seared skate wing atop the wilted leeks. Lay a grilled spring onion carefully on the top side of the skate. Dribble a heavy spoonful of the smoked fish nage at the plate's center, and further garnish with a green herb oil (like a chive oil) and some onion blossoms, if desired.

9. For a family-style presentation, place all of the wilted leeks at the center of the platter, arrange the fish on top in a circular formation, place the grilled onions at the center top, and pool the sauce around the arrangement as a moat.

SWEETS FOR DESSERT, BREAKFAST, AND BRUNCH

CONCORD GRAPE ICE AND MEYER LEMON ICE CREAM WITH CANDIED GINGER

RICH TABLE, SARAH RICH

Just hearing the name "Rich Table" immediately catches the attention of anyone who knows much about the San Francisco dining scene. Since opening in 2012, the restaurant has been nothing short of a sensation—and deservedly so. There are the sardine chips and porcini-dusted doughnuts with raclette. There are the crisp salads and sharp pastas. Any large plate from Evan Rich and his team is well worth ordering. Everything almost always has a clever, kind of eyebrow-raising catch—maybe a texture or an herb or something. And it's always utterly delightful.

And the same goes for the desserts from Sarah Rich! So, we're certainly saving one of the very best complete, start-to-finish restaurant experiences of San Francisco for last here. It's a good reminder to always save room for dessert when dining in this fantastic food-filled city.

I love all of my "ice" desserts; they are my favorites of everything I make at Rich Table. The fresh brightness of the icy fruit means that the dessert stays light and not too overwhelming, and the creaminess of the ice cream keeps it rounded and satisfying. It's the perfect way to end a meal, in my opinion. This particular ice dessert will remind you of childhood with the sweetness of [the] Concord grape. Meyer lemon ice cream mellows it out, and the punch of spicy candied ginger gives it little bursts of excitement that will have you reaching for your next spoonful.

—Chef Sarah Rich

YIELD: 4 servings

CONCORD GRAPE ICE

2 QUARTS CONCORD GRAPES,
STEMMED AND WASHED

1 TO 2 QUARTS WATER

1 TEASPOON CITRIC ACID

½ CUP SUGAR

SALT, TO TASTE

1. Combine all the ingredients in a blender and puree.

2. Check the mixture on a Brix reader; should read 24.

3. Pass through a chinois and freeze.

continued...

MEYER LEMON ICE CREAM

ZEST OF 3 MEYER LEMONS

1 CUP FRESH MEYER LEMON JUICE, STRAINED

4 CUPS WHOLE MILK

2 CUPS HEAVY CREAM

1½ CUPS SUGAR

½ CUP CORN SYRUP

1. Place all of the ingredients in a blender and blend just to mix.

2. Strain and chill.

3. Spin in an ice cream machine until you have the desired texture and freeze until ready to serve.

ASSEMBLY

CANDIED GINGER, CUT INTO SMALL DICE

SLICED RED FLAME GRAPES

TORN FRESH SHISO LEAVES

1. Place the ice cream in a bowl, top it with the grape ice, a knob of candied ginger, 2 to 3 sliced grapes, and shiso leaves, and serve.

MEDJOOL DATE CAKE WITH VANILLA BEAN ICE CREAM AND OKINAWA COOKIE CRUMBLE

GOZU, MARC ZIMMERMAN

You might recall, from a few hundred pages ago, how I mentioned that Gozu includes Wagyu beef throughout its menu in pretty astonishing ways. Well, this is exactly what I meant . . . Get ready for quite the unique and special dessert, folks.

YIELD: About 35 cakes and 2 pints ice cream

MEDJOOL DATE CAKE

225 G MEDJOOL DATES, CHOPPED

10 G BAKING SODA

132 ML BOILING WATER

112 G BUTTER

200 G GRANULATED SUGAR

1 EGG

4 ML VANILLA EXTRACT

180 G ALL-PURPOSE FLOUR

4 G BAKING POWDER

3 G SALT

WAGYU TALLOW, FOR PREPARING THE MOLDS

LIGHT BROWN SUGAR, FOR PREPARING THE MOLDS

1. Robot-coupe the dates until the pieces are small.

2. Place the date pieces and baking soda in a bowl. Add the boiling water and let sit for 10 minutes.

3. In a bowl, cream together the butter and granulated sugar until pale yellow and fluffy. Add the egg and vanilla and beat until combined. Scrape down the side of the bowl.

continued...

4. In another bowl, sift together the flour, baking powder, and salt. Add the flour mixture to the butter mixture in two additions, beating until the batter is fluffy.

5. Add the date mixture and mix until the batter is homogeneous.

6. Preheat the oven to 350°F/177°C in a convection oven (if using a conventional oven, preheat to 375°F/190°C).

7. Melt the tallow.

8. In cylindrical silicone molds, spoon ½ tablespoon of tallow and a sprinkling of light brown sugar into each cavity. Freeze or refrigerate until the tallow solidifies.

9. Pipe 25 g of date cake batter into each cavity.

10. Bake for 20 minutes on Fan 2 until browned.

11. Let the cakes cool to room temperature.

12. Place the molds in the freezer to set the bottoms of the cakes.

13. When frozen, unmold. There should be a lace pattern created from the brown sugar caramelizing with the tallow.

VANILLA BEAN ICE CREAM

640 ML WHOLE MILK

116 ML HEAVY CREAM

2 VANILLA BEANS

70 G EGG YOLKS

138 G GRANULATED SUGAR

2.9 G ICE CREAM STABILIZER

1. In a saucepan, combine the milk and cream. Scrape the seeds from the vanilla beans into the pan. Bring the mixture to a simmer.

2. In a bowl, quickly whisk together the egg yolks, sugar, and ice cream stabilizer so the sugar does not get clumpy.

3. Ladle some of the warm milk mixture into the egg yolks to temper them. Pour all of the egg yolk mixture into the saucepan and heat to 181°F/83°C. Cool the mixture in an ice bath, then freeze in a Pacojet or batch freezer.

OKINAWA COOKIE CRUMBLE

200 G FINE OKINAWA SUGAR

200 G COLD BUTTER, CUBED

200 G ALMOND FLOUR

200 G ALL-PURPOSE FLOUR

60 G COCOA POWDER

4 G FLEUR DE SEL

WAGYU TALLOW, AS NEEDED

1. Preheat the oven to 300°F/149°C. Combine all the ingredients in a stand mixer fitted with the paddle attachment, until the mixture has a consistency that is coarse and sandy.

continued...

2. Transfer to a rimmed baking sheet and bake for 30 minutes, stirring every 5 to 10 minutes.

3. Let cool and Robocoupe, careful not to make the crumble into a paste.

4. Weigh the yield and fold in 10 percent weight melted tallow.

TALLOW CARAMEL

400 G OKINAWA SUGAR

200 ML HEAVY CREAM

8 ML PURE VANILLA EXTRACT

250 G TALLOW (USE BUTTER IF BEEF FAT IS NOT AVAILABLE)

6 G FLEUR DE SEL, OR OTHER COARSE SEAT SALT

1. Combine all of the ingredients together in a large pot and cook over medium heat, whisking continually, until the sugar has dissolved and the caramel has emulsified.

ASSEMBLY

1. Place a tablespoon of the crumble off-center on the right side of the plate. Place the warmed date cake off-center on the left side of the plate.

2. Place a large spoonful of the Tallow Caramel in the center of the plate. Scoop some ice cream onto the crumble and serve.

Q&A, MELISSA CHOU

PASTRY CHEF AND PROPRIETOR, GRAND OPENING

TF: Let's start with your exciting current project, Grand Opening bakery. Can you tell us a bit about the tarts, cakes, and baked goods you're creating for that?

MC: I'm so thrilled to be able to see Grand Opening realized. It's such a personal expression of all the experience and knowledge I've gained over my career working in restaurants in San Francisco, as well as a true representation of my personal tastes. Because I'm Chinese and the bakery is in Chinatown, there is a tendency to label it an Asian bakery, but I think of it as more reflective of the Chinese flavors and textures and sensibility I'm familiar with, coupled with all the Cal-Italian foods and produce I grew up with in San Francisco.

Having spent most of my career in fine dining, it was difficult for me to shed that sensibility in the shift to doing a bakery. So, I think of the tarts and cakes as if they are composed plated desserts, and really, for most of them, the components of each tart could be "deconstructed" onto a plate. It feels like I still get to use those restaurant skills I learned.

But! I also wanted to explore what I could do creatively with baked goods and in the more casual setting of a bakery. I grew up eating of a lot of fruit, and the Bay Area has some of the best fruit in the world, so it is important to me to use it everywhere, in as many applications as possible. Part of the influence of my Chinese roots is that I don't like desserts that are "too sweet," and textures, including soft, fluffy ones, are very important to me. So, these are the foundational ideas behind the way I like to bake.

TF: Grand Opening operates out of Mister Jiu's, where you previously were pastry chef. What was it like opening an acclaimed restaurant that quickly received a Michelin star?

MC: With the opening of Mister Jiu's, there was so much hype and press!! It was over-whelming. I'm a background person, and don't love having so much direct attention on the *potential* of something. I'm so thrilled when something I've made meets or exceeds expectation, and I can only hope that judgments are made organically. But I was thrilled that such an ambitious project as Mister Jiu's was met with so much excitement, because it really showed there was a shift in the way we could experience Chinese food in America. I'm so proud to have been a part of that project.

TF: Prior to Mister Jiu's, San Francisco diners loved your desserts at both Aziza and Mourad. What did you learn as a pastry chef at those two restaurants, and what was your vision running the dessert side at both restaurants?

MC: Aziza was my first pastry chef job, and I was in way over my head. I barely knew anything, so there was a ton of learning on the job. But, because I wasn't in a restaurant that served European food with an established fine dining pastry tradition, there was a huge opportunity to be creative and not be too concerned with a ton of gatekeeping. But I also work really well with parameters, so I found that having to create a dessert menu that could complement Moroccan food was actually incredibly helpful to my development as a chef. If I had been put into that position with no limits, it could have gone off the rails really quickly, but I took very seriously the task of using Moroccan ingredients and the palate, and it helped me to really stretch my creativity.

In a way, my time at Aziza and Mourad really helped me to be able to step into my role at Mister Jiu's. I had the similar task of creating a fine dining pastry menu for a cuisine that people did not typically have a ton of experience with, with regard to plated desserts. Mister Jiu's is much more personal for me, and I am far more familiar with Chinese ingredients than Moroccan ones, but the approach is essentially the same—tons of fruit, lots of texture, not too sweet, and be sure to complement the meal that comes before. It's a team effort.

TF: Growing up in SF, did you always want to be a pastry chef? You initially pursued a career in art, right?

MC: Growing up in a Chinese family in San Francisco means that meals are an essential part of culture and existence. We have the best produce, incredible variety, and boundless amounts of creativity here, and growing up amongst it means food culture is in my bones. I've always loved creating physical things—initially I went to college wanting to be an artist, but realized I wasn't as good at it as I wanted to be, and so I switched to studying art history. Art history is the study of culture, how different conditions of society produced particular expressions of creativity, and I love tracking these same themes in food—it's so interesting to see where food culture has come from, how it has expanded and changed.

TF: What are some of your favorite food memories in SF? Are there any restaurants or bakeries that are personal favorites? Any particular dishes that you seek out again and again?

MC: I love, love pasta and pizza. That feels really SF to me, and I think we have fantastic versions of both. Also tacos, of course. And dim sum. All the SF basics!

My mom loved taking us to eat in all kinds of places—Powell's [Place] fried chicken on Hayes, or The Rotunda at Neiman Marcus for popovers. One of the semiannual things we would do when we were young kids was walk from our house in the Sunset to The Ritz to have high tea—Mom believed in us working for our luxuries! Fantasia Bakery in Laurel Village was a wonderland as a child—they really went all out at Christmas—and they had an orange chocolate tea cake I still sometimes think about.

But I also have a lot of memories of grocery shopping with my dad—he did most of the cooking, and was very particular about where he bought things. We would go to Clement to get all the Chinese produce, and I was slightly traumatized going into the fish shops where my dad always bought fish from the tanks. Additionally, even though we lived in the Sunset, we would drive all the way out to the Marina Safeway, because he believed it was the best one, and it became pretty clear to me early on how important it was to seek out the best, rather than what was the most convenient. My dad also used to lure me to that Marina Safeway with him by promising a slice of the chocolate cake or Dutch apple pie from Just Desserts, which was there around the corner, and seemed to me the top of the tops back then. These days I don't eat a ton of sweets, but I have to say that Colonial Donuts on Lakeshore, near where I live in Oakland (and also my mom's go-to spot when she was growing up in Oakland), has fantastic doughnuts (cake, old-fashioned), and they really do it for me every time.

I also have a very formative memory of eating a prixe fixe lunch at Elisabeth Daniel, where I had my first-ever wine pairing, and it was truly a new way to experience food for me—the way food and wine could speak back and forth to each other and become enhanced in the presence of the other. The idea that food could be made with wine in mind informed, in a way, my approach to designing a dessert menu—it's a complement to the meal, and both savory and sweet courses augment each other.

TF: Finally, I remember hearing somewhere or reading in an article that you're such a big Giants fan that you would actually listen to Jon, Dave, Kruk, and Kuip while getting desserts ready during service. Is this true?!

MC: YES, I *still* listen to games when I'm working! Now that I'm working alone again, I find that it's one of the more reliably entertaining things to keep me occupied—it's a wholesome six-month-long saga! In fact, Dave Flemming and I have become friendly, and I dropped off treats to the broadcast booth during a game the other day!

EGG CUSTARD TARTS

YANK SING

And for dessert, a dim sum favorite from a longtime downtown dining stalwart, Yank Sing. The first Yank Sing location opened in 1958 and switched addresses a bit over the years, until settling into its two current homes in Rincon Center and Stevenson Street. Practically every San Francisco diner has their favorite dim sum dishes, and you can count on Yank Sing to always be one of the most consistently excellent producers of many of those dishes.

YIELD: 12 tarts

PUFF PASTRY

**6 OZ. COLD BUTTER,
CUT INTO 1-INCH CUBES**

**1½ CUPS ALL-PURPOSE FLOUR,
PLUS MORE AS NEEDED**

1 EGG

2 TABLESPOONS WATER

1. Mix the butter and ¾ cup of the flour together to form an "oil dough." Knead the dough into a ball, cover with plastic wrap, and refrigerate for 20 minutes.

2. Meanwhile, mix the egg and water into the remaining ¾ cup flour to form a "water dough." Knead the dough into a ball, cover with plastic wrap, and refrigerate for 20 minutes.

3. Flour a work surface. Roll the water dough out into a large square, about 11 x 11 inches.

4. Spread the oil dough on top of the water dough, leaving a large enough border of the water dough to be able to fold over the oil dough entirely. Fold the sides of the water dough over the oil dough.

continued...

5. Roll the entire dough out to a large square, again aiming for about 11 x 11 inches, and mark it into thirds. Fold each outer third over the center third and roll the folded rectangle out into the center, and then roll the folded rectangle out into a large square again. Repeat two more times.

6. After the third fold, roll out the dough again, and this time mark it into fourths. Fold each outer quarter into the center and then roll the rectangle out. Cover the dough in plastic wrap and place in the refrigerator for at least 20 minutes.

7. On a lightly floured work surface, roll out the dough to a ¼-inch thickness. Cut out disk shapes with a round cutter.

8. Lightly grease the inside of 12 fluted tart molds and press the pastry disks into the molds. Transfer to the refrigerator while you make the filling.

EGG CUSTARD

1 CUP WATER	¼ CUP EVAPORATED MILK
½ CUP SUGAR	½ TEASPOON VANILLA EXTRACT
4 EGGS	PINCH SALT

1. In a saucepan over medium heat, combine the water and sugar and heat until the sugar dissolves, 3 to 5 minutes. Remove the pan from the heat and cool.

2. Whisk the eggs into the cooled sugar syrup. Stir in the evaporated milk, vanilla, and salt. Strain the mixture through a fine-mesh strainer into a container with a pouring lip.

3. Preheat the oven to 350°F/177°C.

4. Fill each of the pastry-lined tart molds three-quarters of the way up with the egg custard.

5. Position the tarts evenly on a baking sheet and place in the oven. Bake until the crust is golden brown and the filling raises to a slight dome, about 45 minutes.

6. Remove from the oven and let cool for 5 to 10 minutes.

7. Carefully tap the molds to remove the tarts.

CORNMEAL PANCAKES

TRUE LAUREL, DAVID BARZELAY

'll admit that I've spent a few *early* mornings at True Laurel. I've also been much later on weekend mornings for the outstanding weekend brunch that often includes these pancakes.

YIELD: about 10 pancakes, 5 inches each

DRY INGREDIENTS

240 G ALL-PURPOSE FLOUR

80 G HEIRLOOM CORNMEAL
(PREFERABLY FROM TIERRA
VEGETABLES)

28 G SUGAR

6 G BAKING POWDER

3 G BAKING SODA

4 G KOSHER SALT

WET INGREDIENTS

2 EGGS

65 G SOUR CREAM

474 ML BUTTERMILK

40 G BUTTER, MELTED

TO FINISH

4 OZ. BUTTER

¾ TO 1 CUP MAPLE SYRUP

1. In a bowl, whisk the dry ingredients together thoroughly.

2. In a separate bowl, whisk the eggs to break them up. Whisk in the sour cream, then the buttermilk, and finally the melted butter. Keep this mixture of wet ingredients chilled until you use it.

3. When you're ready to make breakfast, just add the wet ingredients to the dry ingredients and mix until all the ingredients are moist. The batter is slightly better if it sits for 10 to 20 minutes before cooking the pancakes, but you don't have to wait if you don't want to. Use a ⅓-cup scoop to make 5-inch pancakes.

4. If your pans are nonstick or at least well seasoned, the pancakes brown more evenly if you refrain from using butter or oil for each batch. Instead, just brush the pan or griddle with a tiny bit of butter and then wipe it out before cooking the pancakes. Repeat this process every 2 or 3 batches. That will give the pancakes that perfect, even browning, like they came off a short-order griddle.

5. Even though there is already some melted butter in the recipe, definitely add a generous pat of butter on top of each pancake right after it comes out of the pan. Serve with maple syrup.

PISTACHIO YOGURT PANNA COTTA WITH WATSONVILLE STRAWBERRIES

LA FOLIE, ROLAND PASSOT

La Folie so carefully balanced the best of California produce and the splendor of classical, elegant French cuisine together during its time on Polk Street. This intricate dessert is a terrific representation of that delicious mix.

YIELD: 6 servings

PANNA COTTA

2 CUPS PLAIN ORGANIC GREEK YOGURT

1½ TEASPOONS BRONZE GELATIN

2 TABLESPOONS PISTACHIO OIL OR ¼ CUP PISTACHIO PASTE

¾ CUP HEAVY CREAM

⅓ CUP PLUS 1 TABLESPOON GRANULATED SUGAR

2 BASKETS STRAWBERRIES, HULLED AND SLICED

FRESHLY GROUND BLACK PEPPER, TO TASTE

GRATED ZEST OF 1 LEMON, TO TASTE

1. Place the yogurt in a medium bowl.

2. Place the gelatin in ice water to make it bloom.

3. In a saucepan, combine the pistachio oil, cream, and ⅓ cup of the granulated sugar and bring to a simmer, mixing well. Add the bloomed gelatin.

4. Strain through a fine strainer or chinois and add to the yogurt. Whisk together until thoroughly blended. Pour the panna cotta into 4 soup bowls. Refrigerate for at least 4 hours and up to 24 hours.

5. In a separate bowl, season the strawberries with the remaining 1 tablespoon granulated sugar, pepper, and lemon zest to taste.

PISTACHIO STREUSEL

4 OZ. BUTTER

½ CUP CONFECTIONERS' SUGAR

½ CUP CHOPPED PISTACHIOS

½ CUP ALL-PURPOSE FLOUR

1. Combine all the ingredients until well incorporated, using an electric mixer.

2. Freeze on a rimmed baking sheet.

3. Bake at 375°F/190°C for 15 minutes.

STRAWBERRY FOAM

1½ CUPS STRAWBERRY PUREE

¾ TEASPOON XANTHAN GUM

1½ TEASPOONS
VERSAWHIP "GELATIN"

¼ CUP GRANULATED SUGAR

1. Chill the puree.

2. Add the rest of the ingredients and whip until you get 5 times the volume.

ASSEMBLY

1. When the panna cotta is chilled, top with the strawberries, a sprinkling of the streusel, and four dollops of the Strawberry Foam.

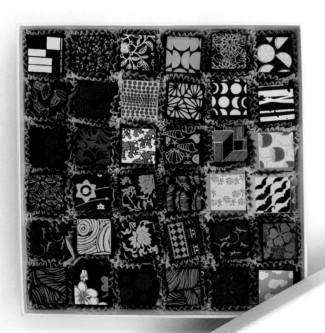

KOKAK
CHOCOLATES

Q&A, CAROL GANCIA

FOUNDER/HEAD CHOCOLATIER, KOKAK CHOCOLATES

TF: Kokak Chocolates opened in June 2020. It's remarkable to think about. And yet here we are, several years after those early pandemic days, and Kokak Chocolates is not only still here but also a citywide favorite for chocolates! The path to starting Kokak for you was hardly "the typical pastry chef learns in school then goes to open a shop" route. Can you tell us about your professional journey to opening?

CG: As a self-taught chocolatier, it was exciting and scary at the same time to launch a new career with Kokak Chocolates. I planned to open Kokak Chocolates before March 2020, but right as we were in the final stages of inspections, all city appointments were canceled when the pandemic started.

The idea of starting a chocolate shop was born from years of searching for work that reflects the next chapter in my life. I started a business as a video producer 20 years ago and built a career in broadcast journalism, television production, and promotional video production. I worked as a journalist for an investigative news program in the Philippines and a TV documentary series. Eight years after running my own video production company, I moved to San Francisco. I joined two television shows at KQED, a PBS station in San Francisco, producing for *Check, Please! Bay Area*, a restaurant television show, and *Jacques Pépin: More Fast Food My Way*, a French cooking show.

After 15 years in video production, I knew I was ready for another challenge. I wanted to feel scared and clueless again. I decided to learn something new. Chocolate has always been a great love within my family. I took some courses and started selling at chocolate salons.

I see the path to opening Kokak Chocolates and all of our obstacles as a blessing in a way. Twenty nineteen was a hard year for me. I signed the contract for the shop in June 2019. My mom passed away less than a month later. Two weeks after she passed on, I was diagnosed with cancer. Throughout the construction of the shop, I went through my healing journey from operation to chemo to radiation. Luckily, it was stage 1 and, with a big change in my daily nutrition, I was able to bounce back in no time. The last day of my radiation was the end of April 2020.

It was pretty challenging to supervise construction, but I was grateful for the distraction and sense of purpose. In a way, it was a blessing that the lockdown gave me more time to complete my treatments and recover.

TF: What has it been like having the shop in such an important, largely residential neighborhood like the Castro?

CG: Starting a chocolate business in San Francisco is both fun and a challenge, and the Castro neighborhood was the ideal location to open. Operating in a residential neighborhood keeps me on my toes. I am an experienced business owner with a 20-year track record, but businesses can be as different as night and day. The business model for my video production agency speaks a different language from how a chocolate shop ticks. After 17 years of running my video production business, I found myself scared and clueless again.

Understanding whom you are selling to, where they are, and how to connect with them [is] often [one] of the challenges of a starting business owner. This is on top of figuring out recipes, labor, ingredients, packaging, rent, equipment, and social media. I found myself overwhelmed a lot during the first couple of years, but one thing that has been a constant is the Castro neighbors who have supported me through each season of the brand's life.

It's during challenging times when you will be thankful that you are doing what you love. Kokak Chocolates brings me so much joy that I almost don't mind the hardships.

TF: How does your Filipino heritage inspire some of your creations?

CG: Kokak means ribbit in Filipino. I chose a name that sounds like an exclamation point. I want people to be excited about the brand and to start a conversation with me about my Filipino culture and heritage. As immigrants, we are taught to blend in. I want to be seen and heard as a Filipino immigrant, an LGBTQ community member, and a woman. My business is so close to my heart, it has to reflect who I am with pride.

Birthing new flavors comes from inspired life experiences in the Philippine islands and California. It's about climbing up a tree to get a guava fruit, enjoying fresh mangoes on weekends with family, and driving with friends to Laguna, a province south of Manila, Philippines, to enjoy a homemade coconut pie.

One of my favorite flavors that honors my heritage is our kalamansi chocolate truffle, shelled in 70 percent single-origin dark chocolate and filled with kalamansi chocolate ganache. Kalamansi is a Philippine citrus fruit with a flavor profile between an orange and a lime. Chocolate is a memory, and kalamansi is about my mom making kalamansi juice for me—hot to soothe me when I'm not feeling well, and cold to keep me cool during the summer.

TF: Why are single-origin chocolates, like the ones at Kokak, so delicious compared to other chocolates, yet we often don't hear much about them in the food media circuit?

CG: While training, I fell in love with using single-origin chocolates called Nacional, a rare cacao variety sourced in Ecuador and protected by the Heirloom Cacao Preservation Fund. Naciónal is a wonderful discovery in flavor and history. This fair-trade variety is farmed sustainably and known to have a complex overall balance with an intense, long, pleasant, and unique flavor. It traces its genetic lineage to the earliest known cacao trees domesticated by humanity 5,300 years ago.

There is so much value in being able to trace where your food comes from and understand what is in it. It's all about accountability. Since there is transparency in the source of our cacao, there is also accountability in the production process and the flavor. Farmers and bean-to-bar makers care that their product is something they can be proud of. As a chocolatier, I care that what I serve customers is "umami" food that comes from a good and delicious source.

We make up our own rules in many of the decisions we make at the shop. This is an expensive chocolate to source, but it has the best flavor. We are a small business that needs to make a profit, but we balance our decision with the commitment to giving customers the best chocolate experience they can have.

TF: Speaking of the food media circuit from earlier, what was it like working for shows like *Check, Please! Bay Area* and Jacques Pépin's programs?

CG: I love sharing stories about things that matter to me. Food is such a big part of our lives as a community and as a family. It was a rare and distinct honor to hear the stories of chefs from all over the San Francisco Bay Area. It gave me such a thrill to watch them work and see how customers were enjoying their food. It's sweat and tears, as I'm learning now, and a lot of passion for what you do.

It was exciting to work with Jacques Pépin and to meet all the back-kitchen chefs working behind the scenes to set up the food for every step of the cooking show's filming. Some of them have become lifelong friends. I'm grateful for the gift of learning how to make French food. It opened my world, and now I'm hooked!

TF: Where else do you enjoy desserts...and savory food...in the city?

CG: I love chocolate...chocolate cake, tiramisu, brownies, bars, and truffles. Victoria Pastry in SF's North Beach has a good tiramisu. Occasionally, I try well-made desserts like the mango sticky rice that has a special umph at Na Ya Dessert Cafe in Hayes Valley. I also buy fresh coconut pie from a friend I met at a pastry class a long time ago.

I love small mom-and-pop restaurants in the city. One of my favorites is this small French-inspired Japanese bistro in the SF Potrero-Mission neighborhood called Bon, Nene. My favorite dish there is [the] mentaiko spaghetti.

I also really enjoy the prawn kimchi quesadilla at Saucy Asian in the SF Castro neighborhood.

Overall, I enjoy savory umami food that makes you think and fantasize about what heavenly ingredients were selected by the chef to create such an impressive orchestra of flavors.

RYE DOUGHNUTS

BIRCH & RYE, ANYA EL-WATTAR

I'm definitely not going to be the one to tell you that you *shouldn't* add a little caviar to your doughnuts! Please feel free to splurge with some caviar accompanying these dessert doughnuts, which is an option at Noe Valley's excellent modern Russian restaurant from Anya El-Wattar, who grew up in Moscow and moved to San Francisco decades ago. With or without caviar, the combination of caramel and soft doughnuts is absolutely irresistible.

A quick note on the current war and being a modern Russian Californian cuisine restaurant: Birch & Rye opened in early 2022, and the restaurant has been very active and eloquent in its support for Ukraine and denouncing the terrible war, including raising over $100,000 for the World Central Kitchen to help with that organization's efforts in Ukraine.

YIELD: 12 doughnuts

¾ CUP WHOLE MILK

1¼ TEASPOONS ACTIVE DRY YEAST

2 TABLESPOONS GRANULATED SUGAR, PLUS ½ CUP FOR TOSSING FINISHED DOUGHNUTS

1½ CUPS ALL-PURPOSE FLOUR

1 CUP WHITE RYE FLOUR

1 EGG

2 OZ. BUTTER, MELTED

½ TEASPOON SALT

RICE BRAN OIL, FOR FRYING

CARAMEL SAUCE, FOR SERVING

1. In a small bowl, heat the milk to no higher than 90°F/32°C. Add the yeast and 2 tablespoons of the sugar. Let sit for 15 minutes.

2. Place both flours in the bowl of a stand mixer. Add the milk mixture, then the egg, butter, and salt. Start the mixer at low speed and, as the ingredients blend, increase the speed slowly to medium. Mix on medium speed for 10 minutes.

3. Remove the dough to a clean work surface and knead it by hand for 3 minutes.

4. Place the dough in an oiled bowl, cover with a clean kitchen towel, and let rest and rise for 1 hour.

5. Portion the dough into 30 g pieces. Roll into balls and gently flatten on an oiled sheet pan.

6. Punch out a hole in the center of each doughnut, cover with plastic wrap, and let rest for another 30 minutes.

7. Heat rice bran oil to 350°F/177°C. Drop in the doughnuts and rotate until golden brown, 1 to 2 minutes total per doughnut. Drain on a paper towel–lined platter.

8. To serve, warm the doughnuts in the oven, then toss in the remaining ½ cup sugar, gently tapping off any excess. Serve with caramel sauce.

APPENDIX

THE "BEST OF" LISTS

Rule number one in food writing is that nothing can truly be "the best." Restaurants change all the time. That being said, there's definitely space for places that are consistently excellent for specific reasons. But, "best of" sounds better than "consistently excellent" for some listicles, so here are the best of the best in SF (and our one and only shout-out to the Bay Area!). Please also keep in mind that all of these are in no particular order, and take everything with a grain of fleur de sel salt, since each category has so many deserving restaurants.

Best Marin County Restaurants

Poggio

Sushi Ran

Buckeye Roadhouse

Village Sake

Picco

The Marshall Store

Copita

Fish

Hog Island Oyster Co. Marshall's Farm/Tony's

Nick's Cove

Cafe Reyes

The Bungalow Kitchen

Lou's Takeaway

Sol Food

Guesthouse

Best Sonoma County Restaurants

Barndiva

Lo + Behold

Willi's Wine Bar

Valley Bar & Bottle

SingleThread

Bravas Bar de Tapas

Diavola

Table Culture Provisions

PizzaLeah

Valette

El Molino Central

Cyrus

Animo

Glen Ellen Star

Little Saint

Best Napa County Restaurants

The French Laundry (yes, it's really good; don't let anyone try to convince you otherwise)

Cook St. Helena

Goose & Gander

Compline

TORC

Mustards Grill

PRESS

The Charter Oak

Bistro Don Giovanni

Ciccio

Angèle

Southside

Auro

Acacia House

Ad Hoc/Addendum

Best East Bay Restaurants

Commis

Chez Panisse (both café and restaurant)

Juanita & Maude

The Cheese Board Collective

Fava

Rose Pizzeria

Tacos Oscar

Raymond's Pizzeria

RAMEN SHOP

Pomella

Bombera

Jo's Modern Thai

DAYTRIP

Snail Bar

Lion Dance Cafe

Best Peninsula Restaurants

Protégé

The Village Pub

Camper

Ethel's Fancy

GINTEI

Sam's Chowder House

Dad's Luncheonette

Vesta

BIRD DOG

Sushi Sam's Edomata

Bevri

Sundance The Steakhouse

Chef Chu's

Vina Enoteca

Breakwater Barbecue

Best South Bay Restaurants

ADEGA

The Bywater

Slice of Homage Pizza

Tasting House

Plumed Horse

Orenchi Ramen

Jubba Somali Restaurant

Zareen's (the original is in Mountain View, which is considered the South Bay by Peninsula native me via the area code geography rule)

Le Papillon

Élyse

LeYou Ethopian

Oak & Rye

Sidecar Modern Tavern

Jang Su Jang

Pho Ga Nha

For San Francisco, I've split the city into six geographic quadrants...some will be dense, and others will not be. It's all subjective, since it's never easy to figure out the best form of organization for this city.

Best NE SF Restaurants

(Russian Hill, Nob Hill, Fisherman's Wharf, Ghirardelli Square, Downtown, Financial District, Lower Nob Hill, Tenderloin, Union Square, SoMa, Embarcadero, Ferry Building—yes, this a gigantic, dense area with tons of great restaurants, so I need to be extra pick . . . and added three extra spaces and combined two related but quite different concepts to moderately help out. I get to determine the rules for this list this time.)

Abacá

Boulevard/Prospect

Liholiho Yacht Club

Sons & Daughters

BIX

Nisei

Saison/Angler

Benu

Gozu

Bodega SF

Tony's Pizza Napoletana

Acquerello

Outta Sight Pizza

Californios

Del Popolo

Swan Oyster Depot

Hilda and Jesse

Eat around the Ferry Building

Best SE SF Restaurants

(Mission, Bernal Heights, Dogpatch, Bayview, Potrero Hill, Mission Bay, Portola)

Lazy Bear

Flour + Water

Delfina

Ungrafted

True Laurel

Piccino

Cellarmaker House of Pizza

The Morris

Rintaro

Tartine Bakery/Tartine Manufactory

Foreign Cinema

Reem's California Mission

Loló

Heirloom Café

Best South-Central SF Restaurants

(Noe Valley, Excelsior, Crocker-Amazon, Glen Park, Balboa Park, Castro, Duboce Park, Upper Haight, Lower Haight, Cole Valley)

Frances

Otra

La Ciccia

Birch & Rye

Mr. Digby's

Saru Sushi

Beit Rima

Gialina

L'Ardoise Bistro

Gentilly

Anchor Oyster Bar

Uma Casa

Pork Store Café

Sandy's

Best North-Central SF Restaurants

(Laurel Heights, Presidio Heights, Marina, Cow Hollow, Japantown, Pacific Heights, Lower Pac Heights, Fillmore, Anza Vista, NoPa/Divisadero, Hayes Valley)

Nopa

Daeho Kalbijjim & Beef Soup

The Anchovy Bar

Sorrel

The Progress

Rich Table

Anomaly

Merchant Roots

State Bird Provisions

SPQR

Robin

A16

Atelier Crenn-Bar Crenn

Spruce

Best NW SF Restaurants

(Presidio, Richmond)

Presidio Social Club

Fiorella (multiple locations)

Aziza

Pearl 6101

Pizzetta 211

Violet's

Dragon Beaux

Burma Superstar

Kitchen Istanbul

Lily

Dalida

Arsicault Bakery

Breadbelly

Mandalay

Noodle in a Haystack

Han Il Kwan

Best SW SF Restaurants

(Sunset, Parkside, Lake Merced, West Portal, Ingleside)

San Tung

Toyose

DamnFine

Hook Fish Co.

Old Mandarin Islamic

Thanh Long

Beep's Burgers

Um.Ma

Palm City

Outerlands

Terra Cotta Warrior

House of Pancakes

Devil's Teeth Baking Company

Gold Mirror

Yo También Cantina

Best Cocktail Bars for Food

Trick Dog

ABV

True Laurel

The Treasury

Heartwood

Bar Iris

Violet's

The Snug

The Beehive

Liliana

Bar Agricole

Macondray

Moongate Lounge

Comstock Saloon

La Mar Bar

Best Wine Bars for Food or Snacks

Ungrafted
20 Spot
High Treason
Palm City
Buddy

GluGlu
Bodega SF
Roaming Goat
Union Larder
Key Klub

Cantina Los Mayas
Linden & Laguna
El Chato
DECANTsf

Best Beer Bars/Breweries for Food

Fort Point Valencia
The Crafty Fox Ale House
The Monk's Kettle

Zeitgeist
Lost Marbles Brewpub
Willkommen

The Willows
Radhaus
The Sycamore

Best Food...with a View!

Waterbar/EPIC Steak
Greens
La Mar
Boulevard
Red's Java House
Hi-Dive

Angler
The Slanted Door and almost anything, really, in the Ferry Building
Coqueta
Scoma's

Cavaña
KAIYŌ Rooftop
Charmaine's
The Ramp
Mission Rock Resort

Best Cafés for Food and Coffee

Café Réveille
Verve Coffee Roasters
SPRO
Poesia Café

Mattina
Le Marais Bakery
Juniper
Scullery

Jane on Larkin
Chalos
Kantine

Best Bakeries/Pastry Shops

Tartine Bakery

The Mill

Arsicault Bakery

Maison Nico

b. Patisserie

Devil's Teeth Baking Company

Maison Danel

Black Jet Baking Co.

Neighbor Bakehouse

Breadbelly

Loquat

Hahdough

Craftsman and Wolves

La Victoria

Kahnfections

Best Proper Brunch/Leisurely Breakfast

Merkado

Fable

Kantine

Causwells

Plow

Hilda and Jesse

Brenda's French Soul Food

Outerlands

Kitchen Story

Foreign Cinema

Presidio Social Club

Wooden Spoon

Zazie

Mama's on Washington Square

Rose's Café

Best for Good Food and Eye-Catching Decor

BIX

Mourad

True Laurel

Angler

Boulevard

Fiorella

Foreign Cinema

House of Prime Rib

Copra

Villon

Eight Tables by George Chen

Acquerello

Spruce

Californios

Akikos

Best Italian and Cal-Italian Restaurants (non-pizza-centric)

Delfina

Acquerello

Flour + Water

Piccino

Itria

Altovino

Trattoria Contadina

SPQR

La Ciccia

54 Mint

Perbacco

Sorella

Sociale

Seven Hills

Che Fico

Best for That Hard-to-Describe, Signature Californian–New American, Seasonal Farm-to-Table Cuisine

Foreign Cinema

Heirloom Café

Boulevard

Prospect

Octavia

Frances

Rich Table

State Bird Provisions

Pearl 6101

The Progress

The Anchovy Bar

Zuni Café

Nopa

The Morris

Lazy Bear

TRIOS OF CUISINE AND DISH RECOMMENDATIONS

Empanadas

Chalos

El Porteño

Chao Pescao

Cioppino

Scoma's

Sotto Mare

Anchor Oyster Bar

Pupusas

Balompié Café #1

Panchita's Pupuseria & Restaurant

D'Maize

Bánh Mì

Saigon Sandwich

Chuck's Takeaway

Banh Mi Viet

Vietnamese (classic)

Mộng Thu Cafe

Thanh Long

Vietnamese (contemporary)

Lily

The Slanted Door

Bodega SF

Ramen

Mensho Tokyo

Marufuku Ramen

Ramenwell

Classic Sandwiches

Molinari Delicatessen

Le Beau Market

Arguello Market

NEW-WAVE Sandwiches

Turner's Kitchen

Lucinda's Deli & More

Deli Board

Specialty Sandwiches

Palm City

Sandy's

La Torta Gorda

Diners/Comfort Food

Orphan Andy's

Blue Plate

Art's Cafe

Bagels

The Laundromat

Schlok's

Dago Bagel

Classic-ish New York–California Pizza

Tommaso's

Outta Sight Pizza

Tony's Pizza Napoletana (various styles)

Neapolitan Pizza

Del Popolo

Flour + Water

Pizzetta 211

Detroit/Square Pizza

Cellarmaker House of Pizza

Square Pie Guys

Golden Boy Pizza

Classic Burgers

Beep's Burgers

WesBurger 'N' More

Roam Artisan Burgers

Upscale Burgers

Wayfare Tavern

Nopa

Zuni Café

Steak House/Steak-Centric

Harris'

House of Prime Rib

Niku Steakhouse

French Bistro/ Brasserie

Routier

La Société

Absinthe Brasserie & Bar

Ice Cream

Bi-Rite Creamery

Mitchell's Ice Cream

Garden Creamery

Doughnuts (not counting beignets)

Dynamo Donut + Coffee

Bob's Donut and Pastries

Johnny Doughnuts

Burritos

Taqueria El Farolito

La Taqueria

Taqueria Cancun

Tacos

La Gallinita Meat Market

El Gallo Giro

La Palma Mexicatessen

Thai

Kin Khao & Nari

Prik Horn

Kin Khao

Lers Ros

Spanish Tapas

Bellota

El Chato

Coqueta

Sushi (omakase high-end)

Omakase

Ju-Ni

Robin

Sushi (more casual)

Saru Sushi Bar

Ebisu

Wako

Izakaya

Rintaro

Izakaya Sozai

PABU Izakaya

Japanese or Japanese-Inspired Sweets/Baked Goods

Yasukochi's Sweet Stop

Uji Time Dessert

Jina Bakes

Filipino

Abacá

Señor Sisig

Pampanguena Cuisine

Korean BBQ

Um.Ma

San Ho Won

Brothers Restaurant

Korean Non-BBQ

Suragan

Daeho Kalbijjim & Beef Soup

Bansang

Food Truck Places

Off the Grid gatherings

SPARK Social/Parklab

District Six

Burmese

Burma Superstar/Burma Love/B Star

Yamo

Mandalay

Poke

Hook Fish Co.

Liholiho Yacht Club

Pa'ina

Turkish

Kitchen Istanbul

Lokma

Taksim

Greek

Estiatorio Ornos

Kokkari

Souvla

BBQ

4505 Burgers & BBQ

Memphis Minnie's BBQ Joint

International Smoke

Plant-Based

Wildseed

Nourish Cafe

Shizen

Dim Sum—Sit-Down

Yank Sing

Dragon Beaux

Hong Kong Lounge

Dim Sum—Take-Out

Good Mong Kok Bakery

Good Luck Dim Sum

Wing Lee Bakery

Indian—More Classic

Pakwan Restaurant

Keeva Indian Kitchen

Roti Indian Bistro

Indian—More Contemporary

Copra

ROOH

Besharam

Brazilian

Cafe de Casa

Sunstream Coffee

Noeteca Wine Bar (for feijoada)

Peruvian/Nikkei

KAIYŌ/ KAIYŌ Rooftop

La Mar/ La Mar Bar

Limón

Fried Chicken

Wayfare Tavern

Nopa

The Front Porch

Fried Chicken (sandwich)

The Bird

Birdbox

Wings

Hot Sauce and Panko to Go

San Tung

Prubechu

Sports Bar with Actually Good Food

Teeth

Foghorn Taproom

The Kezar Pub

Breakfast Sandwich

Devil's Teeth Baking Company

Bandit

Newkirk's

Soul Food

Hard Knox Cafe

Old Skool Cafe

Front Door Cafe

New Orleans

Brenda's French Soul Food

Boug Cali

Gentilly

Great Food with Great Music

BIX

Uccello Lounge

Rite Spot Cafe

Great Restaurant with a Great Cause

Old Skool Cafe

Delancey Street Restaurant

ADDITIONAL SPECIFIC RECOMMENDATIONS

Ukrainian

LELEKA

German

Suppenküche

Radhaus

Portuguese

Uma Casa

Mexican Regions/ Dishes

Contemporary: Loló; Otra

Contemporary (tasting menu): Californios

Oaxacan: Donaji

Yucatan: Poc-Chuc

Tortas: La Torta Gorda; Tahona Mercado

Chinese Regions/ Specialties

Sichuan: Z&Y

Sichuan and Mandarin: Chili House SF

Sichuan noodles: Chong Qing Xiao Mian

Xi'An: Terra Cotta Warrior

Dumplings-centric: Dumpling Home; Yuanbao Jiaozi

Cantonese: R&G Lounge; Capital

Contemporary: Mister Jiu's; Fang

Upscale tasting menu: Eight Tables by George Chen

Wide variety of regions/ specialties: China Live; Begoni Bistro; House of Nanking

Hunan: Henry's Hunan

Rolled savory pancakes: House of Pancakes

Moroccan

Mourad

Aziza; Berber

Khamsa

Persian

Lavash

Komaaj

Middle Eastern

Abu Salim Middle Eastern Grill

Beit Rima

Hummus Bodega

Old Jerusalem

Reem's California Mission and Ferry Building

Sababa

Afghan

Helmand Palace

Uzbek

Halal Dastarkhan

Sri Lankan

1601 Bar & Kitchen

Laotian

Lao Table

Hainan Chicken Rice

Gai Chicken & Rice

Malaysian

Azalina's

Damansara

Jamaican

Peaches Patties

Guamanian

Prubechu

Swiss

Matterhorn Restaurant and Bakery

Chicago/Deep-Dish Pizza

Capo's

Little Star Pizza

Russian—Traditional

Cinderella Russian Bakery & Café

Russian— Contemporary

Birch & Rye

~~~~~~~~~~

GLOSSARY OF KEY HISTORIC NAMES

Here's a handy reference sheet that discusses some restaurants and chefs from the past (both distant and recent) who are either not mentioned or barely mentioned in this book, yet are absolutely critical to know about when looking back at the grand journey of San Francisco's dining history.

Cecilia Chiang

One of the giants of the San Francisco world, Chiang lived to be 100 years old and was a beloved, enormous presence in San Francisco's restaurant community for decades (including into her nineties), until her death in 2020. Her restaurant, The Mandarin (first opened in Russian Hill in 1961; then it moved to Ghirardelli Square), is often credited with introducing San Francisco diners to the true cuisines of different regions of China and what the delicious possibilities of refined Chinese cooking were like—not just the typical Americanized Chinese that San Francisco diners expected. Chiang had so many peers and meant so much to an endless number of people in this city, so I asked one of them, George Chen (owner of Eight Tables by George Chen and China Live), to say something about Cecilia for us: "Known her for nearly 50 years when she first visited my parents' house for mahjong...She was a pioneer woman, especially being Asian back in the day in the rough-and-tumble restaurant world. Tough and outspoken as [could] be...

but her opinions [were] pointed and based on her honest beliefs. I learned a lot from her in my formative years working for her at The Mandarin."

Herb Caen

The longtime *San Francisco Chronicle* columnist was truly the voice of the city's beating heart for much of the twentieth century. He loved his martinis, he loved great restaurants, and he loved San Francisco. Even today, San Franciscans refer to restaurants as a "Herb Caen restaurant," whether it's a classic that he would've dined at in the 1960s and written poetic, savvy prose about, or if it's a restaurant today that truly captures the city's spirit of convivial fun. There has never been a journalist as cherished in the city as Caen, and there probably never will be.

Jeremiah Tower

Did Chez Panisse become arguably the most important restaurant in American culinary history because of Alice Waters, or this incredibly talented chef? Many books and articles have been written about this debate, and the general consensus seems to be they both deserve credit. However, there's no debate needed in terms of how Tower's own SF restaurant, Stars, helped Chez Panisse's California cuisine/farm-to-table influence further grow in the Bay Area in the 1980s and 1990s. The restaurant, located on Redwood Alley near City Hall, was the rare party/see-and-be-seen/outstanding culinary destination combination in this usually somewhat low-key city. By all accounts, Stars could be considered the most pivotal restaurant in San Francisco history, bridging the old days into the modern ones in terms of cuisine and atmosphere. If we could time travel, I would love to go back to 1987 and dine there.

Trou Normand

San Francisco didn't realize how much it loved charcuterie until this SoMa restaurant arrived. The house-made pâtés, charcuterie, and salumi were downright epic—and there were *a lot* of them. Sadly, all the charcuterie closed in 2020, and its amazing space in the historic 140 New Montgomery building still sits empty. No other restaurant in SF has come close to replicating the cured meat program here.

Rubicon

Sure, wine and food go together like San Francisco and fog, but few, if any, restaurants in the city seamlessly paired the two quite like Rubicon. It was one of SF's most prominent downtown restaurants in the late 1990s and 2000s and showcased many great chefs, including Traci Des Jardins, Stuart Brioza, Nicole Krasinski, Dennis Leary, and several other notable names. However, it was equally well-known for its wine program from celebrated sommelier Larry Stone and its rare-in-SF A-list power owners: Drew Nieporent (one of NYC's most well-known restaurateurs), Robin Williams, Robert De Niro, and Francis Ford Coppola.

AQ

You know all about changing the menu with the seasons. But how about the entire decor? That's what this restaurant from Chef Mark Liberman and restaurateur Matt Semmelhack did. Unfortunately, it closed in 2017 (the location is now Birdsong), but it had a profound impact on SF diners not just tasting but also seeing the "seasonal" in seasonal cooking.

Cliff House

There are view restaurants, and then there was the Cliff House. It originally opened near Lands End (by Ocean Beach at the edge of the Outer Richmond) in 1863 and then finally met its demise because of all the classic, infuriating bureaucracy-real estate-pandemic-business-operating San Francisco things. Cliff House recently was purchased by the Hi Neighbor Group, so there will be several concepts from them in that vast, historic space in upcoming months or years.

Chris Cosentino

Cosentino is best known for serving all kinds of offal parts and just about any kind of meaty-meat at his now-closed restaurants Incanto (Cole Valley) and Cockscomb (SoMa), along with winning on the TV show *Top Chef Masters*. And, that's all a little too bad, because Cosentino is just an overall excellent chef, and (as writer Virginia Miller mentions in this book) Incanto was arguably the greatest casual-sophisticated Italian restaurant in town (of its many, many peers) during its dozen-year run that ended in 2014.

Elizabeth Falkner

Though she's a major personality on TV shows these days and has left the San Francisco restaurant scene, the SF-born Falkner had an enormous influence on the city's dessert scene when she opened Citizen Cake in 1997. Before then, she cooked at some of the city's most notable fine dining restaurants, including Elka, Rubicon, and Masa's. She's one of the few chefs who has truly succeeded at bridging the pastry chef–savory chef gap, both opening Citizen Cake and a modern Californian restaurant called Orson.

Daniel Patterson

Patterson recently left the Bay Area dining scene for Los Angeles, but certainly had quite a long run of highly regarded, even trendsetting restaurants while in town. His style of cooking tended to be on the edgier, more modern side of the Californian French cuisine spectrum, which was best experienced at his Coi and Elisabeth Daniel restaurants. Those two made him the rare chef to be at the very top of the fine dining world in San Francisco at two different places in two different decades.

METRIC CONVERSIONS

US Measurement	Approximate Metric Liquid Measurement	Approximate Metric Dry Measurement
1 teaspoon	5 ml	5 g
1 tablespoon or ½ ounce	15 ml	14 g
1 ounce or ⅛ cup	30 ml	29 g
¼ cup or 2 ounces	60 ml	57 g
⅓ cup	80 ml	76 g
½ cup or 4 ounces	120 ml	113 g
⅔ cup	160 ml	151 g
¾ cup or 6 ounces	180 ml	170 g
1 cup or 8 ounces or ½ pint	240 ml	227 g
1½ cups or 12 ounces	350 ml	340 g
2 cups or 1 pint or 16 ounces	475 ml	454 g
3 cups or 1½ pints	700 ml	680 g
4 cups or 2 pints or 1 quart	950 ml	908 g

ABOUT THE AUTHOR

Trevor Felch is a San Francisco-based food, drinks, and travel writer. He grew up on the Peninsula and has called the Bay Area "home" for his entire life, except for a few work or study periods in locales like Ohio, Southern California, and Paris. For a period of the 2010s, he was the Bay Area Editor for *Zagat*, covering the local eats and drinks scene during what many consider the region's modern "golden period" for noteworthy restaurants and bars openings. Today, he's one of the contributors to Fodor's San Francisco guide and writes a monthly wine column for the *Nob Hill Gazette*. Throughout his career, he's covered a wide variety of topics for many different publications including the *San Francisco Chronicle*, *SF Weekly*, *Palo Alto Weekly*, *Serious Eats*, *Thrillist*, *SF GATE*, *Modern Luxury Silicon Valley*, and more. He's an avid swimmer and runner, and always enjoys an afternoon at Oracle Park watching the Giants (or rooting for his other favorite team, the Boston Red Sox, from afar). When he's home by the bay or traveling, he always enjoys exploring with his girlfriend Meg and her dog, Deja.

IMAGE CREDITS

Page 36, Joyce Goldstein; Page 47, Adahlia Cole; Page 50, MINA Group; Pages 44–45, 54, 55, 59, 144–145, 194–195, and 346, Joseph Weaver; Page 60, Brianna Danner; Page 64, Jason Perry; Page 67, Daniel Stumpf; Pages 75 and 109, Krescent Carasso; Page 76, Timofei Osipenko; Pages 83 and 254–255, Ed Anderson; Pages 87 and 337, bread & Butter; Page 89, Anthony Parks and Emilio Salehi, Equal Parts Media; Page 90, Umberto Gibin; Pages 95 and 127, Bonjwing Lee; Pages 98–99, Patricia Chang; Pages 110–111 and 130, Grace Sager; Page 112, Remy Anthes; Page 119, Christine Gatti; Page 139, Tara Rudolph; Page 140, Alanna Hale; Page 151, Wes Rowe; Page 152, Lauren Saira; Page 157, Suemee Osuka; Page 158, Cassava; Page 166, Patrick Michael Chin; Page 177 and 180, Lazy Bear; Page 184, Alina Tyulyu; Page 188, Kelly Puleio; Page 190, Killian Page; page 197, Mariah Tiffany; Pages 200–201 and 313 Melissa de Mata; Page 203, Joanie Simon; Pages 218, 227, and 229, Isabel Baer; Page 220, Pete Sittnick; Page 224, China Live; Page 230, Neetu Laddha Photography; Page 234–235, Kassie Borreson; Page 237, Jordan Wise; Page 239, Jordan Wise; Page 244, Chad Robertson; Page 246, Michael Sugrue; Page 251, Chloe Jackman Studios; Page 258, Andrea Bartley; Page 261, Boris Nemchenok; Page 265, Tony Gemignani; Page 270, Adriano Paganini; Page 274, Alessandro DeSogos; Pages 277 and 278, Albert Law; Page 284, Cafe Zoetrope; Page 285, Gianluca Legrottaglie; Pages 288–289 and 291, Greens; Page 301, Gamma Nine; Page 303, Eric Wolfinger; Page 304, Star Chefs; Page 315, Allison Webber; Page 319, Hardy Wilson; Page 324, Radhaus; Pages 334–335, DeeDee Brown; Pages 340–341, 360, and 361, Kokak Chocolates; Page 343, Kassie Borreson; Page 354, Allie Tong; Page 357, True Laurel; Page 367, Mark Rywelski. All other photos used under official license from Shutterstock.com. Back cover photo by Gordon Mak on Unsplash.

INDEX

– ABOUT CIDER MILL PRESS BOOK PUBLISHERS –

Good ideas ripen with time. From seed to harvest, Cider Mill Press
brings fine reading, information, and entertainment together between
the covers of its creatively crafted books. Our Cider Mill bears fruit
twice a year, publishing a new crop of titles each spring and fall.

"Where Good Books Are Ready for Press"
501 Nelson Place
Nashville, Tennessee 37214

cidermillpress.com